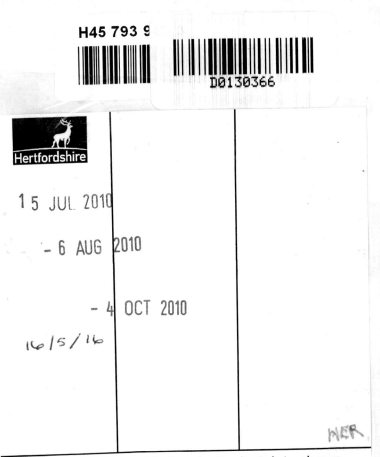

sit back and relax

COVENANT CHILD
Terri Blackstock
0 8499.4301 9

25 appetisers of
summer fiction
to change your life

Sit back and relax

BLESSED CHILD
Bright & Dekker
0 8499.4312 4

THE NOTE
Angela Hunt
0 8499.4284 5

25 appetisers of **summer fiction** to change your life…

THE
RIPPER
CODE

THOMAS TOUGHILL

First published 2008
This edition published 2009

The History Press
The Mill, Brimscombe Port
Stroud, Gloucestershire, GL5 2QG
www.thehistorypress.co.uk

British Library Cataloguing in Publication Data.
A catalogue record for this book is available from the British
Library.

ISBN 978 0 7524 5276 0

Printed in Great Britain

*'Lover and friend has thou put from me
and mine acquaintance into darkness.'*

An extract from the 88th Psalm quoted on the frontispiece of
that most famous of books on the Ripper murders, *The Lodger*,
by Marie Belloc Lowndes, a confidante of Oscar Wilde.

*'Wilde told me how he had saved (Frank) Miles's
bacon but never referred to him again.'*

A statement attributed to Robert Sherard, Oscar Wilde's
intimate friend and biographer.

CONTENTS

ACKNOWLEDGEMENTS

I owe a special debt of gratitude to Robin Odell and Non for the help and encouragement they have given me in this project. My thanks go also to Colin Wilson for his support and enthusiasm.

I am grateful to the following people who have assisted me in my research over the years: Graeme C. Hall, Archivist of the Oxford Union; Jennifer Thorp, Archivist of New College, Oxford; Dr Robin Darwall-Smith, Archivist, Magdalen College, Oxford; Claire Hopkins, Archivist, Trinity College, Oxford; Marcus Risdell of the Garrick Club; Mrs Hatfield, Archivist of Eton College; John Bidwell of the William Andrews Clark Memorial Library, University of California; Paul Davidson, Works of Art Department, Philips of Bond Street; Robert Bowman of Sotheby's; J.S. Williams, Archivist, City of Bristol; Ronald Parkinson, Assistant of Paintings, Victoria & Albert Museum; Paul Goldman, Research Assistant, The British Museum; J.P. Filedt Kok, Curator of Prints, Rijks Museum, Amsterdam; P.K. Escreet, Keeper of Special Collections, Glasgow University Library; Camilla Vignoles, Information Department, Tate Gallery; David Clarke, Department of Fine Arts, University of Hong Kong; Clarissa Schoening Morrison, University of Victoria, British Columbia; Sheila Cooke of the Local Studies Library, Nottingham; and Ralph Gee, Chief Librarian, *Evening Post*, Nottingham.

I wish to express my gratitude to the staff of the following: the Oxfordshire Record Office; the Nottinghamshire County

Record Office; the Public Record Office; the British Library; the Greater London Record Office and History Library; the Royal Academy of Arts; the Printmakers Council; the Mitchell Library, Glasgow; and the Department of English Literature, University of Glasgow.

PAPERBACK EDITION

I would like to thank the following who helped me in the writing of this paperback edition: Graeme C. Hall, Archivist, the Oxford Union; Mrs Elizabeth Boardman, Archivist, Brasenose College, Oxford; Geoffrey Bourne-Taylor, Secretary, Apollo University Lodge no 357, Oxford; Emma Butterfield, Picture Librarian, National Portrait Gallery; Philip Rood, Media Relations Manager, VT Group PLC; P. Hatfield, Eton College; and Hugh McCormick, President, Vincent's Club, Oxford.

Once again, I owe a special debt to Robin Odell and Non. Robin's generosity of spirit and gentlemanly behaviour are rare commodities indeed.

LIST OF PLATES

FOREWORD

This book is the culmination of a project that has evolved and taken shape over two decades. Thomas Toughill first mentioned his ideas to me in the late 1980s and he has been content to let them mature while he acquired further components for his intriguing matrix.

In the intervening years, he has done many things; served as a Special Branch police officer, taught history and written other books. Like any good researcher, he has frequented libraries, archives and hunted down all manner of sources to garner information and supporting detail. *The Ripper Code*, therefore, is not a hurriedly written account intended to capitalise on sensational claims. It is a considered, thoughtful thesis which the author presents to his readers. And it has been worth the wait.

Many books about the Ripper have appeared during this interlude, some airing new suspects, others presenting familiar names in a different guise. A few authors have even aspired to claims of finality with variations on the theme that their theories have allowed the 'case to be closed'. Such claims lack substantiation, but hyperbole has been a strong theme in the history of Ripper literature. Fortunately, this has been balanced to some extent by reliable works of reference which have established a respectable corpus of knowledge and a basis for future research.

Thomas Toughill makes no exaggerated claims for his views; he writes only of having undertaken a quest. He takes a refreshing look at the murders themselves, examining new angles and perspectives and analysing the way events have been interpreted. There is none of the tired old re-hashing of overcooked theories and fiction posing as something more substantial. Of course, he retells the story of the crimes as they unfolded but in a way that establishes them as necessary coordinates for the reader. He avoids any temptation, so prevalent in books on this subject, to swamp the reader with detail.

He takes a new look at some of the touchstones of the Ripper story such as Sir Melville Macnaghten's notes, the murderer's modus operandi and police politics. There are also insights into the nineteenth century world of art and literature which dovetail into his thesis. The author gives the reader sufficient information with which to navigate, while moving the narrative forward in a measured fashion towards its conclusion. This is a skill drawn partly from his background as an historian but also from his instinct as a writer seeking to engage with his reader. As a result, *The Ripper Code* contains no contrived persuasion and no attempts to seduce with shrill, overblown arguments. The style is robust, measured and engagingly matter-of-fact.

Thomas Toughill has constructed a beguiling matrix into which he places the individual he believes to have been Jack the Ripper. Is it the end of the quest to identify the killer whose name has eluded legions of theorists for over a hundred years? Only the reader can judge, but the journey of discovery is certainly worthwhile.

Robin Odell
Author of *Ripperology: A Study of the World's First Serial Killer and a Literary Phenomenon.*

THE SETTING

. . . No one who was living in London that autumn will forget the terror created by these murders. Even now I can recall the foggy evenings, and hear again the raucous cries of the newspaper boys: 'Another horrible murder, murder, mutilation, Whitechapel!' Such was the burden of their ghastly song; and, when the double murder of 30th September took place the exasperation of the public at the non-discovery of the perpetrator knew no bounds, and no servant-maid deemed her life safe if she ventured out to post a letter after ten o'clock at night. And yet this panic was quite unreasonable. The victims, without exception, belonged to the lowest dregs of female humanity, who avoid the police and exercise every ingenuity in order to remain in the darkest corners of the most deserted alleys.

This is how Melville Leslie Macnaghten recalled the autumn of 1888 when Jack the Ripper, the most infamous and mysterious murderer in British history, carried out his brief but terrible vendetta against the female sex. Near panic there certainly was. 'Horror ran through the land', proclaimed one contemporary account. Yet in that year, Macnaghten, who as a senior Metropolitan Police officer was destined to play a major role in the Ripper case, lived in Chelsea in the West End of London, some six safe miles from Whitechapel, the squalid slum-ridden area the murderer chose as his hunting ground.

Whitechapel, named after the parish church of St Mary Matfellon which was painted white in the Middle Ages, stands to the east of the ancient City of London. Traditionally a home for hard working emigrants, the district prospered for many years under foreign influence and industry. When the Jews were allowed to re-enter England by Oliver Cromwell in the 1650s, after a ban of several centuries, many of them settled there, as did later the exiled Huguenots, the skilled and well-educated French Protestants. Over the years many of the people who came to Britain to enjoy its religious and political tolerance took up residence in Whitechapel, thus giving the area a strong cosmopolitan appearance. However, the industrial revolution and the immense growth in the population of London in the early nineteenth century had a profound and lasting effect on the district. By the 1880s, the once proud name of Whitechapel had long become a byword for poverty, disease, prostitution, and crime. It was, according to local clergyman, Samuel Barnett, 'the evil square mile', inhabited by, in the words of writer Jack London, 'the people of the abyss.'

When Mrs Barnett moved with her husband to St Jude's, Whitechapel in 1873, she had difficulty in believing what she found there; a dark crowded maze of filthy evil-smelling alleys and courts; an environment so unhealthy that more than half the local children died before their fifth birthday; a district so deprived that over a third of the population was classed as living in poverty or want and where great numbers of women were forced to sell themselves openly for a few pence or a loaf of bread; an atmosphere so denuded of hope that drink represented for many the only escape from an unbearable reality, and senseless violence accepted as a part of daily life; and an area so dangerous and crime-ridden that the police routinely patrolled it in pairs.

At the bottom of the heap were 'the dossers', the homeless who were forced to sleep rough in the streets, churchyards, or parks, unless they had the 4d it cost to hire a bed for the night in one of the 233 common lodging houses in the area. Jack London observed a group of these down and outs in Christchurch Garden, otherwise known as 'Itchy Park':

A chill raw wind was blowing, and these creatures huddled there in their rags, sleeping for the most part, or trying to sleep. Here were a dozen women, ranging in age from twenty years to seventy. Next a babe, possibly of nine months, lying asleep, flat on the hard bench, with neither pillow nor covering, nor with anyone looking after it. Next half-a-dozen men, sleeping bolt upright or leaning against one another in their sleep. In one place a family group, a child asleep in its sleeping mother's arms, and the husband (or male mate) clumsily mending a dilapidated shoe. On another bench a woman trimming the frayed strips of her rags with a knife, and another woman, with thread and needle sewing up rents. Adjoining, a man holding a sleeping woman in his arms. Farther on, a man, his clothing caked with gutter mud, asleep, with head in the lap of a woman, not more than twenty five years old, and also asleep.

It was from women of this class that the Ripper selected his victims. Why he restricted himself to Whitechapel is not known. In 1888 there were several other parts of London where low class prostitutes were to be had, but the Ripper chose not to operate there, perhaps because, as one newspaper said, Whitechapel provided favourable opportunities for 'both perpetration and escape'.

If the murders were restricted to the East End, the fear they engendered was not, as Melville Macnaghten makes clear. In fact, the Ripper scare extended well beyond the West End of London and indeed the shores of the United Kingdom. Stories spread that the Ripper had moved to America or the Continent. The reason for all of this was the unprecedented nature of the case itself. The murder of five East End whores was in itself a matter of little public concern; after all violent death in that area was almost commonplace. The Ripper killings however represented a new and, to contemporary minds, a deeply disturbing form of murder. Killing for revenge or gain was one thing, but that a man should kill prostitutes for the opportunity to cut open their bodies, tear out their innards and run off with 'certain parts of their anatomy' was something which the Victorian mind could not easily grasp.

In short, the Ripper murders constituted an open, and almost certainly deliberate, challenge to the solidity and hypocrisy of Victorian society. The Ripper did not try to conceal his victims; on the contrary he left them butchered in a public place for all the world to see. True, he killed his last victim in a room, but only because the streets had become too dangerous for him to work in. And by way of compensation, he used the privacy to indulge his satanic urges to the full and leave the woman barely recognisable as a human being.

In a sense, the Ripper is reminiscent of Sawney Bean, the fifteenth century Scottish cannibal who lived with his incestuous family in a cave from which they emerged to rob, kill, and eventually eat anyone unfortunate enough to pass by. When these crimes were uncovered (because one would-be victim escaped) the whole of Scotland was so shocked that the King himself led the hunt which culminated in Bean's arrest and execution. Closer to the Ripper in time and character is Jean Lacenaire, the early nineteenth-century French murderer. He was not a serial killer; in fact he was a rather unsuccessful petty criminal. But, as he made clear in his *Memoirs* which he wrote while awaiting execution, he was a loner and a rebel who regarded his activities as a calculated assault on the society which produced him and which he had grown to hate. There is of course one important difference between Lacenaire and the Ripper; the Frenchman was caught, whereas the Ripper was not. His name remains a mystery, hence the need for this book.

Over the years a great deal has been written about the identity of Jack the Ripper. However, as shall be seen, practically all of it can be safely dismissed. Moreover, many, if not most, students of the case seem to believe that the Ripper was a deranged East Ender, a man who lived his life in obscurity, save for his brief notoriety in the autumn of 1888.

The fact remains though that the prime suspect in the Ripper files is a Montague John Druitt, an Oxford educated barrister, who had attended Winchester, one of the most exclusive Public schools in England. What makes this particularly meaningful, given the rigid class structure of Victorian England, is that the police officer who accused Druitt was Melville Macnaghten, himself an Old Etonion.

At first glance, it appears that Macnaghten snatched Druitt's name out of the ether. There is no known police file on Druitt, who committed suicide in early December 1888, and no other police officer refers to him. However, it is clear that Macnaghten must have had a very good reason for listing Druitt as his prime suspect and in particular for including the following sentence in an official document which was meant for the eyes of his political masters:

(Druitt) was sexually insane and from private information I have little doubt but that his own family believed him to have been the murderer.

If Macnaghten's report, which has become known as the 'Macnaghten Memorandum', is the most important document in the Ripper files, then that sentence is the most important in the memorandum itself. What exactly did Macnaghten mean by 'sexually insane' and who was the source of his 'private information'? The way forward in this case is to answer these questions, for therein lies the path to the Ripper's identity, be that Druitt *or someone else*.

That Macnaghten should accuse another Public schoolboy is not as surprising as it at first seems. If the Ripper was a 'new' type of murderer, one who had the imagination and the sheer gall to use murder as a means of avenging himself on society, then it is indeed likely that he was an educated man from a privileged background who knew the East End well from his frequent visits there (probably in disguise) in pursuit of sex and drugs.

The logic here is the Ripper murders stemmed from the corrupting power of vice, the unrestrained pursuit of physical pleasure and carnal gratification by someone from an Establishment background who, as a result of the gross inequalities in Victorian society, was able to find what he craved easily, cheaply, and *anonymously* in the brothels, opium dens and slums of the East End. The Ripper then, far from being a deranged local, is more likely to have been a 'toff' from outside, a man who regarded Whitechapel as his hunting ground, for that, in another form, is what the district had been to him before his addiction pushed him into madness.

The Ripper killings must be seen in their proper historical context if they are to be understood. Here, it is necessary to mention the Cleveland Street Scandal of 1889, the year after the Ripper struck. In that year, the police learned that certain upper class gentlemen, aristocrats, politicians and the like, were frequenting a house in London's Cleveland Street for the purpose of having sex with low class rent boys. The police though were apparently prevented by the government from arresting the guilty parties, the most prominent of whom were allowed to leave the country. Indeed the only person to receive a lengthy prison sentence was a journalist who tried to bring out the truth about the case only to be punished for his efforts with 12 months' imprisonment for criminal libel. Recently released government files indicate that the reason for the cover up in this scandal was the involvement of Queen Victoria's grandson, the Duke of Clarence, who was apparently named as a frequenter of the male brothel. Here was a raw display of what power and justice meant in late Victorian Britain. (Clarence has been named as a Ripper suspect himself. The charge is absurd, but, given the argument presented here, it is important to note that the accusation was made.)

When Oscar Wilde published the first edition of his only novel, *The Picture of Dorian Gray* in 1890, he was savaged in the press for producing a book which was suitable for 'none but outlawed noblemen and perverted telegraph boys', a clear reference to the Cleveland Street Scandal, in which many believed Wilde had been involved, although no evidence to that effect has ever been found.

The press though did have a point. Dorian Gray's relationship with his friends and the general atmosphere of decadence which pervades the novel are strongly redolent of the Cleveland Street Scandal. It is surprising therefore that, until now, no one has studied *The Picture of Dorian Gray* more deeply and seen the similarities therein with another case which had shocked Victorian Britain much more profoundly, the Ripper murders.

Central to the theory put forward here is the claim that the Ripper murders inspired Wilde's novel which is essentially the story of a wealthy man whose life of vice in the stews of the East End turns him into a murderer. Naturally, there is no suggestion whatsoever that Wilde had anything to do with the murders themselves, merely that he came to learn that the killer was a former lover of his and that he dropped clear hints about this in his novel. In addition, this author suggests that, as appears to have happened in the Cleveland Street Scandal, the truth about Jack the Ripper was suppressed in order to protect a member of the Royal family.

As for Montague John Druitt, this author has carried out original research which enables him to provide convincing answers to the vital questions cited above. Simply put, these are that Oscar Wilde, *who spent two years at Oxford with Druitt*, was one source of Macnaghten's 'private information' and that by 'sexually insane', *a phrase Wilde used to describe the urges which led to his own imprisonment in*

1895 *for gross indecency with young men*, Macnaghten, *quoting medical opinion*, meant that Druitt was a vice-driven 'boy-worshipper.' Druitt, it is now clear, was the sort of man who would have been involved in the Cleveland Street Scandal, had he still been alive, which would explain why he worked not just as a barrister, but as a teacher in a boarding school for boys, and why one of his legal colleagues, a solicitor called Edward Henslow Bedford, played a leading role in securing the prosecution of the journalist who tried to reveal the truth about the case.

However, Druitt was not, it seems, the Ripper. As will be argued in due course, that mantle belongs to another vice-driven 'friend' of Oscar Wilde, which returns us full circle to Melville Macnaghten for, if the following theory is correct, *he and Jack the Ripper lived in the same street.*

THE MURDERS

PRELUDE

'Now the Whitechapel murderer had five victims and five victims only.' So wrote Sir Melville Macnaghten, who joined the Metropolitan Police as an Assistant Chief Constable in 1889, several months after the last of those murders, that of Mary Jane Kelly, which took place on 9 November 1888. Not all students of the Ripper case agree with this figure. Some, like Dr Forbes Winslow, an amateur detective who played an active role in the hunt for the killer, have suggested that the first murder took place not in the second half of 1888 but on 26 December 1887.

This victim is unidentified other than by the fanciful name 'Fairy Fay'. In listing the Ripper killings, *The Scotsman* said on 10 November 1888, 'Last Christmas week, an unknown woman found murdered near Osborne and Wentworth Street, Whitechapel.' According to Tom Cullen in his *The Crimes and Times of Jack the Ripper*, '"Fairy Fay" lost her life as a result of a wrong decision; she decided to take a short cut home when the pub in Mitre Square where she had been drinking all evening closed after midnight, and in the dim warrens behind Commercial Road she was struck down and carved up by an unknown assassin.'

A contemporary broadsheet entitled *An Account of the Fearful Atrocities* contains some details on this killing:

The first of this series of horrible murders which are believed to be the work of the same man, was committed so far back as last Christmas, when the body of a woman was found with a stick or iron instrument thrust into her body. In this case the woman was never identified and no particular sensation was caused, the death being generally assumed to be the result of a drunken freak on the part of the nameless ruffians who swarm about Whitechapel.

The killing of Emma Smith, a common prostitute, on 3 April 1888 must be dismissed as a Ripper murder. Smith was taken alive to the London Hospital where she stated before expiring that she had been attacked by four men. Moreover no attempt had been made to cut her throat, the Ripper's hallmark. She died in fact from peritonitis which developed as a result of having a foreign object, not a knife, rammed into her vagina.

Martha Turner (or Tabrams), a married prostitute, is unlikely to have been a victim of the Ripper. Turner's body, which was found on a staircase in George Yard Buildings at 3 a.m. on Tuesday 7 August, had not been mutilated, another of the Ripper's hallmarks, and, as in the Smith case, her throat had not been cut. Her body had been pierced thirty-nine times, probably by a bayonet, and possibly, according to the examining doctor, by two weapons, a theory which is the foundation of the belief that the Ripper was ambidextrous. Turner had been seen earlier that night in the company of two soldiers and another prostitute. Macnaghten was emphatic about what ensued. 'These men were arrested, but the second prostitute failed, or refused, to identify, and the soldiers were accordingly discharged.' The inquest into Turner's death, which opened on 10 August, returned a verdict of murder against a person or persons unknown.

Commenting on the above three crimes, Colin Wilson, who has probably had more to say about the Ripper case than any other writer, finds it worth noting that 'the murders of 'Fairy Fay', Emma Smith, and Martha Turner occurred on holidays –

Boxing Day, Easter Monday and August Bank Holiday, when many murders took place in London.' If then these killings were not the work of the Ripper – and for want of evidence, that of 'Fairy Fay' must remain an open question – they at least set the scene for the terror that was to engulf the East End of London in the autumn of 1888.

MARY ANN NICHOLS

Mary Ann, or Polly, Nichols was a typical Whitechapel whore, a gin-sodden derelict who routinely sold her body in any convenient staircase, alley or court for the price of a night's lodging. At the age of 42 in 1888, she stood 5ft 2in tall and had most of her front teeth missing. She had been married for over twenty years and had five children, but she was separated from her family. Her husband, William Nichols, a printer's machinist, had got fed up with her drinking habits and left her eight years before, taking the children with him. He initially made financial provision for his estranged wife, but discontinued this when he found out that she had taken to prostitution. For several years Nichols drifted from one London workhouse to another. In early 1888, she was staying in the Lambeth Workhouse in south London. She took a job as a servant in a house on Wordsworth Common, but any hopes she may have had of finding long term security there vanished when, after only a few months, she was dismissed for stealing £3, apparently to buy drink. After this she slipped back to the stews of Whitechapel where by August she was sharing a room with three women in a common lodging house at No. 18 Thrawl Street.

Nichols was last seen alive by a friend, Emily Holland, who bumped into her at 2.30 a.m. on Friday 31 August at the corner of Osborne Street and Whitechapel Road. Holland was sure of the time because as she spoke to Nichols, the clock of the Whitechapel Church struck. Nichols was the worse for drink and penniless. She declared that she had had her lodging money three times that day and spent it. Holland wanted her to come back with him, but she declined and headed off towards Whitechapel. As she did so she said, 'It won't be long before I'll be back. See what a jolly bonnet I've got now,' implying that this adornment would help her find custom. Unfortunately for her, it did.

Bucks Row was a better than average East End street. It was a fairly wide thoroughfare with a warehouse on one side and on the other a row of terraced houses which were occupied for the most part by relatively well off tradesmen. It was however badly lit, with only one gas lamp servicing the whole street. Between the house and a board school there was a closed gateway to some stables. Some time within an hour of leaving her friend, Nichols picked up a man and went with him to this suitably dark and secluded spot to earn the 4d she needed for her lodging.

Nichols' body was discovered between 3.30 a.m. and 3.45 a.m. by Charles Cross, a market porter, on his way to work. So bad was the lighting that he at first mistook her crumpled form for a piece of tarpaulin which had fallen from a cart. On discovering that this was a woman, he sought assistance from another porter, John Paul, who happened to pass by at that moment. The two men argued over what to do, and eventually concluded that the woman had been raped and that she may still be alive. After pulling down her disarranged clothing, they set off in search of a policeman.

A few moments after the porters left the scene, PC Neil of J Division came across Nichols' supine body and with the aid of his lamp saw immediately what Cross and Paul had missed – the woman's throat had been cut from ear to ear. He also saw that, disturbingly, her eyes were wide open. Her bonnet lay close to her left hand. Neil felt her arms and found them quite warm from the joints up. Seeing another constable pass in the next street, Neil called him over and asked him to summon Dr

Llewellyn, the police surgeon, who lived nearby. The doctor arrived within a quarter of an hour and after a cursory examination, pronounced Nichols dead and gave instructions for her body to be taken to the mortuary.

Nichols' clothes had soaked up most of the blood which had leaked from her wounds, but a little had drained onto the ground. This was promptly washed away with a bucket of water and by daylight the only signs of where the murder had taken place were faint dark stains between the paving stones.

Mortuary is too grand a word for the place to which Nichols' body, in its official iron shell, was taken. Described by *The Daily Telegraph* as 'a disgraceful hole and corner hovel' which provided surgeons 'with the most incomplete appliances for carrying out their delicate and difficult duty', it was simply a shed behind the Old Montague Street workhouse. Nichols' body lay in the yard outside this shed until the two workhouse inmates, Robert Mann and James Hatfield, had their breakfast. Then and only then did the undressing and washing of the corpse take place. It is not clear whether this was started under police supervision, as should have been the case, but around 7 a.m. Inspector Spratling, who was taking an inventory of Nichols' clothing, lifted up the woman's skirt and made the shocking discovery that this was no ordinary murder. Nichols' stomach had been ripped open.

On being called to the mortuary in the wake of this news, Dr Llewellyn immediately carried out a full post-mortem, or at least as full as was possible given the lack of facilities and equipment. His findings, which he gave in evidence at the inquest into Nichols' death, are reproduced below. It was this testimony which gave birth to two contentious points about the Ripper – whether he was left-handed and whether he possessed any anatomical knowledge:

On the right side of the face there was a recent and strongly marked bruise . . . caused by a blow from a fist or the pressure of a thumb. On the left side a circular bruise might have been produced by the pressure of the fingers. There were two cuts in the throat, one four inches long, the other eight. The large vessels of the neck on both sides were severed. The incisions also completely severed all the tissues down to the vertebrae which had also been penetrated . . . There were several incisions running across the abdomen. On the right side there were also three or four similar cuts running downwards. . . As far as the throat is concerned the weapon appeared to have been held in the left hand of the person who used it. Similarly the wounds in the abdomen ran from left to right and might have been done by a left handed person. The murderer must also have had some rough anatomical knowledge. He seems to have attacked all the vital parts. . . I would say that the murder might have occupied four or five minutes.

As for the weapon itself, the doctor reckoned that it was stout-backed and pointed, like a cork cutter's or cobbler's, with a blade six to eight inches long.

The police had initial difficulty in identifying the body, the only clue being the mark of the Lambeth workhouse on Nichols' petticoats. The matron of the workhouse though failed to recognise either the body or the clothes. However as word of the murder spread, some occupants of Nichols' lodging house came forward. Their identification of the body was corroborated by an inmate of the Lambeth workhouse some days later and formally at the inquest by Nichols' father, Edward Walker, a smith from Camberwell. He recognised his daughter by a missing tooth and a mark on her forehead. He produced a letter which she had sent to him the previous Easter from Wandsworth where she was working as a servant. This read, 'You will be glad to know I am settled in a new place. My people went out yesterday and have not returned, so I am left in charge. They are teetotallers and are very nice people and I have not much to do.' Walker conceded that his daughter was fond of drink but maintained that her only fault was that she was too good to others and not to herself. Her husband did not agree; while staring down at her in her coffin, he is said to have melodramatically forgiven her for the life she had led him.

In 1888 there was no proper coroner's court in the East End of London and inquests were usually held in any suitable location that was available, which in practice usually meant a public house. However the committee of the Working Lads' Institute, displaying a fine sense of the historical moment, offered the use of their premises in Whitechapel Road and it was there on Saturday 1 September that the inquest into the death of Mary Nichols began, presided over by Mr Wynne Baxter, the Coroner for the South Eastern Division of Middlesex County.

Wynne Baxter was destined to play a major role in the Ripper case, not as a sleuth but as a penetrating critic of police methods and official attitudes towards the East End. He handled the first three Ripper inquests which fell within the Metropolitan area and by rights he should have been responsible for the fourth and last. But as shall be seen, it would appear that the authorities, smarting from his earlier comments, thought otherwise.

Baxter started as he intended to continue. He clearly disbelieved the police account of the treatment of Nichols' body in the mortuary and closely questioned the attendants, Mann and Hatfield, with a view to revealing discrepancies between the two versions:

Q.: (the Coroner): The police were not present? (when the undressing of the body began).
A.: No, there was no one present.

Q.: Had you been told to touch the body?

A.: No.

Q.: Who gave you instructions to do all this?

A.: No one gave us any. We did it so as to have the body ready.

Q.: Who told you the doctor was coming?

A.: I heard someone talking about it.

Not content with this, Baxter resorted to raw sarcasm:

Q.: Having finished, did you make the post-mortem examination?

A.: No, the police came.

Q.: Oh, the police came did they? And so it was no longer necessary for you to go on with the post-mortem?

In his conclusions, Baxter called for the establishment of public mortuaries under the charge of experienced keepers, an arrangement he felt would ensure that bodies were attended to only in the presence of doctors and that hygiene in the area would be improved. 'Surely', he said, 'if mortuaries are found necessary in the West End, there must be stronger reasons for them in the midst of so much squalid crowding.' He did not agree though with the foreman of the jury who accused the government of indifference towards the poor because it had not offered a reward for the arrest of the murderer:

Foreman: It is my opinion, and the opinion of the rest of us, that the government ought to offer a reward – and a big one. If it had been a rich person that was murdered there would have been a reward of £1,000 offered but just because it is a poor 'unfortunate' there is hardly any notice taken.

Coroner: I think you are altogether wrong and have no right to make such statements. For some time past the offering of rewards has been discontinued, no distinction made between rich and poor.

Foreman: Nevertheless I am glad to see the inhabitants are going to offer a reward and I will give £25 myself.

The evidence given at the inquest shed no light on the identity of the murderer, his motive, or on how he managed to kill his victim so quietly and escape undetected. There were at least three watchmen in Bucks Row and neither they, nor the patrolling policemen, saw or heard anything suspicious. The murder was committed almost underneath the window of Mrs Emma Green. She stated that, although a light sleeper, she heard nothing during the night until the police woke her at about 4 a.m. to question her. Similarly, Mr Walker Purkis, who lived opposite the murder site, said that although he had slept fitfully during the night he heard nothing until the police knocked on his door shortly after finding Nichols' body. In fact, so difficult was it to believe that the murderer could have escaped unseen and unheard that some suggested that Nichols had been murdered elsewhere and her body dumped in Bucks Row from a cart. The medical evidence however ruled out this possibility.

It was this uncanny – almost supernatural – stealth of the murderer, coupled with his apparent lack of motive, which chilled the hearts of Londoners. The East End was a very violent area, with murders almost commonplace in some places. But these killings always had a motive – robbery, revenge, drink, jealousy, or whatever. The murder of Nichols was different. It was apparently done for its own sake, that is to say, to cut a woman's throat and rip open her stomach. This was a concept which Victorians, occupants of a far simpler and more 'natural' world than that of the modern age, could not easily envisage. This is borne out by the fact that, as shall be seen, even such a figure as Coroner Baxter continued to seek a material explanation for the murders.

Mary Ann Nichols was buried in Ilford cemetery on 6 September. A few weeks later the occupants of Bucks Row succeeded in their petition to change the by then notorious name of their street. It became known as Durward Street.

* * * * *

The people of London were doubly unfortunate in that the Ripper murders took place when the Metropolitan Police was in internal disarray and public confidence in the Force was at a low ebb. Most writers on the Ripper case have placed the blame for this sorry state of affairs on the Commissioner of Police, Sir Charles Warren, a Major General in the Royal Engineers, who had made his name handling the Bantu in Grinqualand West and who was summoned from Egypt in 1886 to bolster faith in a government which felt itself threatened by a rising tide of social unrest. He was the third choice for the job, the first two men, Sir Redvers Buller and Lord Charles Beresford, having turned it down.

Once behind his desk, Warren acted as his background would suggest. He treated the police force as if it were the army, and more disturbingly, the lower orders of British society like troublesome natives. His staffing of senior police positions with military appointees, his contempt for the Criminal Investigation Department (which according to Tom Cullen he did not even mention in his 1887 Annual Report) and his concern for matters of little relevance to proper policing angered and demoralised the professional police officers who worked under him. His handling too of the so-called 'Bloody Sunday' disturbances of November 1887 in which he deployed against a mob of unemployed descending upon Trafalgar Square, a force of four thousand constables, three hundred mounted life guards, three armed foot guards, and three hundred mounted policemen, in an action which, not surprisingly, turned into the worst display of violence seen in the capital since the Gordon riots of 1780, dismayed many policemen who were all too aware that this event would serve only to alienate the public further.

And yet a degree of blame must be directed against the system which then existed, a system which allowed a totally unsuitable man like Warren to be appointed in the first place and which allowed the Home Secretary, Henry Matthews, to interfere in the internal affairs of the Force without reference to the Commissioner. Warren was particularly, and some would say rightly, incensed at the 'special relationship' which had grown up between Matthews and the Head of the CID, James Monro, a Scotsman who had seen twenty-six years' service in India before taking up this post in 1884, and who was widely respected for his ability. Matthews took to writing direct to Monro who in turn claimed that his department was independent of the Commissioner and answerable only to the Home Office. Clearly, Warren could not tolerate this behaviour and on 31 August, the day Mary Nichols was murdered, he secured the resignation of Monro.

If Monro's departure is diplomatically understandable, it nevertheless caused morale within the CID to slump further, just as the Ripper investigation was about to begin in earnest. Robert Anderson, an Irish barrister, and himself an admirer of Monro, was chosen as the Head of the department. It is a measure of his enthusiasm for the job that he accepted it only on condition that he received a month's sick leave in Switzerland.

On the very day that Anderson left London for the therapeutic Alpine air, the Whitechapel murderer struck again.

ANNIE CHAPMAN

Annie Chapman, or Dark Annie, was a woman who had known better days. She had been married to John Chapman, a coachman, by whom she had three children, and she lived for a while with her family in West London. However, around 1882, she left her husband and the respectable life he gave her and drifted into the squalor of Whitechapel. It is not known why she did this but there are strong grounds for believing drink to be responsible.

She lived for some time with a sieve maker in Spitalfields, a relationship which led her to adopt the alias Annie Siffey or Sievey. She initially enjoyed a separation allowance of 10s from her husband, but this ended on his death in 1886. To eke out a living, she turned her hand to hawking, crochet work, and whenever the need arose, which was doubtless often, to walking the streets. Her lifestyle was summed up by her friend, Amelia Farmer:

I am afraid she used to earn her living partly on the streets. She was a straightforward woman when she was sober, clever and industrious with the needle. But she could not take too much drink. She had been living a very irregular life all the time I've known her.

The wonder is that Chapman made any success at all out of whoring. At 48 years old in 1888, she looked much older and the effects of the tuberculosis and malnutrition which were slowly killing her were already etched on her face. She was only 5ft tall and she had two of her front teeth missing. The clothes she was wearing when she was murdered were described as 'old and dirty'.

Chapman spent the last night of her life, Friday 7 September 1888, in the kitchen of Crossingham's lodging house in Dorset Street, which then had the reputation of being one of the most lawless thoroughfares in London. By rights, she should have been denied entry, but the keeper, Timothy Donovan, knew her as a long-time resident who had left the lodging house only the week before, and had allowed her to stay. She was doubtless grateful for this kindness, for the previous week had been a hard one. She had got into a fight with a woman over a bar of soap and had come off second best, sustaining bruises to her chest and face. She had also fallen ill and despite a visit to the infirmary had been unable to throw off her ailment. When she spoke to her friend, Amelia Farmer, earlier that Friday evening she had complained of being too tired to do anything.

At around 2 a.m. on the morning of 8 September, Donovan reminded Chapman of the house regulations and told her that she must either pay for a bed at once or leave. Chapman took this well enough. As she stepped into the night, she asked Donovan to hold a bed for her. 'I haven't any money now, but don't let the bed. I will be back soon' he quoted her as saying.

Hanbury Street, only half a mile from the scene of the Nichols' murder, had once been a proud area, built to house the Spitalfield weavers. However, the industrial revolution had swept away their looms and with them the prosperity of the district. *The Daily Telegraph* painted a depressing picture of the street as it was to be found in September 1888:

The neighbourhood is described as a very rough one and respectable people are accustomed to avoid it. It is inhabited by dock labourers, market porters, the tenants of common lodging houses, and a certain number of cabinet-makers who supply the furniture establishments of Curtain Road.

. . . In these squalid parts of the metropolis, aggravated assaults, attended by flesh wounds from knives are frequently met with, and men and women become accustomed to scenes of violence.

The people do not, however, appear to interfere with each other unless provoked. Late at night there are many scenes of degradations and immorality. . .

Shortly before 5 a.m. on 8 September, John Richardson, a porter in Spitalfields market, who helped his mother with her packing case business at No. 29 Hanbury Street, entered the passageway of the two-storeyed house and walked through to the unpaved backyard which was separated from its neighbours by a wooden fence 5½ft high. He did not actually enter the yard but sat on the doorstep while he trimmed a piece of leather from his boot. There were at least seventeen people living at No. 29; people who, for a variety of reasons, came and went at all hours of the day and night. For this reason the doors to the passageway were never locked, a fact known to local prostitutes. Richardson later testified that he frequently removed couples from the yard who had gone there for immoral purposes, but on this morning he saw nobody and after a few minutes he left.

As the nearby brewer's clock was striking 5.30 a.m., Mrs Elizabeth Long passed by the entrance to No. 29 where she saw a man and a woman standing together on the pavement, apparently haggling. She heard the man ask, 'Will you?', and the woman reply, 'Yes.' The man had his back to her and she did not see his face, but she described him as taller than the woman, over 40 years of age and foreign in appearance. She also said that he had a shabby genteel appearance and that he was wearing a brown deerstalker and, she thought, a dark coat. His companion she did see clearly and later, when taken to the mortuary, had no hesitation in identifying her as the latest victim of the Whitechapel murderer.

Shortly after Mrs Long walked on, Chapman went with a man, presumably the one described above, through the passageway of No. 29 and down the two steps into the backyard.

Albert Cadoche, a carpenter, who lived next door at No. 27, entered his backyard at about 5.20 a.m. to go to the lavatory. As he returned to the house, he heard a woman's voice from the backyard of No. 29 say 'No'. On re-entering his backyard a few moments later, he heard something fall against the fence. Cadoche, however, took no notice and simply made his way to work. This lack of inquisitiveness was unfortunate for there can be little doubt that what Cadoche heard was Annie Chapman being murdered. If he had chosen to look over the fence, he would have caught Jack the Ripper literally red-handed.

The sun was well up when, shortly before 6 a.m., John Davis, a porter, who lived at No. 29, pushed open the door to the backyard and stopped short. There, only a few feet beneath him, between the steps and the fence, lay the body of Annie Chapman, her clothes pulled up to her chest and her innards open to the world.

Chapman lay on her back, with her legs drawn up and her knees turned outwards. Her hands were raised as if she had made a vain attempt to protect her throat. This had been so savagely cut that she appeared at first glance to have been decapitated. A handkerchief was wound tightly around the neck, which gave rise to the false belief that the Ripper had used it to tie his victim's head back on. Her stomach had been cut open from groin to midriff and her intestines lifted out and draped over her right shoulder.

The first police officer on the scene was Inspector Joseph Chandler who arrived there at 6.10 a.m. A small crowd had already gathered around the house. Drawing on reinforcements, he cleared the passageway and entered the yard, which he found empty except for the body. With people gaping on from any suitable vantage point the surrounding buildings provided, he proceeded to carry out an inspection of the yard.

He found no sign of a struggle or that anyone had climbed over the fence. He saw no bloodstains outside the yard and within it only a very few near the body. He did notice a piece of coarse muslin and a small hair comb lying near the foot of the woman. Further away from the body, near the tap, he discovered a nail box, a piece of flat steel, which Mrs Richardson claimed, and a leather apron. He ensured that the body was not touched until the police surgeon arrived and in the meantime draped a piece of tarpaulin over it.

The Divisional Police surgeon, Dr George Bagster Phillips, arrived at 6.30 a.m. Phillips, a man with twenty-two years' experience, pronounced Chapman dead after a brief examination and gave instructions for her body to be taken to the mortuary. This was done in the very same metal shell which had been used to transport Nichols' body only a few days before. Phillips also carried out his own search of the yard. He saw the piece of cloth and comb and formed the opinion that they had been placed there by design. He also saw smears of blood on the fence close to the woman's head. Some accounts say that he also found a part of an envelope bearing the seal of the Sussex Regiment and on the front the letter 'M' and the postmark 'London 28 August 1888'. (This promising clue came to nothing when it was revealed at the Inquest that Chapman had found the envelope in her lodging house and used it to wrap her pills in.) Phillips arrived at the mortuary at 2 p.m. to carry out his post-mortem. To his anger he discovered that, as appears to have occurred in the Nichols' case, the body had already been touched. In this case it had already been stripped and washed by two nurses. At the inquest, Phillips protested about this and the circumstances under which he was forced to work, pointing out that 'there are no adequate conveniences whatsoever for carrying out a post-mortem examination.' He went on, 'Indeed in summer weather, that shed (i.e. the mortuary) is dangerous to the health of the operator.'

Meanwhile in Hanbury Street, the enterprising occupants of the house adjoining No. 29 began to charge a one penny admission fee to the many people anxious to view the murder site. A rumour spread that the killer had left a chalked message on the wall of one back garden which read, 'I have now done three, and intend to do nine more and give myself up and at the same time give my reasons for doing the murders.' The discovery by a young girl of blood-like marks in the backyard of No. 25 raised the possibility that the killer had escaped by climbing over the backyard fences. An investigation showed however that the marks were not blood.

If Mary Nichols' death stunned people, the Chapman murder shocked them, for there was now no question but that a habitual killer, of an unprecedented type, was at large. When Mrs Mary Burridge, a dealer in floor clothes who lived in Blackfriars Road, read about Chapman's murder in *The Star* newspaper on the afternoon of the murder, she fell into a fit and died. Mrs Sodeaux, a silk weaver's wife who lived in Hanbury Street itself, became so depressed by the nearby killing that she committed suicide. Doubtless the press played a large part in generating an atmosphere of fear and apprehension. *The Star* spoke of the killer as a 'ghoul-like creature . . . stalking down his victims like a Pawnee Indian . . . simply drunk with blood.' This treatment was not restricted to London. Hundreds of miles away, *The Glasgow Herald* informed its readers that the assailant 'comes as unseen and vanishes as quickly as Frankenstein's monster when engaged on a similar work of destruction. His whole action, indeed, is suggestive of some unnatural creature, with the savagery of a wild beast and the brain of a human being.'

Wild hyperbole such as this only served to exacerbate the situation. If the killer was to be caught, or at least stopped, what was needed was concrete action and constructive advice. To this end, a group of East End tradesmen, worried about the fall in business caused by the killings, formed on 10 September the 'Whitechapel Vigilance Committee' under the chairmanship of businessman George Lusk. This organisation raised money which was used to pay unemployed men to patrol the streets of Whitechapel at night in organised beats. Soon other committees of a similar nature sprang up. After the Chapman murder there began also a stream of letters to the police and press with proposals and recommendations on how the investigation should be conducted. Particularly pointed comments came from Dr Forbes-Winslow in a letter to *The Times* on 12 September. Winslow, the son of a resident physician in a Hammersmith asylum, believed the killer to be 'of the upper class of society' and maintained that:

> . . . the murders have been committed by a lunatic lately discharged from some asylum, or by one who has escaped. If the former, doubtless one who though suffering from the effects of homicidal mania, is apparently sane on the surface, and consequently has been liberated, and is following out the inclinations of his morbid imaginations by wholesale genocide. I think that the advice given by me is a sound one – to apply for an immediate return from all asylums who have discharged such individuals, with a view to ascertaining their whereabouts.

Winslow was not content though with this contribution. He developed an almost obsessive interest in the murders, even to the point of becoming personally involved in the hunt for the murderer, a practice which apparently led some detectives to suspect him of being the killer. He also recommended that Scotland Yard should place the following advertisement in the personal column of a London newspaper and question everyone who replied:

> A gentleman who is strongly opposed to the presence of fallen women on the streets of London would like

to co-operate with someone with a view to their suppression.

To his disgust, the police refused to entertain this suggestion.

Beneath all this advice and activity lay a profound and undisguised lack of confidence in the police. The Vigilance Committee issued the following public notice:

Finding that, in spite of murders being committed in our midst our police force is inadequate to discover the author or authors of the late atrocities, we the undersigned have formed ourselves into a committee and intend offering a substantial reward to anyone, citizens or otherwise, who shall give such information as will be the means of bringing the murderer or murderers to justice.

The Reverend Samuel Barnett, Vicar of St Jude's, Whitechapel, called in *The Times* for 'greater police supervision' arguing that there were never 'enough policemen to do anything more than to contain crime within certain areas.' The press too did not pull any punches. Calls were made for the resignation of the Home Secretary and the rumour that Warren was to be posted to the colonies was applauded. *The Daily Telegraph* stated that the CID was in 'an utterly hopeless and worthless condition' and that if it were headed by a competent man 'the scandalous exhibition of stupidity and ineptitude revealed at the East End inquests and the immunity enjoyed by criminals, murder after murder, would not anger and disgust the public feeling as it has undoubtedly done.' Despite this criticism, Robert Anderson, the newly appointed Head of CID, did not hurry back to his desk, although towards the end of September he moved from Switzerland to Paris, so, it is said, that he could keep in closer touch with his office.

The police handling of the Chapman case was certainly open to criticism. At the inquest, Coroner Baxter was not even provided with plans indicating where the body was found. To his anger, Baxter learned that two men who saw Chapman's body immediately after Davies had not been identified. One witness stated that he had told a policeman of the murder and that the officer had refused to leave his post to investigate. And yet in all fairness it must be said that the police were dealing with a new type of case with no guidelines to follow. It is important to remember that the whole gamut of forensic and scientific aids which a modern police force uses routinely simply did not exist in 1888. DNA, fingerprints, blood groupings, fibre tests, radio communications for patrolling officers, computer records, street cameras etc were not available to Warren's men, who had no alternative but to rely on traditional investigative methods which, in practice, meant painstaking door-to-door inquiries, and the questioning of large numbers of people, backed up by the local knowledge of experienced officers and a network of informers.

According to Inspector Frederick Abberline of Scotland Yard – the man who led the hunt for the Ripper at street level – every common lodging house within half a mile of Hanbury Street, numbering over two hundred, was checked, and the name taken of every man who entered them after 2 a.m. on the morning of the murder. That this produced no hard evidence did not surprise Abberline. In a statement on these searches, he pointed out that people entering lodging houses in the early hours of the morning were little noticed. They were, as he said, simply asked for their money and then shown to their beds up poorly lit staircases. Also, and this was an important point if the blood on the murderer's hands was to be seen, washing facilities in those houses were shared and the water poured down the sink straight away.

Nevertheless, in the days immediately after Chapman's death, the police questioned, detained and arrested many suspects, but to no avail. Two of these arrests though are worth mentioning for they led in each case to a short-lived belief that the murderer had been caught.

The first suspect was William Henry Piggott, a mentally disturbed man who was arrested in Gravesend, over twenty miles from London, on the day after Chapman's murder. When questioned, Piggott, who was found in possession of blood-stained clothing, replied in a rambling, incoherent manner, but eventually admitted that he had been near to Hanbury Street on the previous morning. Abberline travelled to Gravesend and was so struck by Piggott's resemblance to a man who was reported to have acted suspiciously in a Whitechapel public house only hours after the murder that he decided to bring him back to London for further questioning. Word of this soon spread and when Abberline arrived back in London the following morning, he found a large crowd, which grew during the day, outside the Commercial Street police station, hoping to catch a glimpse of the suspect. They were to be disappointed for the witnesses who had seen the suspicious character in the public house did not recognise Piggott in an identification parade. Also, Piggott's shaky mental condition collapsed under this ordeal and after a medical examination he was declared to be a lunatic and sent to an asylum. The later Ripper murders left no doubt as to his innocence. The blood-stained clothing however was never explained.

Of greater importance was the arrest on 10 September of the elusive 'Leather Apron'. The excitement caused by this was such that within a few hours of its taking place a broadsheet was being sold on the streets of London proclaiming:

They've captured Leather Apron now, if guilty you'll agree,
He'll have to meet a murderer's doom and hang upon a tree.

'Leather Apron' was the alleged nickname of John Pizer, a Polish Jew, who, it was said, gained his soubriquet by virtue of his trade, shoe mending. According to some, he had the reputation of being cruel to prostitutes and for this reason he was named as a suspect after the murder of Mary Nichols. The police, however, had been unable to locate him. The nickname though was seized upon by the press and public alike, and it quickly became a byword for the murderer, whoever he was. For example, when Piggott was arrested, *The Times* asserted that 'he resembles in some aspects Leather Apron'. Unfortunately, this confusion led people to presume Pizer's guilt, and some newspapers, very unwisely, to name him as the killer.

It was not the discovery of the leather apron in the backyard of No. 29 Hanbury Street which prompted the police to redouble their efforts to locate Pizer, for that garment's presence in the yard was entirely coincidental, but disclosures made to the press by Timothy Donovan, the lodging housekeeper, that he had ejected Pizer from his premises a few months earlier for mistreating a woman, and that the Pole was in the habit of wearing a deerstalker, like the man seen with Chapman by Mrs Long. Police traced the suspect to a house in Mulberry Street and arrested him there on the morning of Monday 10 September. Pizer protested his innocence, but went quietly to the police station.

Initially the case against Pizer seemed very strong. When arrested he was found to be in possession of several knives. It was discovered that he made hats, a possible link with Mary Nichols via the new bonnet she acquired shortly before her death. Most damning of all, a witness, a half-Spaniard half-Bulgarian by the name of Emanuel Violenia, came forward, claiming that he had seen Pizer stab Chapman with a knife in Hanbury Street. However, on closer examination, the case collapsed. It transpired that Pizer anticipated accusation and had gone out of his way to secure an alibi at all times. This meant that he could prove that he had not left his place in Mulberry Street since the previous Thursday. He was also able to provide an alibi for the night Nichols was murdered. In addition, Violenia's story did not stand up to much scrutiny. As *The Times* put it, 'cross examination so discredited Violenia's evidence that it was wholly distrusted by the police'. Pizer was freed the following day and given a public clearing by the police. At the inquest, Coroner Baxter made it plain that the Pole had no connection with the murders, thus clearing the way for 'Leather Apron' to take legal action against those who had libelled him.

The inquest into Chapman's death was the longest in the Ripper case. It opened on 10 September in the premises of the Working Lads' Institute and lasted through five sittings until the 26th, thirteen days after the deceased was buried. Again no light was thrown on the killer's identity, or how, if the murder took place at around 5.30 a.m. as the evidence suggested, the assailant managed to walk through the streets in near broad daylight without his blood-stained clothing attracting attention.

Reflecting on this point, *The Times* suggested that the culprit did not come from the lower orders, but was more likely to be 'a man lodging in a comparatively decent house in the district, to which he is able to retire quickly and in which, once it was reached, he would be able at his leisure to remove from his person all traces of his hideous crime.' *The Glasgow Herald* believed though that the killer was 'probably a stranger and not a sojourner in the locality', and argued that a 'man with a thirst for blood such as seems to possess this wretch would not be likely to seek gratification at his own door' and 'would naturally go to a place like Whitechapel where opportunities for both perpetration and escape are favourable'.

In his evidence at the inquest, Dr Phillips stated his opinion that Chapman had been dead for two hours when he examined her at 6.30 a.m. He admitted though that the cold and the loss of blood could easily have upset his calculations. He estimated that the weapon used was a 'very sharp knife with a thin narrow blade at least six to eight inches long.' He was sure that it could not have been a bayonet but thought that it could have been a post-mortem knife or a slaughterman's knife 'well ground down.' He also believed that the killer possessed some anatomical knowledge.

With regard to the injuries on the body, Phillips was distinctly reticent. He said that Chapman's tongue and face were swollen and that she had a bruise over her right temple with 'two distinct bruises each the size of the top of a man's thumb on the forepart of the top of the chest.' The throat had been cut twice 'as though an attempt had been made to separate the bones of the neck.' He disclosed that certain portions of the abdomen were missing but declined to elaborate on this or on the mutilations other than to say that all the injuries inflicted on Chapman would have taken at least fifteen minutes to carry out. However, the coroner and the jury refused to accept this treatment and a lively exchange with the doctor ensued:

Dr Phillips: I still feel that in giving these details to the public you are thwarting the ends of justice.

Foreman: We are of the opinion that the evidence should be heard.

Several Jurymen: Hear, Hear.

Coroner: I have carefully considered this matter and I have never before heard of any evidence being kept back.

Phillips: I have not kept it back. I have only considered whether it should be given or not.

Coroner: We have withheld taking this evidence as long as possible because you said the interests of justice might be served by keeping it back.

Phillips: I am of the opinion that what I am about to describe took place after death, so that it could not affect the cause of death, into which you are inquiring.

Coroner: That is only your opinion and might be
repudiated by other medical opinion.

Phillips: Very well. I will give you the results of my post-
mortem.

No newspaper published these details but the medical
journal, *The Lancet*, did:

The abdomen had been entirely laid open; the intestines,
severed from their mesenteric attachments, had been
lifted out of the body, and placed on the shoulder of the
corpse; whilst from the pelvis the uterus and its
appendages with the upper portion of the vagina and the
posterior two-thirds of the bladder, had been entirely
removed. No trace of these parts could be found, and the
incisions were cleanly cut, avoiding the rectum, and
dividing the vagina low enough to avoid injury to the
cervix uteri. . . . Obviously the work was that of an expert
– of one, at least, who had such knowledge of anatomical
or pathological examinations as to be enabled to secure
the pelvic organs with one sweep of the knife. . .

Without question, the most dramatic part of the inquest
was the coroner's summary which was given on 26
September. Baxter began with his version of how the
murderer carried out his attack. Baxter reckoned that 'Judas-
like' the murderer grabbed Chapman by the chin and
suffocated her silently. Baxter also reckoned that the killer
took an organ from the body in a manner which implied
anatomical knowledge and skill in the use of a knife. This
organ and Chapman's rings, which had been wrenched from
her fingers, were still missing.

This was uncontroversial enough, but what Baxter said next
stunned his listeners. He had reached the conclusion that the
killer, far from being a lunatic, had removed the uterus for the

purpose of selling it to an interested party. He explained that within a few hours of the publication in the press of the medical evidence given at the inquest, he had been informed by a leading medical school that some months previously an American had approached a staff member there with a view to obtaining an unspecified number of the type of organs taken from Chapman's body. The American, who was known to have approached another medical school with this request, was willing to pay £20 for each specimen. It was this financial reward, Baxter believed, which was the killer's motive.

The Times took this variation of a Burke and Hare theory seriously and the following day carried an editorial urging the police to investigate Baxter's information. However very soon the letter page of that newspaper was filled with condemnation of the allegations made against the medical profession. *The Lancet* too joined in, calling Baxter's theory 'highly improbable'. Very quickly, the mercenary theory, although a bombshell when disclosed, faded into obscurity, never to be heard of again. Unfortunately, the same could not be said of the killer.

On 19 September, *The Times* carried a report that on the day of the Chapman murder, 'a man changed his clothes in the lavatory of the City News Room, Ludgate Circus, and left hurriedly, leaving behind a shirt, a pair of trousers, and a pair of socks. The attendant threw the discarded clothes into the dustbin and they were taken away in the City sewers cart on the following Monday. The police are said to be endeavouring to trace these clothes but decline to give information on the subject.'

No corroboration of this report, or the result of the police search, can be found. But coincidence or not, a letter, purportedly from the killer and addressed to 'The Boss, Central News Agency, London City' was posted in East London on 27 September. This letter, which is dated 25 September and written in red ink, reads as follows:

Dear Boss,

I keep on hearing the police have caught me but they won't fix me just yet. I have laughed when they look so clever and talk about being on the <u>right</u> track. That joke about Leather Apron gave me real fits. I am down on whores and I shant quit ripping them till I do get buckled. Grand work the last job was. I gave the lady no time to squeal. How can they catch me now. I love my work and want to start again. You will soon hear of me with my funny little games. I saved some of the proper <u>red</u> stuff in a ginger beer bottle over the last job to write with but it went thick like glue and I cant use it. Red ink is fit enough I hope <u>ha</u>. The next job I do I shall clip the ladys ears off and send to the police officers just for jolly wouldnt you. Keep this letter back till I do a bit more work then give it out straight. My knife's so nice and sharp I want to get to work right away if I get a chance. Good Luck.

Yours truly
Jack the Ripper

Dont mind me giving the trade name.

wasnt good enough to post this before I got all the red ink off my hands curse it.

No luck yet. They say I'm a doctor now *ha ha*.

This letter was passed to Scotland Yard which, in accordance with the author's request, decided to keep its existence confidential until or in case the murderer struck again. The police did not have long to wait.

DOUBLE EVENT

The events of 30 September 1888 are among the most remarkable in the annals of British crime. Despite the general furore and public alertness created by the earlier murders and the resultant increased police activity, the Ripper succeeded by 2 a.m. that morning in killing two women, in separate attacks, and escaping once more into the back streets of Whitechapel. He was disturbed after slitting the throat of his first victim, Elizabeth Stride, in Berner Street about 12.45 a.m. and, furious at being deprived of his opportunity to mutilate her, he hurried west towards Aldgate and the City of London. At some point on his journey he met Catherine Eddowes who had just been released from Bishopsgate police station where she had spent several hours sobering up. He murdered her in Mitre Square and then indulged the frenzy which had built up inside him. PC Watkins of the City of London Police found Eddowes' body at 1.45 a.m. looking, as he described her, like 'a pig cut up for market.'

The following day, 1 October, a postcard was sent to the Central News Agency. Partly obscured by what appeared to be bloodstains, it read:

I was not codding dear old Boss when I gave you the tip. Youll hear about saucy Jackys work tomorrow. Double Event this time. Number one squealed a bit. Couldnt finish straight off. Had no time to get ears for police. Thanks for keeping last letter back till I got to work again.
    Jack the Ripper

Elizabeth Stride, known also because of her gangling frame as 'Long Liz', was born Elizabeth Gustafsdotter in Gothenburg, Sweden on 27 November 1843. In the late 1860s she moved to England to work as a domestic servant for a family in the West End of London. In 1869 she married at Sheerness a carpenter by the name of John Thomas Stride. At this point it becomes difficult to discern fact from fiction in Stride's life. She claimed that she had nine children and that she was widowed in September 1878 when the *Princess Alice*, a pleasure steamer, collided with another vessel in the Thames and sank with the loss of over 500 passengers, including her husband and two of her children. Stride claimed that she saved herself by climbing up a rope as the vessel was sinking and that as she did so, another passenger accidentally kicked her in the mouth, knocking out her front teeth. However the evidence suggests that this story is untrue. The name 'Stride' does not appear on the passenger list of the *Princess Alice* and the only father to drown with two children was an accountant called Bell. Also, when Sven Olssen, the clerk of the Swedish Church in Princes Square, St George in the East, told the inquest into her death that although he had known Stride for seventeen years, he had never heard of her having children. It is also worth noting that although her upper front teeth were indeed missing at the time of her death, the post-mortem showed that they had not been removed by a blow to the mouth.

It seems more likely then that Stride invented the *Princess Alice* story to disguise her separation from her husband and to explain away her descent during the 1870s and early 1880s into alcoholism and East End destitution. She spent the last three years of her life as the common-law wife of an Irish labourer by the name of Michael Kidney. She made some living out of cleaning and sewing, but her love of drink got the better of her and this weakness caused her to leave Kidney several times, periods when she doubtless supported herself by prostitution. Kidney was however a tolerant man. He never went after Stride but waited for her to return, which she always did, and believed that she liked him more than any other man. He last saw her alive on the Tuesday before her death. They parted in Commercial Road when Kidney went to work. On returning that night to the lodging house, he found that Stride had gone. He never found out why she had suddenly left him, but he did not think that it was because of another man. His feelings for her seemed to be genuine enough. After identifying her body in the parish mortuary of St Georges in the East, he went out and got

41

drunk. Later that night he stormed into Leman Street police station and astonished the desk officer by declaring, 'If Long Liz had been murdered on my beat, I'd bloody well go out and shoot myself.'

Since 1882, Stride had lived on and off in a lodging house at No. 32 Flower and Dean Street. One day in September 1888, Dr Barnardo, the philanthropist and founder of the boys' home, visited the kitchen of this house and got into conversation with some of the women he found there. The main topic was the murders. Barnardo was struck by the feelings of resignation and despair which the killings had produced. One woman, apparently the worse for drink, stated bitterly, 'No one cares what becomes of us. Perhaps one of us will be killed next.' Barnardo went to view Strides' remains in the mortuary and was shocked to recognise her as one of the frightened creatures who had stood around him in the kitchen that day.

Stride spent the early part of her last evening alive in the company of the deputy of her lodging house, Mrs Elizabeth Tanner, in the Queen's Head public house in Commercial Street. At about 6.30 p.m. the two women walked back to the lodging house where they separated, Stride going to the kitchen and Tanner going elsewhere in the building. Stride was seen later that evening by several people, three of whom gave evidence at the inquest into her death.

The earliest sighting was made by William Marshall, a warehouse labourer. He was standing outside his home in Berner Street at 11.45 p.m. when he saw Stride, whom he recognised in the mortuary both by 'face and dress', talking to a man three doors away. Marshall did not see the man in the dark but he appeared to be middle aged with 'a small black coat and dark trousers.' He heard the man say to the woman in a mild, educated voice, 'You would say anything but your prayers', after which the couple went off together down the street. Stride was seen in Berner Street at around

12.30 a.m. by PC 452 H. William Smith. After viewing Stride in the mortuary he was certain of his identification. He saw the man clearly and provided a description of him which was later circulated by Scotland Yard. The third witness was James Brown, a boxmaker. As he was crossing Berner Street at around 12.45 a.m. to buy some supper from a chandler's shop, he saw a man and woman standing close to the wall of the Board School in Fairclough Street which passed close to the murder site. He looked around when he heard the woman say, 'No, not tonight, some other time', and saw that the man was leaning against the wall over the woman. Strides' companion was wearing a long coat which almost reached his ankles. He appeared to be of stoutish build and around 5ft 7in tall. Brown took no further notice of the couple, but about a quarter of an hour later, while he was still eating his supper, he heard screams of 'Murder!' and 'Police!'.

The various descriptions of the Ripper will be discussed later. It is sufficient to say now that between 12.45 a.m. and 1 a.m., Stride accompanied a man to No. 40 Berners Street, an address which was also known as Dutfields Yard. This was a court off the main street and separated from it by high walls and a pair of large wooden gates, one of which was fitted with a wicket door for ease of entry when the main gates were closed, which was rare. On the night of the murder, the gates were open. At the time of the murder the houses on the left of the court were quiet. These were terraced cottages and the occupants, mostly tailors and cigarette makers, had already turned in. The building on the right, the socialist International Working Men's Educational Club, was still active and noisy. A debate entitled 'The Necessity for Socialism Amongst Jews' had been held earlier that evening and this had been followed by an impromptu party which carried on into Sunday morning. The lights from this party, which was held on the upper storey of the club, were the only illumination in the court. These lights fell onto the cottages directly opposite, but left the rest of the yard in inky darkness. On the night of the murder, Berner Street too was unlit. In describing the entrance to the yard, *The Times* said that for 'a distance of 18ft or 20ft from the street there is a dead wall on each side of the court, the effect of which is to enshroud the intervening space in absolute darkness after sunset.' This was obviously a suitable place for a street prostitute to take a client and it was here that Stride and the Ripper went together, but with very different purposes in mind.

The steward of the International Working Men's Club was Louis Diemschutz. He lived on the premises with his wife. She assisted in the running of the club, for Diemschutz was also a traveller in cheap costume jewellery which he hawked from the back of his pony-drawn cart. He had spent Saturday at a market in Crystal Palace and did not return home until 1 a.m. on Sunday morning. He was sure of the time for he checked the clock in the baker's shop at the corner of Berner Street as he passed. When he turned into the yard however his pony suddenly shied to the left and refused to go forward. He peered into the darkness to his right but managed only to make out a vague shape on the ground. He prodded it with the handle of his whip, but to no effect. He dismounted and lit a match which in the windy night was blown out almost straight away. The brief flash of light was sufficient though to show Diemschutz that what lay at his feet was a woman who was either drunk or dead.

Anxious about his wife, Diemschutz rushed into the club. After finding her safe in the kitchen, he picked up a candle and went back into the yard with some members. They found that the woman's throat had been cut and that a large quantity of blood – Diemschutz reckoned about two quarts – had flowed onto the cobblestones. The men lifted Stride's head and shoulders from the ground. As they did so, they found that her body was still warm, although her clothes were damp from the rain. They also saw that in one hand she still gripped a bag of cachous. She also had a small bunch of flowers attached to her black fur-trimmed jacket.

Alerted by cries from the club, the police were on the scene within minutes. They quickly sealed off the yard and carried out a thorough search of the court and all the buildings in it. This failed though to produce any sign of the killer. An examination of the hands and clothes of the people found in the yard and a search of their person also proved negative. Everyone in the yard was questioned and made to give their names and addresses. This was an arduous process as far as the socialist club members were concerned, for many of the twenty-eight members present that night were newly-arrived immigrants from Eastern Europe with only limited knowledge of English and the police did not finish their immediate inquiries in the yard until 5 a.m., half an hour after Strides' body was taken to the mortuary.

This questioning at least established that Stride could not have entered the yard until about 12.45 a.m. William West, a printer and club member, said that he walked through the yard at 12.30 a.m. and saw nothing suspicious then. Morris Eagle, another club member, returned to the club at 12.45 a.m., but saw nothing out of the ordinary. At 12.45 a.m., a Russian member called Joseph Lave walked over to the very spot where Strides' body was found fifteen minutes later. He was quoted as saying, 'The court was very dark, and so I had to grope my way along the right hand wall. I would have stumbled over the body if it had been there at the time.'

The time of death suggested by the above evidence was confirmed by the first doctor to examine Strides' body, Frederick William Blackwell of the nearby London Hospital. Arriving in the yard at 1.10 a.m., he estimated that Stride had been dead for about twenty minutes to half an hour. He found that her throat had been cut by a single sweep of the knife, but that no mutilations had been made to her body.

Clearly the Ripper had been interrupted by Diemschutz. But how had he escaped from the yard undetected? As far as is known, access to the court could only be made via the gateway. It is unlikely that the Ripper scaled the walls of the yard and a police examination the following day indicated that no one had done so. It seems almost certain then that as Diemschutz suddenly turned into the yard, the Ripper withdrew into the darkness and waited until the salesman rushed into the club before sneaking through the gateway into Berner Street. Indeed it has been suggested that it was not Stride's body and freshly split blood which caused the pony to shy, but the malicious presence of the murderer.

If this reconstruction is correct, then the Ripper was, once again, very lucky. A Mrs Mortimer, who lived only four doors from the murder site stood outside her house between 12.30 and 1 a.m. She saw nothing unusual and did not notice anyone enter No. 40. It would appear that she re-entered her house only a few minutes before Diemschutz arrived home, flushing the Ripper out of the yard. If Mrs Mortimer had remained outside her house a little longer, she would surely have caught sight of the murderer fleeing from the scene of the crime.

On leaving Berner street, the Ripper chose to travel west towards the eastern boundary of the City of London. At about the same time as he began this 10–15 minute journey, Catherine Eddowes, a tiny bird-like woman, was released from Bishopsgate police station in the City. Eddowes was 43 years old, but looked far older in consequence of her love of drink and the Bright's disease which was ravaging her body. She had been taken into police custody at a quarter to nine the previous evening by PC 931 who found her drunk in a street in Aldgate. She was impersonating a fire engine and had attracted a crowd. The constable had tried to stand her against a wall but she kept falling down. On arrival at the station, she refused to give her name and address and was placed in a cell.

It was then the normal policy of the City police, unlike its Metropolitan counterpart, to release drunks once they had sobered up, and not to bring them before a Magistrate. By 1 a.m. Eddowes was thought fit to be released. On departure she gave her name as Mary Ann Kelly of 6 Fashion Street, Spitalfields, and with a 'Good night, old cock' to the duty officer, she left the station in the direction of Houndsditch and Mitre Square which were only a few hundred yards away.

It is not known when the Ripper and Eddowes met, but from what has been said above, it could not have been much before 1.15 a.m. Nor is it known if they met in Mitre Square or went there together after meeting elsewhere. All that can be said with certainty is that Eddowes' grossly mutilated body was found in the south-west corner of that small square at 1.45 a.m. by PC Watkins who swore that the corpse had not been there when he inspected the area fifteen minutes before.

The sight was indeed difficult to miss. The woman lay on her back with her head turned to the left. Her right leg was bent but her left leg lay extended straight from her body. Her arms were outstretched away from her body. Her face was a mass of cuts. A large gash extended from the side of her nose to her jaw. Her upper lip had been sliced through and both her eyelids nicked. An attempt had apparently been made to sever her right ear. Her throat had been cut from left to right for a length of about six inches. Her clothes had been pulled up and her stomach ripped open upwards from groin to sternum. Some of her intestines had been lifted from her stomach and draped over her right shoulder. Another piece of intestine had been placed between the left arm and the body.

The Ripper was nothing if not bold, but in killing Eddowes in Mitre Square he threw all caution to the wind, a clear sign of his desperate state of mind. The square, which lies just north of the Minories and west of the Aldgate, had three entrances in 1888, a main thoroughfare to Mitre Street and two passages leading respectively to Duke Street and St James Place. It was patrolled by a policeman every fifteen minutes. There was a watchman on duty on the night of the murder, an employee of Kearley and Tonge whose warehouse lined two sides of the square. PC Richard Pearse lived directly opposite the spot where Eddowes was found, but he heard nothing during the night. Despite these risks, the Ripper struck once more in a public place and escaped without detection. On this occasion he took with him as he hurried towards Whitechapel the uterus and left kidney of his victim, together with a piece of her apron which he apparently used to clean the blade of his knife.

On finding the body of Eddowes, PC Watkins rushed immediately to the warehouse watchman for help. The woman was obviously dead and the constable's first duty was to raise the alarm, for the killer could only have left the Square a few minutes before. The watchman, George James Morris, was an ex-policeman and therefore knew what action to take. After briefly viewing the body, he rushed up Mitre Street blowing his whistle, a more effective means of attracting attention than the rattle with which Watkins was equipped. Morris saw nobody suspicious and two policemen soon answered his whistle. In this way, word of the murder was spread.

In the autumn of 1888, the City Police, which was responsible for its ancient square mile charge to the Corporation of the City of London and not to the Home Office as was the case with the much larger Metropolitan Police, was under the actual command of the Assistant Commissioner, Major Henry Smith, the Commissioner, Sir James Fraser, then being on the verge of retirement. Smith was a very different man from Charles Warren. Popular and possessed of a sense of humour (his memoirs are subtitled, *The Story of Sixty Years, Most of them Misspent*), he had a flexible and practical approach to his work as can be seen from the measures he said he took during the Ripper investigation. In an attempt to find out as much as possible about the murders he put nearly a third of his force into plain clothes. 'It was subversive of discipline', he admitted, 'but I had them well supervised by the senior officers'. With regard to his men's enquiries, he wrote, 'The weather was lovely and I have little doubt that they enjoyed themselves, sitting on door steps, smoking their pipes, hanging about public houses, and gossiping with all and sundry.' He also took two other steps; he made discreet enquiries into the butchers and slaughtermen working in the City and he gave instructions that every man and woman seen together after midnight were to be stopped and questioned. If this last order had been heeded, Eddowes might not have been murdered.

The night of the murder found Smith in the Cloak Lane police station close to Southwark Bridge. He had gone to bed but the combination of the noise from the railway depot in front of the station and the stench from the furriers to the rear had made sleep impossible. In the weeks since Chapman's murder, Smith had begun to think that the killer had either gone abroad or given up his work. However, when the bell next to his bed rang at 2 a.m., any such thoughts were immediately dispelled. There had been another murder: this time in the City. Within minutes he was dressed and on his way to Mitre Square in a hansom cab with a fifteen-stone Superintendent beside him and three detectives clinging to the back, the whole carriage rolling 'like a "seventy four" in a gale', in Smith's own graphic phrase.

Smith's journey that night did not end in Mitre Square. After inspecting Eddowes' body, he led his men in hot pursuit of the killer across the City boundary into Whitechapel. Part of the Ripper's flight could be traced. From Mitre Square, he had gone north east across Houndsditch into Goulston Street where in the passageway of a dwelling house he dropped the piece of apron he had taken from the victim, and, apparently, chalked a message on the wall. He had then made his way to a public sink in Dorset Street where he cleaned the night's work from his hands. Not all the bloodstained water had drained away when Smith arrived on the scene. But after that the trail went cold. Smith travelled around the area until daybreak, hoping in vain for an arrest. At 6 a.m. he gave up the ghost and went to bed feeling 'completely defeated'. It is unfortunate that before retiring he did not visit the scene of 'the writing on the wall' in Goulston Street, for if he had he might have been able to dissuade Sir Charles Warren from destroying this potentially important piece of evidence.

The piece of apron, a bloodsoaked rag in appearance, was found by PC 254 Long at 2.55 a.m. in the passageway of Nos 118–19 Goulston Street. (According to the autopsy report, the seams of this fragment corresponded with the rest of Eddowes' apron, virtually confirming that the portion was genuine.) On the dado wall above it, there was written in what has been described as a 'round schoolboy hand' the chalked message:

> The Juwes are
> The men that
> will not
> be Blamed
> for nothing

The constable searched the staircase but on finding no one hurried to Commercial Road police station with the piece of apron and news of the message. On learning of this, Major Smith sent Detective Sergeant Halse of the City Police to Goulston Street with instructions to photograph the writing when there was sufficient light. Goulston Street was however the responsibility of the Metropolitan Police and Superintendent Arnold, who was in charge of the Whitechapel Division, saw the writing as an incitement against the Jewish population. He wanted the writing erased but did not wish to take the responsibility for doing so. He sent an Inspector to the site to stand by with a sponge awaiting a decision from a senior officer. (In Arnold's defence it must be remembered that he was dealing simultaneously with enquiries into Stride's murder).

Shortly after 5 a.m. Warren himself arrived at Goulston Street. Suggestions were put to him that only the top line of the message, or even the single word 'Juwes' should be rubbed out, or that the area should be cordoned off. Halse asked for the erasing to be deferred until dawn, only an hour or so away, so that a photograph could be taken. But Warren would have none of this. He ordered the writing to be copied down and then immediately scrubbed clean. Smith claims that Warren obliterated the message with his hand. Warren went later to the headquarters of the City Police to explain his action. Smith was however already asleep and Warren was met instead by the head of the City CID, Mr McWilliams, who told him bluntly that the erasure was a mistake.

This was a verdict with which Smith concurred. As he wrote later, 'The writing on the wall may have been – and, I think, probably was written – to throw the police off the scent, to divert suspicion from the Gentiles and throw it upon the Jews. It may have been written by the murderer, or it may not. To obliterate the words that might have given us a most valuable clue, more especially after I had sent a man to stand over them until they were photographed, was not only indiscreet, but unwarrantable.' Sir Robert Anderson, Head of the Metropolitan CID, also condemned the erasure, although he did not actually name the officer responsible. 'It was done by officers of the uniformed branch in the division upon an order issued by one of my colleagues.'

To his credit, Warren accepted full responsibility for the removal of the message. In a letter to the Home Secretary explaining his actions, he stated his belief that the message had been written to turn the local people against the Jews and that if the words, which he did not think could have been satisfactorily concealed from the public, had still been in place when daylight broke, riots could have ensued. It is true that the Ripper murders had created a wave of anti-semitism throughout the East End. John Pizer, the original 'Leather Apron', was a Polish Jew and he had been forced to remain in police custody even after establishing his alibi for fear that a mob which had gathered outside the police station would have lynched him, innocent or not. Warren therefore had some justification in fearing that the message would cause an outbreak of violence against the Jewish population. However it is difficult to believe that a compromise could not have been reached and that the passageway could not have been cordoned off from the public until there was sufficient light for a photograph to be taken.

* * * * *

After being examined in site by the City Surgeon, Frederick Gordon Brown, and his assistant, George W. Sequeira, Eddowes' body was taken to the City mortuary in Golden Lane where it was prepared for the post-mortem. The immediate problem facing the police was identification, there being nothing on the body which linked it directly to the woman who had earlier been released from Bishopsgate police station. The victim had the appearance of a common lodging-house dweller. These people were in the habit of carrying their world possessions about with them and this seemed to be with the case with the murdered woman. *The Times* carried the following inventory of her personal effects:

> . . . a piece of string, a common white handkerchief with a red border, a match box with cotton on it, a white linen pocket containing a white bone handle table knife, very

blunt (with no blood on it) two short clay pipes, a red cigarette case with white metal fittings . . . a check pocket containing five pieces of soap, a small tin box containing tea and sugar, a portion of a pair of spectacles, a three-cornered check handkerchief, and a large white linen pocket containing a small comb, a red mitten and a ball of worsted.

However it was none of these objects which led to the identification of Eddowes, but two pawn tickets in a tin box which were found beside her corpse. One of the pawn tickets, for a pair of men's boots which had fetched 1s 6d, was made out in the name of Kelly. These details were published in the press and read on the following Tuesday by John Kelly, the man with whom Eddowes had been living for the past seven years. He identified the body and provided the police with information on Eddowes' background.

Catherine Eddowes, the daughter of a tinplate worker, was born in the Midlands but grew up in London. When she was nineteen, she ran away from home with a soldier by the name of Thomas Conway, whose initials she had tattooed on her forearm. She stayed with Conway for eleven years and had three children by him, but, as far as Kelly knew, the couple never married. They split up because of Eddowes' drinking habits. It later transpired that Conway and the children took steps to avoid Eddowes. Conway changed his name to Quinn and the children apparently moved without leaving forwarding addresses.

Kelly and Eddowes paired up after they were thrown together several times in the lodging house where they stayed. Kelly was an odd job worker in the market and Eddowes occasionally charred. She drank, but Kelly at least did not find her behaviour troublesome. To augment their income during the summer, the couple went hop picking in the neighbouring counties. They had not done well that year and they had decided to walk back to London from Kent on the Thursday before Eddowes' death. They arrived back penniless and Kelly was forced to pawn his boots so that he could buy something to eat. The following day Kelly earned a sixpence. He wished to buy food with it, but at Eddowes' insistence spent 4*d* on a bed for himself in the lodging house. Eddowes passed the night at the Mile End casual ward where the bed took up the remaining 2*d*. Kelly last saw Eddowes at 2 p.m. on the day before she was murdered. Eddowes said that she intended to visit her daughter in Bermondsey and that she hoped to be back by 4 p.m. Kelly later heard that she had been locked up for drunkenness, but made no enquiries about her as he felt sure that she would turn up the following day.

* * * * *

The inquest into the death of Elizabeth Stride was held in the vestry hall in Cable Street under Coroner Baxter. The medical evidence was given by Dr Blackwell, the first doctor to examine Stride, and Dr George Phillips who assisted Blackwell in the post-mortem and who, it will be recalled, had handled the Chapman autopsy.

As previously mentioned, Dr Blackwell estimated that Stride had been dead for about twenty minutes to half an hour when he arrived in the yard off Berner Street. He found Stride lying obliquely across the passage on her left side but looking towards the right wall. Her legs were drawn up with her feet close to the right wall of the court. The top of her dress had been unfastened around the neck. Her open right hand was lying on her chest smeared with blood. Her left hand was on the ground clutching a small packet of cachous wrapped in tissue paper. Her face appeared placid. Around her neck there was a silk scarf, the bow of which had been pulled very tight to the left. Blackwell thought that the murderer had done this in order to pull Stride backwards and cut her throat. The incision in her throat ran from left to right. It severed the blood vessels on the left and sliced the windpipe completely in two. It ran exactly along the lower edge of the scarf, which had been slightly frayed in the process. Blackwell could not say whether Stride's throat was cut as she had been falling or when she was on the ground. He pointed out though that the blood would have spurted out in a stream if her throat had been cut while she was standing up. He also pointed out that Stride would have bled to death comparatively slowly because the vessels had been cut on only one side of the neck and the artery had not been completely severed.

Dr Phillips testified that in his opinion the murderer had seized Stride by the shoulders and forced her to the ground. This was indicated by the bruising over both of her shoulders and beneath her collar bone. From the bloodstains he thought it obvious that Strides' throat was not cut until she was lying down. With regard to the rest of the examination, he had found that Stride had once had tuberculosis and that her right leg had been badly set after a fracture and was slightly deformed. At the time of death, her stomach was full and contained partly digested cheese, potatoes, and farinaceous powder. He had found no trace of poison, ruling out the theory that the Ripper first drugged his victims. All the teeth in Strides' lower jaw were missing.

A knife had been found in Whitechapel Road at 12.30 a.m. on the night of the murder by Thomas Coram, a warehouse employee, who drew the attention of a passing policeman to it. The knife, which had a dagger-shaped blade about 9–10 inches long, was lying in a doorway with a bloodstained handkerchief tied around the handle with string. The doctors remarked on the knife's rounded point which meant that it would have been unsuitable for the purpose Strides' killer had in mind. They conceded though that it could have been used to cut her throat. (It is not at all clear why so much importance was attached to this knife; it was after all found before the estimated time of Strides' death.)

The inquest into the death of Catherine Eddowes was held at the Golden Lane mortuary in the City of London. It opened on 4th October and was presided over by the City Coroner, Mr. S.F. Langham. The deceased was formally identified by her sister, Eliza Gold, who gave Eddowes a good character reference, describing her as of 'sober habits.' Frederick Wilkinson, the keeper of Eddowes' lodging house, also spoke well of her. She did drink, he admitted, but she was a jolly, well-liked person. And he had never heard of being intimate with anyone other than John Kelly. As far as he knew, she had not been in the habit of walking the streets.

At this inquest, there was no reticence about giving the full findings of the post-mortem, and Dr Brown, the surgeon of the City of London police, gave a very detailed report on the wounds suffered by Eddowes. In the cross-examination, Dr Brown stated that the cause of death was loss of blood from the cut in the throat and that this was done when the victim was on the ground. He did not think that there had been any struggle and attributed the silence with which the murderer killed his victim to the instantaneous severing of her throat. He also said that the mutilations, which he reckoned took at least five minutes to complete, were made after death with a sharp-pointed knife whose blade was at least 6in long. He believed the murderer acted alone and that he would not have had much blood on his person. He was of the opinion that the removal of Eddowes' kidney indicated that the murderer had some medical knowledge. He had no explanation though as to why the killer should wish to take this kidney and the uterus with him. He also believed that the killer carried out the mutilations while kneeling between Eddowes' legs.

A commercial traveller by the name of Joseph Lawende testified that at about 1.35 a.m. on the night of the murder, he saw a man and a woman standing together in Church Passage which leads to Mitre Square. The woman was three or four inches shorter than her companion who wore a peaked cloth cap. Lawende saw the woman place her hand on the man but not to shove him away. He did not see the woman's face but believed that her clothes were identical to those he saw later on the deceased in the mortuary. With the permission of the jury, the coroner prevented the witness from describing the man on the grounds that this disclosure may hinder subsequent police enquiries. A description based on Lawende's evidence later appeared in the *Police Gazette* and this will be discussed in due course.

The two inquests returned the by now familiar verdict, wilful murder against a person or persons unknown. Elizabeth Stride was buried in a pauper's grave. Eddowes, by contrast, was interred with much ceremony in the City of London cemetery at Ilford on 8 October. Her coffin received a police escort and the route was lined with bystanders, many of whom stood bareheaded. Two mourning coaches followed the hearse and behind came a large wagon carrying women, 'the majority of whom', in the words of the *East London Advertiser*, 'were attired in a style not at all befitting to the occasion.' John Kelly and Eddowes' four sisters walked behind the coffin to the graveside. Eddowes' husband, Thomas Conway, did not attend. He had not come forward after the murder and he was not located by the police until the middle of October. His excuse for not presenting himself earlier was that he had not been reading the newspapers.

WAR ON WARREN

The double murder brought the East End to the verge of boiling point. It was not simply fear that the inhabitants felt, although this was understandably the dominant emotion.

There was anger too at the incompetence of the police, resentment at the refusal of the government to offer a reward for the capture of the killer, and worry by local merchants and innkeepers at the damage being done by the murders to late night business. There was shame too in some quarters at the notoriety which had befallen the area.

Naturally blame for this sorry state of affairs was laid squarely at the feet of the Home Secretary, Henry Matthews, and the Commissioner of Police, Sir Charles Warren, and very soon there were renewed calls for their resignation from both press and public. As far as the East End was concerned, Warren was by far the main target for abuse. He was already hated for his attitude towards the lower orders, and people in the East End needed little encouragement to attack him. At least five meetings were held in the district on the afternoon of Sunday 30 September, the day of the double murders. All called for the resignation of Warren. One speaker described Warren as the enemy of the working classes and declared that if the Commissioner set foot in the East End he would be hanged from the nearest lamp post.

Warren could have helped himself greatly if he had tried to make use of the press. However, he made no serious attempt to improve his relations with the Fourth Estate. Far from taking the press into his confidence and explaining his conduct of the hunt for the Ripper, he refused to allow any of his officers to talk to journalists. The press responded in kind, taking every opportunity to criticise and ridicule him. It was, declared *The Star*, 'War on Warren'.

The release of the 'Jack the Ripper' letter and postcard on 2 October increased tension still further. The boastful contempt of the author for the police and his spine-chilling name sent shock waves throughout the whole country. The missives were reproduced in facsimile form and posted up around London together with a request for anyone recognising the handwriting to contact the police. As far as is known this step produced no worthwhile leads. These original communications were however soon followed by a stream of others purporting to come from the killer. Some but not all were signed 'Jack the Ripper'. Some were written in verse, although most were in prose. The Ripper correspondence will be discussed in detail later, but one letter, a package in fact, should be mentioned here.

On the evening of 16 October, Mr George Lusk, the Chairman of the Whitechapel Vigilance Committee, received at his home in Alderney Road, Mile End, a small cardboard box through the post. The box gave off an offensive odour and on opening it, Lusk found something which looked like a bodily organ, and a letter which read:

Mr Lusk   From Hell

Sir I send you half the kidne I took from one woman praesarved it for you tother piece I fried and ate it was very nise I may send you the bloody knif that took it out if you only wate a whil longer

Signed   Catch me while you can Mishter Lusk

Lusk, who had already received at least one letter supposedly from the killer, thought at first that this was a hoax. However after consulting his colleagues on the Vigilance Committee, he took the box and its contents to Mr F.S. Reed, a local doctor. Reed thought the fleshy substance to be half of a human kidney which had been divided longitudinally and asked Dr Openshaw, the pathological curator at the London Hospital for his opinion. Openshaw found by the use of his microscope that the object was indeed part of a left human kidney which had been taken from the body of an adult. In view of the fact that Eddowes' left kidney was known to have been removed by the murderer, the package was handed over to the City Police. The press, perhaps unwilling to believe the worst, treated this development with scepticism and claimed that the kidney came from an animal or a corpse which had been dissected in a hospital for medical research. As shall be seen, Major Smith thought otherwise.

The air of panic which then existed in Whitechapel was made vivid by Walter Dew, the policeman who became famous as the man who arrested Dr Crippen, but who during the Ripper murders was a constable in the East End. One day while on plain clothes duty with another officer named Stacey, Dew spotted a wanted and violent criminal who was known as 'Squibby'. Before he could be detained though, Squibby turned and ran off down Commercial Street, with Dew and his friend in pursuit, truncheons drawn. On seeing this, spectators jumped to conclusions. They started to shout 'Jack the Ripper! Jack the Ripper!', and joined in the chase. As Dew chased his suspect, he heard hundreds of people running behind him. Squibby was a notoriously tough character and when the two policeman eventually cornered him in the upstairs of a house, they prepared themselves for a fight. They were astonished then when they found him trembling with fear. They soon realised though that he was not frightened of them, but of the mob which had gathered outside and was calling for him to be lynched.

The crowd refused to be calmed or to listen to police calls that Squibby was not the Ripper. It saw the arrival of police reinforcements as proof of his guilt and became even more insistent in its demands for his blood. When Squibby finally left the house for the police station, the crowd made a determined, and nearly successful, attempt to break through his police escort and grab him. He travelled part of the way in a 'four wheeler' carriage, but this had to be abandoned when the crowd showed that it was quite capable of overturning it. Even after Squibby reached the station, the crowd refused to give up and several times tried to storm the building. It was many hours before order was restored and the crowd persuaded to disperse.

It would not be surprising if Squibby was carrying a bag when he was first spotted by the mob, because word had spread that the Ripper carried his knife in a black bag (or Gladstone bag). So deeply entrenched did this image of the bag as a symbol of murder become that it has remained a firm part of the Ripper legend over the years. It is not known though how this association arose for, as will be seen later, no mention of a bag appears in any of the descriptions of the killer. As far as can be seen though the link with the bag stems from the statement made by Mrs Mortimer who stood in Berner Street from 12.30 a.m. to 1 a.m. on the night of Strides' death. She saw a man, aged about 30 and carrying a black bag, hurry down the street towards Ellen Street. However this man was later identified as a member of the socialist club who had nothing to do with the murders. Another possible explanation for the bag link may lie in the evidence of Albert Backer of Newnham Street, Whitechapel. On the night before the double murder, Backer got into conversation with a man in the Three Nuns Hotel in Aldgate. The man, whom Backer thought to be shifty and up to no good, wished to know what sort of women used the hotel bar and where they went afterwards. In his description of the man, Backer said he wore black clothes, a black hat, and carried a black bag.

However the genesis of the bag legend may lie elsewhere, for a man carrying a Gladstone bag was taken into police custody on the night of the double murder, according to Robert Clifford Spicer of Saville Row who, in a letter to *The Daily Express* on 16 March 1931, claimed that as a young constable he captured Jack the Ripper that night and took him to Commercial Street police station only to see him released by the Inspectors handling the Ripper investigation.

In his letter, Spicer said that on the night of the double murder, he decided to walk his beat backwards, a ruse commonly used in those days to make life more difficult for criminals. At around 1.45 a.m. in an alley off Henage Street, he saw a man and a woman sitting together on a brick-built dustbin. He recognised the woman as 'Rosy', a known prostitute. She had a two shilling piece in her hand. Spicer had never seen the man before but he felt instantly that he was the murderer. He was well dressed with a 'high hat, black suit with silk facings, and a gold watch and chain', but he had blood on the cuffs of his shirt. He was carrying a Gladstone bag. He refused to explain his presence in the alley with Rosy, telling Spicer that this was none of his business. Spicer disagreed and led him to Commercial Street police station with Rosy in tow. The suspect remained calm and offered no resistance. The arrest though attracted attention and on the way to the station, people began to cheer and shout that the killer had been caught. Some women, in Spicer's words, 'were so excited that they ran half naked into the street'.

However any hopes of fame and glory Spicer may have had were dashed when he reached the station. Eight Inspectors attached to the Ripper case were on duty at the time and they were not impressed by Spicer's action. They accepted the suspect's story that he was a Brixton doctor and, on learning that Rosy had no complaint about him, released him without asking him to explain the blood on his cuffs or to open his bag for inspection. Spicer was in fact reprimanded by the Duty Inspector for detaining a respectable doctor. In reply, Spicer asked rhetorically what a respectable doctor was doing with a prostitute in an alley in the early hours of the morning.

This incident so disillusioned Spicer that he left the Metropolitan Police some months later. He saw the 'doctor' on several subsequent occasions at Liverpool Street station accosting women and always carrying his bag. Spicer used to shout, 'Hello, Jack. Still after them?', at which the man would immediately flee. Spicer described him as 'about 5ft 8in or 9in and about twelve stone, fair moustache, high forehead and rosy cheeks.

The double murder brought renewed calls for the offer of a reward for the capture of the murderer. The principle of a reward was an important one for the inhabitants of the East End, many of whom attributed government policy to simple class distinction. But there were also strong financial considerations. The murders were seriously damaging late night business throughout the district and it is no coincidence that most of the leading figures in the campaign for the offer of a reward, and in the various Vigilance Committees which sprang up, were local tradesmen, shopkeepers, and merchants.

George Lusk, the recipient of the purported Eddowes' kidney, was such a man. On behalf of the Whitechapel Vigilance Committee, he submitted a petition to Queen Victoria calling for the introduction of a reward. The Queen however declined to accept the petition on the advice of the Home Secretary who informed her that it was not the policy of her government to offer rewards. The government had in fact outlined that policy in a letter to the Mile End Vigilance Committee which had sought the offer of a government reward after the Chapman murder:

I am directed by the Secretary of State to acknowledge receipt of your letter of 16th, with reference to the question of the offer of a reward for the discovery of the perpetrators of the recent murders in Whitechapel, and I am to inform you that had the Secretary of State considered the case a proper one for the offer of a reward, he would at once have offered one on behalf of the Government, but that the practice of offering rewards for the discovery of criminals was discontinued some years ago, because experience showed that such offers of reward tended to produce more harm than good. And the Secretary of State is satisfied that there is nothing in the circumstances of the present case to justify a departure from this rule.

I am, Sir,
Your Obedient Servant,
G. Leigh Pemberton

Warren in fact pressed the Home Secretary to issue a reward. It certainly would not have been difficult for the government to justify an exception being made of the Ripper case. The murders were without precedent and were already assuming the proportions of a national scare. Moreover, it is highly unlikely that anyone could ever have been framed for the Ripper murders. There was certainly a recent precedent for offering a reward in respect of a particularly outrageous crime. In May 1882, Lord Frederick Cavendish, the Chief Secretary of Ireland, and his senior civil servant, Thomas Henry Burke, were murdered by Irish terrorists in Phoenix Park in Dublin. The government offered the very large sum of £10,000 for information leading to the capture of the assassins. Cavendish was not just a Lord; he was also the nephew of the then Prime Minister, William Gladstone. These were facts which were not lost on George Lusk, but it was in vain that he wrote to *The Times* arguing that a generous reward would 'convince the poor and humble residents of our East End that the government authorities are as much anxious to avenge the blood of these unfortunate victims as they were the assassination of Lord Cavendish and Mr. Burke.'

The offer of a reward might have generated a much-needed feeling of empathy between Whitechapel and Whitehall. Whether it would have led to the arrest of Jack the Ripper is an entirely different matter. If there is one certainty about the Ripper it is that he was a loner. He worked alone and in all probability lived alone. Only a close relative or friend was likely to have known his identity and such a person would probably not have been persuaded by the promise of financial gain to turn him over to the authorities. Support for this view can be found in the lack of response to the rewards which were offered. Within a day of Eddowes' death, the City of London offered £500. Simon Montagu, an East End MP, put up another £500 from his own pocket. A further £100 was offered by the Tower Hamlets Battalion. These were substantial sums of money in 1888, but they did not elicit one serious claim.

While the East End businessmen were worried about financial matters, local women sought to repair the damage done to the reputation of their district. In the three days after the double murder a petition, which was largely organised by the wife of Reverend Barnett, was signed by over 4,000 East End women and sent to the Queen through the Home Secretary. The petition read:

To Our Most Gracious Lady Queen Victoria

Madam:
We, the women of East London, feel horror at the dreadful sins that have been lately committed in our midst and grief because of the shame that has befallen the neighbourhood. By the facts which have come out in the inquests, we have learned much of the lives of those of our sisters who have lost a firm hold on goodness and who are living sad and degraded lives. We call on your servants in authority and bid them put the law which already exists in motion to close bad houses within whose walls such wickedness is done, and men and women ruined in body and soul.

We are, Madam, your loyal and humble subjects.

Queen Victoria did not need this petition to bring the murders to her attention for, as shall be seen, she was already taking an active interest in them. This was an interest which her subjects shared. The stream of letters on the murders to the press and the police which started in earnest after the Chapman killing turned into a torrent after the 'double event'. According to Warren's biographer, Watkin Williams, Scotland Yard received 1,200 letters a day on the killings. In the correspondence pages of the London newspapers, the murders became the dominant subject.

The letters varied in nature and intent. A few writers offered their assistance in the hunt for the killer. Many letters were concerned with the Ripper's identity, some merely stating the sort of man the killer had to be, others actually naming a suspect. Richard Mansfield, the American actor who played the title roles in the stage production of *Dr Jekyll and Mr Hyde* which was then showing in London, was one man so named, the accuser being convinced that Mansfield's performance was too realistic to be an act. Most letters though carried suggestions about how the murders could be prevented or the Ripper captured.

Some were sensible, such as that street lighting in the area should be improved and that Whitechapel should be patrolled by policemen on bicycles. Other ideas were worth consideration, for example that armed policemen should be disguised as women and used as decoys. One correspondent to *The Times*, Frances Power-Cobbe, went further and called for the introduction of female detectives. She argued that such women would be able not only to move quietly and without suspicion throughout Whitechapel, but also to 'extract gossip freely.' In her opinion, a female detective 'would be in a position to employ for whatever it may be worth that gift of intuitive quickness and 'mother wit' with which her sex is commonly credited.'

Many letters were clearly the work of pranksters or mentally unbalanced people. One writer claimed that the purpose of the murders was the overthrow of the Empire and its replacement by a republic. Another declared that the murders were carried out by Germans who disguised themselves by gluing the skins of dead people over their own. At least these Germans were not republicans, for their objective was to obtain the Crown of England as well as the Colonies, India, and the New World.

There is no evidence that, for all their number and variety, these letters produced any worthwhile lead in the murder hunt and it would seem that the greatest effect they had was the additional strain they placed on police resources through having to be read, processed, answered, and investigated. There was though one suggestion which the police adopted, or at least agreed with. This was to deaden the noise made by their boots. F.P. Wensley, who rose to become the Head of the Metropolitan CID, was a plodding constable in Whitechapel during the murders. He recalls in his memoirs, *Detective Days*, that he and his colleagues nailed strips of rubber, usually cut from old bicycle tyres, to the soles of their boots.

The most visible measure taken by the police after the 'double event' was to flood the East End with men, both plain clothed and uniformed officers (Wensley was himself such a draftee). *The Daily Chronicle* on 8 October described the scene in and around Whitechapel on the first Saturday night after the double slaying when, following the receipt of another (and still unidentified) Jack the Ripper letter, it was widely feared that the killer would strike again, and the whole area was in a state of great agitation.

A *Daily Chronicle* reporter visiting the East End at 11 p.m. that night was impressed by the police activity he witnessed. He found the yard of Leman Street police station to be crammed with uniformed constables drawn from every division in London. The constables were parading to receive their orders before going on patrol, and so numerous were they that this process lasted until midnight. Hundreds of plain clothes men were already on the streets, but others were still in the station awaiting instructions. The journalist wondered when there had last been such an assembly of detectives and was struck by the resolve of the officers to catch the killer.

So strong was the police presence that, according to the article, it seemed impossible for the Ripper to appear without detection. In the quieter streets the only men seen were plain clothes officers. The City Police had more than doubled their patrols, thereby ensuring that every spot in the various beats, however obscure, was inspected every five minutes. The City force also positioned men at fixed distances with orders to look out for suspicious characters and, if necessary, to follow them. The article assured readers that these special arrangements applied equally to other parts of the Metropolis in case the Ripper, on finding the East End too dangerous to operate in, decided to move to another district. In particular the parks, where the journalist believed the Ripper would easily find a victim, were being well patrolled.

The police enquiries into the Stride murder were outlined in a report to the Home Secretary by Chief Inspector Swanson. Dated 19 October, this report was accompanied by a letter from Warren who, in somewhat strained language, stated, 'Very numerous and searching inquiries have been made in all directions and with regard to all kind of suggestions which have been made. These have had no tangible result as far as the Whitechapel murders.'

The report itself contained the following information:

. . . 80,000 pamphlets to occupiers were issued and a house to house enquiry made not only involving the result of enquiries from the occupiers but also a search made by police and with a few exceptions – but not such as to convey suspicion – covered the area bounded by the City Police boundary on the one hand, Lamb St, Commercial St., Great Eastern Railway and Buxton St., then by Albert St., Dunk St., Chicksand St., and Great Garden St., to Whitechapel Road and then to the City boundary. Under this head also Common Lodging Houses were visited and over 2,000 lodgers were examined.

Enquiry was also made by Thames Police as to sailors on board ships in Docks or river and extended enquiry as to Asiatics present in London. About 80 persons have been detained at the different police stations in the Metropolis and their statements taken and verified by police and enquiry has been made into the movements of a number of persons estimated at upwards of 300 respecting whom communications were received by police and such enquiries are being continued. Seventy-six butchers and slaughterers have been visited and the characters of the men employed enquired into, this embraces all servants who have been employed for the past six months.

Enquiries have also been made as to the alleged presence in London of Greek Gipsies, but it was found that they had not been in London during the times of the various murders.

Three of the persons calling themselves Cowboys who belonged to the American Exhibition were traced and satisfactorily accounted for themselves.

Up to date although the number of letters daily is considerably lessened, the other enquiries respecting alleged suspicious persons continues as numerous.

All of this was very well, but it did little help to help the beleaguered Warren. He defended himself at length in the press on 4 October against charges that his handling of the Ripper case had led to a drop in policing standards. But this was far from enough to alleviate his position. If he wished the confidence of the press and the public at large, nothing less than the capture of the Ripper would suffice. It was against this background that he decided to investigate the use of bloodhounds in the search for the killer.

The Home Office files show that the idea of using bloodhounds in this way was suggested to Warren as early as 12 September by a Mr J.H. Ashforth of Belgravia Square, Nottingham. The subject soon became a hot topic in the press. In an editorial, *The Times* pointed out that twelve years before a bloodhound had helped solve a murder at Blackburn and wondered why the same could not be done in Whitechapel. The Master of a Sussex hunt wrote asking that he be given carte blanche to track down the Ripper in the East End. More seriously, Percy Lindley, a breeder of bloodhounds, wrote to *The Times* stating his professional opinion that a bloodhound could track the Ripper if placed on his fresh scent and suggesting that the police should keep trained dogs on hand ready for immediate use.

On 4 October, Mr Edwin Brough, a noted breeder of bloodhounds from Wyndegate near Scarborough, was invited by Warren to travel to London with two of his best dogs for trials. The bloodhounds, Champion Barnaby and Burgho, were described by *The Times* as 'magnificent animals.' Barnaby was the better known of the two dogs as a show animal, but Burgho, a black and tan with a head 12in long, was the more suitable for police purposes. He had been trained from a puppy to hunt 'the clean shoe', that is to sniff out the scent of a man whose shoes had not been treated with blood or aniseed. Barnaby on the other hand had only started such training when he was 12 years old.

Two trials were held on Monday 8 October, one in the morning in Regents Park and a second at night in Hyde Park. Warren attended the first trial which began at 7 a.m. with the ground still bearing a thick coat of frost. A young man who was given a fifteen minute start was successfully tracked over a distance of one mile. At night the dogs were used on a leash, as they would be if they were ever deployed in Whitechapel. A third trial was held the following morning, again at 7 a.m. Warren not only attended on this occasion, but acted on two of the six runs as the hunted man. Conditions were thought to be better for trailing on this second morning, but this did not prove to be the case. All in all, the results of the trial were disappointing.

Commenting on this episode in his memoirs, Sir Melville Macnaghten remarked:

> I cannot conceive of a more impossible locality in which to expect hounds to work or how any sane individual could ever have dreamt of success in this direction. Certain it is, however, that the notion did find some favour with a highly placed police official, and that he himself arranged to be hunted by Bloodhounds in Hyde Park. The thing appeared in the papers, and just ridicule incurred. It was incurred too when the 'man in blue' stood none too high in the public estimation.

It is important to state clearly though where Warren's culpability for the bloodhound fiasco lay. As shown above the idea of using them did not originate with him and in carrying out the trials he was bowing not just to public opinion, but also *expert* opinion. Moreover, he cannot be accused of wasting government money on the dogs, for the Home Office refused to grant him the money he estimated would be needed for the purchase or hire of the dogs and their food and accommodation. Where Warren can be criticised is in not clarifying to the public, the press, and his own subordinates the exact status of the dogs and what decision had been reached about their use.

When the dogs arrived in London for their trials, the press stated categorically that they had been purchased by the police. *The Daily Telegraph* even reported on 9 October that an instruction had been issued by Scotland Yard that in the event of another murder, the body of the victim was not to be disturbed until the bloodhounds were brought to the scene. Warren did not correct these statements. Nor did he rush to correct press reports that the dogs had got lost during further trials in Tooting Common. In fact the police had requested the use of the dogs in a matter entirely unrelated to the Ripper murders – the killing of a sheep – and reported them as missing when the person in charge of them could not be located. The word 'missing' was misconstrued by the press which subsequently reported that the hounds had got lost in a fog.

Burgho was not even in London when the above incident took place. Mr Brough had got fed up waiting for the police to make a decision about employing the dogs and he went back home, taking Burgho with him. He left Barnaby in the charge of a friend, Mr W.K. Taunton, for a while but angrily demanded its return when he discovered that the animal had been used to investigate the possibility that the burglary of a shop near Mitre Square on the night of Eddowes' death was connected with the murders. This was an impossible task; any scent left by the culprit would long since have been obliterated. However, Brough's greatest worry was that Barnaby would be poisoned by criminals if they learned that it was being used in this way, and that he would not be compensated, as no formal agreement had been reached with the police over the employment of the animal. By the beginning of November therefore, both bloodhounds were back in Scarborough with their master. Unfortunately, Warren did not see fit to disseminate this fact to the press or the officers handling the Ripper investigation.

The sojourn abroad of Robert Anderson, Head of the CID, did not long survive the 'double event'. He arrived in Paris from Switzerland on the night of the murders and was ordered home the following day by the Home Secretary. On his return, he prepared himself for a lengthy meeting with Matthews and Warren by spending his first day in London and half the following night studying the Ripper case. At this meeting Matthews made it clear that he held Anderson responsible for the capture of the murderer. But the wily CID chief was in no mood for subservience or to be used as a scapegoat. He pointed out in reply that he considered himself responsible for taking all legitimate means to find the murderer and went on to call the measures already taken 'wholly indefensible and scandalous' because in his opinion 'these wretched women were plying their trade under definite police protection'. In his opinion, prostitutes should be warned that they would not receive police protection and that any woman found soliciting after midnight should be arrested. He conceded that the second suggestion was too drastic to be implemented, but wished the first to be adopted.

It is significant that Anderson was ordered home by the Home Secretary and not by Warren. It has already been explained that a struggle existed between the Commissioner and the Home Office over control of the CID and that in August Warren had won a round in that battle by forcing the resignation of James Monro as Head of the CID and replacing him by the less formidable Anderson. Monro however did not retire from public life but in fact moved to the Home Office where, thanks to the respect he commanded within the force and his (erstwhile) good relationship with Matthews, he continued to exercise influence over his old department. Anderson's return increased this influence, for the two men were close friends. Very soon they and senior CID officers were holding conferences at the Home Office and keeping Warren very much in the dark about what was discussed.

So angry did Warren become at this undermining of his authority that he decided to state his views publicly. In the November edition of *Murray's Magazine* he wrote an article entitled *The Police of the Metropolis* in which he asserted:

It was clearly intended that he (the Head of the CID) should be subordinate to the Commissioner of Police, and everyone who knows anything of police duties must be aware that it was quite impracticable for police work to be done efficiently under two heads, the one independent of the other.

Not content with this, Warren took the opportunity to lash out at his political opponents:

It is to be deplored that successive governments have not had the courage to make a stand against the more noisy section of the people representing a small minority, and have given way before the tumultuous proceedings which have exercised a terrorism over peaceful and law abiding citizens, and it is still more to be regretted that ex-ministers, while in opposition, have not hesitated to embarrass those in power by smiling on the insurgent mob.

These comments and others like them caused uproar, and left the Home Secretary no alternative but to censure Warren. He wrote to Warren abruptly reminding him that under a Home Office circular of May 1879, he was forbidden to publish anything about his work without the permission of the Home Office. Warren's reply was blunt. Had he known of the existence of this circular, he would not have accepted the post of Commissioner of Police. In fact, he felt that he could not continue in office without the power to answer his critics and for that reason he wished to tender his resignation.

Warren submitted his resignation on 8 November. By one of those twists of fate which no writer of fiction would dare invent, Jack the Ripper chose that very night to carry out his last and most appalling murder. In the early hours of 9

November, he picked up Mary Jane Kelly, a still attractive 25-year-old prostitute, and went back with her to her room at No. 13 Miller's Court, where, availing himself of the privacy and time afforded him there, he indulged his dark urges to the full. When he was satisfied with the destruction he had wrought on Kelly's body, he secured the door of her room behind him and stepped off into history and legend.

MARY JANE KELLY

Dorset Street was only a few hundred yards from the scene of Annie Chapman's death. Despite its evil reputation, it was a well lit street, busy at all times of the day and night, thanks mainly to the large number of lodging houses it contained. The biggest of these, with about 300 beds, was probably Crossingham's which stood at No. 35 on the south side of the street close to Commercial Street. This, it will be recalled, was the lodging house from which Chapman was evicted on the night of her death because she was unable to pay for her bed. Directly opposite this house was No. 26 Dorset Street, behind which lay Miller's Court.

Miller's Court, which was about 30ft long by about ten broad, consisted of a number of rooms which were leased by John McCarthy and known collectively as 'McCarthy's rents'. Many, though apparently not all, of these rooms were occupied by prostitutes. Access to the court was by an arched passageway barely 3ft wide. The passageway was unlit but a street lamp hung close to the entrance in Dorset Street. The left-hand side of the passageway was taken up by McCarthy's chandler shop at No. 27 Dorset Street. At the bottom of the passageway on the right was No. 13 Miller's Court. This had originally been the back parlour of No. 26 Dorset Street, but had been partitioned off to form, with its own door, a separate 'rent'. For this tiny room, barely 12ft square, McCarthy charged 4s 6d per week.

Mary Kelly, a tall stoutish woman with a fine head of long black hair, moved into this room with her common-law husband, Joseph Barnett, in February or March 1888. According to Barnett, on whom researchers into Kelly are forced to rely heavily, she was born in Limerick, Ireland and moved as a young girl to Carmarthern in Wales where her father worked as a foreman in an iron works. She married a collier by the name of Davis, but he was killed in an explosion. Deprived of financial support, Kelly took to walking the streets first in Cardiff and then in London, to which she moved in 1884. She told Barnett that she lived initially in a 'gay' house (i.e. a bordello) in the West End and travelled to France with a gentleman. The truth of this has never been established, but it is worth noting here that Kelly liked to be called Marie Jeannette and that she was buried under that name. In any event Kelly, within a short time, was living in the East End with a man called Morganstone, near the gas works close to Ratcliffe Highway, and later with a mason in Bethnal Green by the name of Fleming. She met Barnett at Easter 1887, but continued to see this Fleming from time to time.

Barnett and Kelly lived in several places before Miller's Court. The reason for moving appears to have been Kelly's drinking habits and their inability to pay the rent, factors which were no doubt connected. On 30 October 1888, they had a violent quarrel in which a window in the room was broken. After this Barnett went to live in a doss house in Bishopsgate, although he returned each day to see Kelly and give her any money he could afford. He was a porter at Billingsgate market, but he was frequently out of work. He last saw Kelly alive on the evening of 8 November when he called to tell her that he had no money to give her. He found her in the company of Maria Harvey, another prostitute.

Why Kelly and Barnett split up has never been satisfactorily explained. In one statement, Barnett said he left because Kelly allowed Harvey to come and live with them. Harvey did indeed spend a few nights in Kelly's room in early November. There is evidence that yet another prostitute shared the room with Kelly after Barnett moved out. However in a statement to Inspector Abberline, Barnett said that 'in consequence of not earning enough money to give her and her resorting to prostitution, I resolved on leaving her. . .'

By the evening of 8 November, Kelly was in an unenviable position. She was living alone, while the Ripper was still on the prowl. She owed over 30s to McCarthy, and, in the absence of assistance from Barnett, had only one way of repaying this money. According to her young friend, Lizzie Allbrook, Kelly was so depressed and worried that she was planning to go back to her mother in Wales.

After Barnett and Harvey left her that evening, Kelly visited the local public houses looking for custom. Mary Ann Cox, a prostitute who lived at No. 5 Miller's Court, saw Kelly return with a man around 11.45 p.m. The man had a blotchy face, a thick carrotty moustache, and side whiskers. He was dressed in shabby dark clothes, and was carrying a quart of beer. Cox reckoned that he was about 36 years old and about 5ft 5in tall. Kelly was so drunk that she could barely return Cox's greeting. She managed though a rendition of 'I plucked a violet for my mother's grave' as she entered the room with her companion. Cox went to her room and stayed there until midnight when she went out (presumably to seek business herself). She came back for a minute at 1 a.m. to warm her hands and Kelly was then still singing. When she returned home for the last time that night, at around 3 a.m., Kelly's room was silent and in darkness.

Elizabeth Prater, who was separated from her husband, lived directly above Kelly in Room 20. She left home at about 9 p.m. on the evening of the 8th and returned about 1 a.m. the following morning. She stood at the entrance to Miller's Court talking to McCarthy until 1.30 a.m. when she went to bed. No one entered the court during that time. There was no light in No. 13 when she passed. She barricaded herself into her room with two tables against the door (a damning comment on the neighbourhood) and fell asleep with her clothes on. At about 3.30 or 4 a.m., she was wakened by a kitten which crawled across her neck. Just then she heard a cry of murder, two or three times. The building was so flimsy that she could hear when a person walked about in Kelly's room, but she could not make out where these cries were coming from. In any case, such cries were not uncommon in Miller's Court. She woke again at 5 a.m. and went to the Ten Bells public house for a drink.

A single cry of murder from a young woman was heard at around 4 a.m. by Sarah Lewis, of No. 24 Great Pearl Street in Spitalfields. Lewis was visiting Mrs Keyler who lived at No. 2 Miller's Court which was opposite Kelly's room. She had fallen asleep in a chair but had been wakened by the chimes of a church clock. The cry came from nearby but Lewis did not look out of the window to investigate. She was probably in any case already on edge; two nights before, she and a female friend had been accosted in Bethnal Green by a man carrying a black bag. Earlier that evening she had spotted the same man again.

When Lewis arrived at Miller's Court that night, which was about 2.30 a.m., she noticed a man standing against the wall of the lodging house across the street. She was unable to describe this man other than to say that he was stout, not very tall, and wore a wideawake hat. This man is likely to have been George Hutchinson, an unemployed labourer and acquaintance of Kelly. He is also probably the most important witness in the entire Ripper case, for if his statement to the police is true, and Inspector Abberline thought that it was, then the man seen with Kelly earlier that night by Mrs Cox must be cleared of suspicion. This is because Hutchinson claimed to have seen Kelly pick up a man in Thrawl Street around 2 a.m. and return with him to her room.

Hutchinson said that he bumped into Kelly at 2 a.m., just as he was passing Thrawl Street. She was desperate for money and asked him for sixpence. She had received money from him in the past, but whether or not this was for services rendered is not known. On this occasion though he had none to give. He had used up the last of his money on the journey from Romford. On learning this Kelly bade him good night and walked away, saying that she had to find some money.

As she walked down Thrawl Street, a man carrying a 'small parcel in his left hand with a kind of strap around it' appeared from the opposite direction, tapped Kelly on the shoulder and said something to her which caused the pair to burst out laughing. Kelly said, 'Alright' to the man and he replied, 'You will be alright for what I have told you'. With his right hand around Kelly's shoulders, the couple walked off together. Hutchinson stood under the lamp outside the Queen's Head public house and watched them pass. The man, who had his hat over his eyes, dipped his head. Not to be outdone, Hutchinson bent down and stared the man in the face. He glowered back sternly.

Hutchinson followed Kelly and her new companion to the corner of Dorset Street where they stopped for about three minutes. The man said something to Kelly who replied, with a kiss. 'Alright my dear. Come along. You will be comfortable'. Kelly said that she had lost her handkerchief. At this the man pulled out a large red handkerchief and presented it to Kelly with a flourish. They then went to Kelly's room. Hutchinson waited outside the entrance to the court to see if they would come back out, but after waiting for about three quarters of an hour he went away in search of a bed for what was left of the night.

Mrs Cox heard a man walk down the court at 6.15 a.m., which, as she pointed out in her evidence at the inquest, was too late for anyone going to work in the market. She admitted though that as she did not hear a door being closed. The man could have been a policemen. He could also have been Jack the Ripper, leaving behind the butchered body of Mary Kelly.

The 9th of November was an auspicious day. It was the birthday of the Prince of Wales and the date chosen that year to hold the Lord Mayor's Parade, the most colourful and popular annual event in the capital. But the murder of Kelly pushed both these occasions into the background. The suspicion that this was the aim of the Ripper was held by *The Star*. 'The murderer chose his time well. . . He got his sensation. While the well-stuffed calves of the City footmen were paraded for the laughter of London, his victim was lying cold in a foul dimly lit court in Whitechapel.'

At 10.45 that morning, McCarthy told his assistant, Thomas Bowyer, to go to Kelly's room and obtain some money from her. Bowyer walked from McCarthy's shop through the arched passageway to No. 13 and knocked on the door. On receiving no reply, he tried to open the door, but found he could not. He looked through the keyhole, but saw no key. He went round to the front of the room where two sets of windows overlooked the court. He knew that Kelly stuffed rags into the frame of the window which had been broken during her argument with Barnett. He pulled these rags out, pushed aside the makeshift curtain and peered into the room. He had been a soldier for twenty years and had seen service in India, but that did not prepare him for what he saw. There was blood on the floor and on the walls. Lumps of flesh were on the table next to the door. Beyond that, on the bed lay the body of a woman who had been mutilated beyond recognition.

When Bowyer managed to stop his knees from knocking together, he ran to McCarthy and told him what he had seen. 'Good God, do you mean that Harry?' was McCarthy's first response. They rushed back to Kelly's room where McCarthy looked through the broken window for himself. The sight sickened him. 'It was more the work of a devil than a man', he was later quoted as saying. The two men hurried to Commercial Street police station where they found Inspector Beck on duty. He returned with them to Miller's Court, and after confirming their story sent word to Superintendent Arnold. Abberline arrived from Scotland Yard soon after and took charge of the investigation. He sealed off the yard, allowing no one in or out without the permission of the police. Dr Phillips, who was quickly on the scene, declared Kelly beyond medical help. He also advised Abberline not to break down the door but to await the arrival of the bloodhounds.

Warren must be held to blame for the delay in entering Kelly's room. It is not true to say, as some writers have, that Warren had already resigned and that he no longer had anything to do with the Ripper case. He had merely tendered his resignation, which he had done before, and which he had possibly done this time as a political manoeuvre against Matthews. Moreover, he was in his office that morning. Official records show that he informed the Home Office at 12.30 p.m. that another murder had taken place and that 'the matter [had] been placed in the hands of Mr Anderson, Assistant Commissioner'. Unfortunately, Warren did not take action to ensure that his state of limbo did not paralyse the upper levels of the Metropolitan Police. As a result, confusion reigned at Scotland Yard for a few hours that day and no word was dispatched to Abberline that the dogs he was expecting were over two hundred miles away in Yorkshire.

One of the officers waiting outside Miller's Court with Abberline was young Walter Dew. He had known Kelly by sight and he had often noticed her 'parading along' the streets of the districts 'usually in the company of two or three of her kind, fairly neatly dressed and invariably wearing a clean white apron, but no hat'. On arriving at Miller's Court, he was advised by Inspector Beck not to look into the room, but he could not resist the temptation, much to his horror as he later recorded. 'What I saw when I pushed back an old coat and peeped through a broken pane of glass into the sordid little room which Kelly called her home was too harrowing to be described. It remains with me – and always will remain – as the most gruesome sight of the whole of my police career.'

At 1.30 p.m., nearly three hours after the discovery of Kelly's body, Superintendent Arnold arrived at Miller's Court. He said the instructions about the bloodhounds had been discontinued and gave orders for the door to be forced. He first had a window, apparently the larger of the two, removed so that the room could be better examined and a photograph taken.

After this was done, Arnold authorised McCarthy to smash down the door with his pickaxe. The room was so small that when the door swung open, it knocked against the table containing the lumps of Kelly's flesh. As Dew entered, he slipped on the blood-covered floor and fell.

The butcher's shambles which awaited the police was described in the *Illustrated Police News*:

The throat had been cut right across with a knife, nearly severing the head from the body. The abdomen had been partially ripped open, and both of the breasts had been cut from the body, the left arm, like the head, hung to the body by the skin only. The nose had been cut off, the forehead skinned, and the thighs, down to the feet, stripped of the flesh. The abdomen had been slashed with a knife across downwards, and the liver and entrails wrenched away. The entrails and other portions of the frame were missing, but the liver etc., it is said, was found placed between the feet of this poor victim. The flesh from the thighs and legs, together with the breasts and nose, had been placed by the murderer on the table, and one of the hands of the dead woman had been pushed into her stomach.

The room itself was sparsely furnished. Apart from the bed it contained only two tables and a chair, on which Kelly's clothes lay neatly folded. There was a fireplace in the wall facing the door. Between this and the partitioned wall, there was a cupboard which was bare apart from some empty ginger beer bottles, a few pieces of crockery and some bread. Above the fire there hung a print of *The Fisherman's Widow*. According to some reports, the murderer had draped pieces of flesh over the picture nails.

The bed was immediately to the right of the door, hard against the partitioned wall. Dr Phillips found Kelly's body lying close to the edge of the bed nearest the door. However, the location of the bloodstains on the bed, mattress, and sheet indicated to Phillips that Kelly had been on the far side of the bed when she was killed – by having her right carotid artery severed – and that she was moved after death (presumably to facilitate mutilation). The body was dressed only in a lined undergarment. The bedclothes had been turned down, apparently by the killer.

Dr Thomas Bond, a lecturer in Forensic Medicine and a consulting surgeon to 'A' Division of the Metropolitan Police and to the Great Western Railway, arrived at 2 p.m. to assist Phillips. Bond, who also took part in Kelly's post-mortem, wrote a report on the murders which is to be found in the official Ripper papers. In this he supported Phillips' view that the body was moved after death by pointing to the blood which 'had flowed down on the right side of the woman and spurted onto the wall', and suggested that Kelly's face was covered with the bed sheet when she was attacked. Bond also explained how he came to estimate the time of death:

Rigor mortis had set in but increased during the progress of the examination. From this it is difficult to say with any degree of certainty the exact time that elapsed since death as the period varies from six to twelve hours before rigidity sets in. The body was comparatively cold at two o'clock and the remains of a recently taken meal were found in the stomach and scattered about over the intestines. It is therefore pretty certain that the woman must have been dead about twelve hours and the partly digested food would indicate that death took place about three or four hours after food was taken, so one or two o'clock in the morning would be the probable time of the murder.

The only part of Kelly's face which the murderer left untouched was the eyes, which were wide open when the body was found. Walter Dew records that they seemed to be staring at him in terror. In Victorian times some scientists believed that the eyes of a corpse maintain a picture of the last thing seen and that this image could be reproduced in a photograph. (In fact, earlier that year *The British Journal of Photography* carried an article claiming that a murderer in France had been convicted using such a technique). According to Walter Dew, the police did indeed photograph Kelly's eyeballs some time that afternoon. However, apart from the official statement that this photograph was taken, no more was ever said about this episode by the police.

When the police entered the room, they found the still warm remains of a large fire in the grate. At its height the fire had been so hot that it melted the spout and handle of a kettle. Among the ashes were found the remnants of a straw hat and pieces of woman's clothing. These had almost certainly belonged to Maria Harvey, the prostitute who lived in Kelly's room for a few days. She testified that she had left behind '. . . two dirty cotton shirts, a boy's shirt, and a girl's white petticoat and a black crepe bonnet.' These items were not found in the room.

It has long been suspected that something else was found in the fire and that the authorities kept the fact secret. For example, *The Sunday Times* reported on 11 November that

Dr Phillips had returned to the murder room the day before to sift through the ashes and scrutinise them. According to the newspaper, nothing of any value was found.

What was the purpose of the fire? At the inquest into Kelly's death, Abberline said that in his opinion the murderer used the fire to enable him to see what he was doing. It has also been suggested that the Ripper simply used the fire to heat the room on a cold November morning. Neither explanation is satisfactory. There was a candle in the room. Why did the killer not use that if he wished to light the room? Moreover, this was a very intense fire, capable of melting the spout off a kettle. Clothes alone could not have generated enough heat to do this. Neither, for that matter, could coal or coke under normal circumstances. It appears then that the Ripper added something to the fire, something which he had brought with him to Kelly's room. And if he took the trouble to do this, it is reasonable to say that the fire played a central, and not an incidental, role in the murder.

Shortly after 4 p.m. on the afternoon of 9 November, a one-horse carrier's cart arrived in Dorset Street to convey Kelly's body to the mortuary under the direction of Dr Phillips. News of this brought a great rush of people to the scene and an attempt was made by the crowd to break through the police cordon. Proper respect was shown though when the remains were brought out of Miller's Court. 'The crowd which pressed round the van was of the very humblest class', reported *The Daily Chronicle*, 'but the demeanour of the people was all that could be desired. Ragged caps were doffed, and slatternly-looking women shed tears, as the shell, covered with a ragged looking cloth, was placed in the van.' After the body was taken away, the police boarded up the windows of the murder room, padlocked the door, and posted a guard outside.

The body was transported not to the mortuary in Old Montague Street, as was done with the previous Ripper victims killed in the Metropolitan area, but to Shoreditch mortuary next to St Leonard's Church. The significance of this was that, in terms of legal jurisdiction, Shoreditch lay in North East Middlesex, which meant that the inquest would be handled not by Wynne Baxter, but by Dr Roderick MacDonald MP, the coroner for that area. The suspicion has naturally arisen that Kelly's body was taken to another mortuary so that the critical Baxter would be replaced by another man who, being a former police surgeon, would be more 'understanding' of the problems facing the authorities in the hunt for the Ripper. Certainly, MacDonald's handling of the Kelly inquest shows that such an interpretation cannot be readily dismissed.

At the mortuary, the police surgeons, who estimated that it had taken the Ripper about two hours to carry out the mutilations, spent three times as long re-assembling Kelly's body. An official statement was made that all of Kelly's organs were accounted for and that the killer had taken no part of her with him. This however was treated with open scepticism. *The Times* reported, 'We are enabled to state on good authority that notwithstanding all that has been said to the contrary, a portion of the bodily organs was missing. The police, and with them the divisional surgeon, have arrived at the conclusion that it is in the interest of justice not to disclose the details of the professional inquiry.' The mistaken belief that Kelly was pregnant led to the rumour that the missing organ was in fact the uterus containing the foetus.

In addition to his general report on the Ripper murders, Dr Thomas Bond produced a detailed separate report on the Kelly killing. This document, which was at some stage removed from the Ripper files and returned to Scotland Yard only as late as 1987, sets the record straight on a number of important points concerning the Kelly killing. For example, Kelly's breasts were not found on the table beside her head, but in fact on the bed. Moreover, Kelly was not pregnant and her uterus was found under her head. However, irrespective of what the authorities said in public, Kelly's heart *was* absent. It is not clear though if the Ripper took the organ with him, or whether he burned it in the fire.

This, easily the most horrific of the Ripper crimes, shook the country. The day after it occurred, the Queen sent a message to her Prime Minister, Lord Salisbury. 'This new most ghastly murder shows the absolute necessity for some very decided action. All these courts must be lit, and our detectives must be improved. They are not what they should be. You promised when the first murder took place, to consult with your colleagues about it.' A few days later, the Queen again addressed her government on the murders. 'Have the cattle boats been examined? Has any investigation been made as to the number of single men occupying rooms to themselves? The murderer's clothes must be saturated with blood and must be kept somewhere. Is there sufficient surveillance at night?'

The government did not take long to take the Royal Hint. Within hours of the first missive from the Queen, the cabinet met and approved the following notice:

MURDER PARDON

Whereas on the 8th or 9th in Miller's Court, Dorset Street, Spitalfields, Mary Jane Kelly was murdered by some person or persons unknown, the Secretary of State will advise the grant of Her Majesty's pardon to any accomplice not being a person who contrived or actually committed the murder who shall give such information and evidence as shall lead to the discovery and conviction of the person or persons who committed the murder.

(Signed) Charles Warren
Commissioner of Police
of the Metropolis.

Metropolitan Police
4 Whitehall Place,   10th November 1888

The offer of a pardon was a remarkable event and a clear indication of the near panic which was then gripping London. News of the murder had helped spark trouble among the crowd on Ludgate Hill which had gathered to watch the Lord Mayor's parade. Dozens of arrests ensued. On the night of the murder large groups of people gathered in Dorset Street and in front of the local police stations, excitedly awaiting any word of the Ripper's arrest. There were several instances where innocent men were denounced as the Ripper and pursued through the streets. A sure way to invite such treatment was to carry a black bag in the area. Even doctors attached to the London Hospital came under suspicion.

One man carrying such a bag was arrested and taken to Leman Street police station. He was found to have nothing to do with the murders and released. Mrs Paumier, who sold chestnuts near Miller's Court, claimed that on the day of the murder a man with a black bag stopped beside her and announced that he knew more about the murder than she did. She said the man was about 5ft 6in tall with a black moustache and was dressed in a black silk hat, black coat, and speckled trousers. She was sure that the same man had frightened three of her friends the night before by claiming that his bag contained something 'that the ladies don't like'.

In a bizarre event on Saturday night, a man with his face blackened, appeared at the corner of Wentworth and Commercial Streets and proclaimed himself to be Jack the Ripper. Not surprisingly, he was immediately seized by passers-by. A crowd gathered quickly and began to beat him. Cries of 'Lynch him!' were heard. Fortunately for the man, the police arrived quickly and led him off to the safety of the Leman Street police station, where he refused to identify himself other than as a doctor at St George's Hospital (although *The Globe* newspaper later named him as a Dr Holt). According to *The Times*, the police attached great importance to this arrest as the man's appearance answered their description of the Ripper. The doctor was described as 'about 35 years of age, 5 ft. 7 in. in height, of dark complexion, with a dark moustache, and . . . spectacles'. There is no further information available on this man, but there is no reason to doubt that, like all the others who were detained that weekend on suspicion of being the Ripper, he was released after questioning.

The Kelly inquest, which took place on Monday 12 November, was both short and stormy. It began with an acrimonious exchange between Coroner MacDonald and the jury over whether the inquest should be held in Shoreditch at all.

Juror: I do not see why we should have the inquest thrown on our shoulders when the murder did not happen in our district, but in Whitechapel.

Coroner's Officer (severely): It did not happen in Whitechapel.

Coroner: Do you not think that we do not know what we are doing here? The jury are summoned in the ordinary way, and they have no business to object. If they persist in their objection I shall know how to deal with them. Does any juror persist?

Juror: We are summoned for the Shoreditch district. This happened in Spitalfields.

Coroner: It happened within my district.

Another Juryman: This is not my district. I come from Whitechapel, and Mr. Baxter is my coroner.

Coroner: I am not going to discuss this subject with the jurymen at all. If any juryman says he distinctly objects, let him say so. (After a pause) I may tell the jurymen that jurisdiction lies where the body lies, not where it is found.

After putting the jurors firmly in their place, MacDonald sent them to view Kelly's body and the murder room. The jurors were at least spared the sight of Kelly's mutilations for her body was covered up to her neck with a dirty sheet. The face though was horrible enough. According to the *Pall Mall Gazette*, it resembled 'one of those horrible wax anatomical specimens.' Continuing, the paper said: 'The eyes were the only vestiges of humanity. The rest was so splashed and scarred that it was impossible to say where the flesh began and the cuts ended.'

The subsequent evidence soon indicated that Kelly died about 4 a.m. However, Mrs Maxwell, the wife of the lodging house keeper at No. 14 Dorset Street which stood opposite Miller's Court, struck a discordant note. She testified that she not only saw Kelly between 8 and 8.30 a.m. on the morning of the murder, but that she actually spoke to her. Needless to say, she was closely questioned by the Coroner:

Coroner: Did you speak to her?

Maxwell: Yes. It was unusual to see her up at that hour. I spoke across the street, 'What brings you up so early?' She said, 'Oh, Carrie, I do feel so bad.'

Coroner: And yet you say you had only spoken to her twice previously? You knew her name, and she knew yours?

Maxwell: Oh, yes, by being about in the lodging house.

Coroner: What did she say?

Maxwell: She said, 'I've had a glass of beer, and I've brought it up again.' I imagine she had been in the Britannia beer shop on the corner. I left her saying that I could pity her feelings.

Coroner: Then what did you do?

Maxwell: I went to Bishopsgate Street to get my husband's breakfast.

Coroner: Did you see Kelly again?

Maxwell: When I returned I saw her outside the Britannia public talking to a man.

Coroner: This would be about what time?

Maxwell: This would be about a quarter to nine.

Coroner: What description can you give of the man?

Maxwell: I could not give you any, as they were at some distance.

Inspector Abberline (interrupting): The distance is about 16 yards.

Maxwell: I am sure it was the deceased. I am willing to swear to it.

Coroner: You are sworn now. Was he a tall man?

Coroner: No, he was a little taller than me and stout.

Inspector Abberline: On consideration, I should say the distance at 25 yards.

Coroner: What clothes had the man?

Maxwell: Dark clothes. He seemed to have a plaid coat on. I could not say what sort of hat he had.

Coroner: What sort of dress had the deceased?

Maxwell: A dark shirt, a velvet body, a maroon shawl, and no hat.

Coroner: Have you ever seen her the worse for drink?

Maxwell: I have seen her in drink, but she was not a notorious character.

Mrs Maxwell's testimony remains a mystery. It is difficult to see how she could have been wrong about the date of her sighting, especially as the murder occurred only three days before the inquest, and on the same day as the Lord Mayor's parade. And yet, she is flatly contradicted by the medical evidence which states that Kelly died in the early hours of the morning, and with partly digested food in her stomach, *which would not have been there if she had vomited in the street.* Also, it is significant that no one in the Britannia public house saw Kelly on the morning of the 9th. Maxwell may well have invented this whole story, but on balance it is more likely that she was just mistaken.

In his testimony, Abberline sought to correct the impression which had gone abroad that the Ripper, after murdering Kelly, locked the door of her room and took the key with him. Quoting Barnett, he stated that the key to the door had been lost for some time and that after the pane of glass was smashed in the argument on 30 October, Kelly had adopted the habit of bolting the door through the window when she left. Abberline pointed out that this could be easily done. It would appear that Bowyer and the police, being unable to open Kelly's door and knowing nothing about the bolt arrangement, merely *assumed* that it was locked. The murderer would have learned about the bolt when he accompanied Kelly back to her room and would thus have been able to secure the door with it when he left.

Towards the end of the morning, Dr Phillips gave his evidence. At the request of the coroner, Phillips did not go into detail and simply said that the cause of death was the severing of the right carotid artery. The jury, under the impression that a fuller statement would follow at a later time, asked no questions. However, shortly afterwards, MacDonald suddenly announced that he did not wish to hear any more evidence and asked the members of the jury if they were ready to return a verdict. The foreman of the jury, doubtless astonished at this turn of events, agreed that he and his colleagues had heard enough to return a verdict of wilful murder against some person or persons unknown.

At the close of proceedings, MacDonald stated, 'There is other evidence which I do not propose to call, for if we at once make public every fact brought forward in connection with this terrible murder the ends of justice might be retarded.' This is an extraordinary statement, *in effect an admission that evidence was being suppressed*, which understandably has led to a great deal of speculation. Unfortunately, the nature of this evidence has never been revealed. Was there something found in the fire after all? Did the Ripper do something to Kelly before killing or mutilating her? Was there something in Kelly's past which the authorities did not wish to be made public?

The termination of the inquest after only half a day was criticised by the press. *The Daily Telegraph* expressed surprise that a verdict should be delivered before one of Kelly's relatives could be brought from Ireland to identify the body, and called for the Attorney General to order a new inquiry. It also pointed out that the opportunity had been lost to have witnesses produce sworn statements while their memory was still fresh. This was a valid comment; George Hutchinson for example was not called as a witness and had he not approached the police of his own free will, his important evidence would have been lost.

Warren's resignation was officially accepted on 12 November. To his undoubted chagrin, the government appointed Monro as his successor. Punch parodied the situation with a new version of a traditional nursery verse:

> Who chased COCK WARREN?
> 'I,' said the Home Sparrow,
> 'With my views cramped and narrow,
> I chased COCK WARREN.'

> And who'll fill his place?
> 'I,' said Monro,
> 'I'm the right man, I know,
> And I'll fill his place.'

> And who'll tie your hands?
> 'I,' said Routine,
> 'That my business has been,
> So I'll tie his hands.'

Who'll see fair play?
'I,' said John Bull,
'For I'm quite a fool;
I'll see fair play.'

No relative came forward to claim Kelly's body. It was saved from a pauper's grave only by the generosity of Mr Henry Wilton, the long-serving sexton of the Shoreditch Church, who agreed to pay for the funeral out of his own pocket. In a polished elm and oak coffin with metal mounts and a plaque reading, 'Marie Jeannette Kelly, died 9 November 1888, aged 25 years', the body was put to rest in the Roman Catholic cemetery at Leytonstone on 18 November. No contemporary heeded the appeal by Mr Wilton for a tombstone and the grave remained unmarked until the 1990s when a simple headstone was erected.

POSTSCRIPT

Commenting on the theory that after the Kelly murder the Ripper took a rational decision to stop his killings, at least for the time being, Macnaghten wrote:

It will be noticed that the fury of the mutilations *increased* in each case, and, seemingly, the appetite only became sharpened by indulgence. It seems, then, highly improbable that the murderer would have suddenly stopped in November '88, and been content to recommence operations (some years later). A much more rational theory is that the murderer's brain gave way altogether after his awful glut in Miller's Court, and that he immediately committed suicide, or, as a possible alternative, was found to be so hopelessly mad by his relations, that he was by them confined in some asylum. (original emphasis)

A study of other sex murderers strongly supports Macnaghten's assessment. Sex murderers do not give up or lose interest; they carry on killing until death or capture stops them. This would have been especially true of the Ripper. The rate at which he murdered – five women in ten weeks – and the reckless daring he displayed in doing so show that he was in the grip of a particularly pressing obsession, one that would certainly have come to outweigh his natural instinct for survival. Nevertheless some students of the Ripper case have added two other women to his list of victims and for that reason they are mentioned here.

The first was 'Claypipe Alice', whose body was found in Castle Alley, Whitechapel at around 1 a.m. on 17 July 1889 by PC 272H Walter Andrew. With a blow of his whistle, he summoned his Sergeant, whom he had just left, and the two men bent over to inspect the body. McKenzie was lying on her right side with her clothes pulled up to the waist. Her throat had been cut and blood had gathered in a pool around her neck. There were two stab wounds in her lower stomach. Despite a slight drizzle, the body was still warm.

Beneath the body, the police found a farthing and a claypipe. This last item led to the woman's early identification. It was soon learned that she had been living with a labourer called John McCormack for the past six or seven years. For the last year, the couple had been staying in a common lodging house in Gun Street. McCormack last saw McKenzie alive a few hours before her death. He had come home from work at around 4 p.m. and had given her some money. He then went to bed, but on waking up at sometime between 10 and 11 p.m., he found that she had gone out. He was unable to provide much information about the victim other than that she came from the town of Peterborough and that she had two sons who lived abroad. He maintained that she was a decent woman who supported herself by charring and casual work. The police though considered her a prostitute. That she was a heavy drinker was not in dispute.

Dr Bagster Phillips was the first medical man on the scene and he, together with Dr Gordon Brown, the City Police surgeon, carried out the post-mortem later that day. They concluded that the woman had died as a result of being stabbed in the throat, apparently while being held down on the ground. These injuries, which extended to the genitals, were in fact a series of cuts which did not penetrate the abdominal cavity. Phillips also believed that the knife used in the killings was smaller than that (or those) which had been used in the murders he had examined the year before.

All of this indicated that McKenzie was not a victim of Jack the Ripper. For some reason though, which has never been made clear, Robert Anderson, Head of the CID, was not satisfied with the finding of this post-mortem and asked Dr Bond to carry out his own examination. This Bond did on 18 July in the presence of Dr Phillips. He concluded:

I see in this murder evidence of similar design to the former Whitechapel murders, viz, sudden onslaught on the prostrate woman, the throat skilfully and resolutely cut with subsequent mutilation, each mutilation indicating sexual thoughts and a desire to mutilate the abdomen and sexual organs.

I am of the opinion that the murder was performed by the same person who committed the former series of Whitechapel murders.

Phillips disagreed with this conclusion and with Bond's contention, also stated in the above report, that the murderer was left-handed. In his own findings, Phillips stated, 'After careful and long deliberation I cannot satisfy myself on purely anatomical and professional grounds that the perpetrator of all the 'Whitechapel Murders' is one man. I am on the contrary impelled to a contrary conclusion – this noting the mode of procedure and the character of the mutilations and forgoing of motive in connection with the latter.' This, it must be noted, is the considered opinion of the doctor most clearly involved with the Ripper crimes, having examined, or carried out the post-mortem on, all the victims except Mary Nichols.

The second woman was found in Swallow Gardens, a railway arch close to Royal Mint Street, in the early hours of 13 February 1891 by PC Ernest Thomson. Her clothing was disarranged. There was a wound in her throat and severe injuries had been inflicted to her abdomen. Thomson had only been in the police force a few weeks and he was doubtless relieved when his whistle elicited prompt assistance in the form of PC Leeson, a man who was later to achieve fame during the Siege of Sydney Street in 1911.

Leeson immediately recognised the victim as 'Carrotty Nell' or Francis Cole, a local prostitute. She was in fact still alive when found (a strong indication that she was not a Ripper victim), but clearly dying. She could not speak and she succumbed without uttering a word. It is more than likely that the killer was disturbed by PC Thomson.

Coles was found to possess two hats, an old one attached to her belt and a new one lying nearby in the gutter. This was traced to a shop in Baker's Row, Spitalfields. The owner of the shop remembered selling the hat to Coles the previous afternoon. He also recalled the man who bought it for her and was able to give a description of him to the police. The suspect was quickly identified as James Sadler, a fireman sailor on the SS *Fez* berthed in London docks. He was arrested, taken to Leman Street police station and charged with murder. A crowd gathered outside the station and called for the blood of the man they believed to be Jack the Ripper, even if the police did not share that opinion.

Sadler denied killing Coles although he did admit picking her up on the evening of the 11th when he was discharged from his ship, and spending most of the following day in her company. The time, out of bed, had been spent mostly in public houses. However, shortly after buying Coles her hat, Sadler was mugged in Thrawl Street and robbed of his money and watch. When the robbers ran away, he threatened to kill Coles for not helping him fight them off. He left Coles in their lodging house around 12.40 a.m. on the morning of the murder. When he returned some twenty minutes later, she was gone. He returned once more at 3 a.m., but this time he was in a highly agitated state and he was covered in blood. He claimed that he had been robbed again. The lodging housekeeper had his doubts about this explanation and he refused Sadler entry, directing him instead to the London Hospital for treatment.

The case against Sadler seemed strong, albeit circumstantial, and he was placed in Holloway Prison awaiting trial. However the police failed to find any direct evidence linking him to Coles' death and after a month the government reluctantly ordered his release. The police though remained certain of his guilt. Indeed Macnaghten in his notes clearly suspected that Sadler had murdered both Coles and McKenzie:

(2) Alice McKenzie was found with her throat cut (or rather stabbed) in Castle Alley on 17th July 1889: no evidence was forthcoming and no arrests were made in connection with this case. The stab in the throat was of the same nature as in the case of the murder of
(3) Frances Cole in Swallow gardens, on 13th February 1891 – for which Thomas Sadler (sic), a fireman, was arrested, and, after several remands, discharged. It was

ascertained at the time that Sadler had sailed for the Baltic on 19th July '89 and was in Whitechapel on the night of 17th idem. He was a man of ungovernable temper and entirely addicted to drink and the company of the lowest prostitutes.

* * * * *

THE EVIDENCE

'Knowledge, observation, deduction', counselled Sherlock Holmes. The purpose of this section is to analyse the facts of the Ripper case in an attempt to draw conclusions and valid inferences about the killer and the murders. What did he look like? Did he possess any medical knowledge? Did he write the Jack the Ripper letters? Was he left-handed? Did the murders possess any ritualistic element? It is only on the answers to these, and other questions, that a serious theory on the Ripper's identity can be based.

THE DESCRIPTIONS

What value can be placed on the various descriptions of the Ripper? None at all, if Macnaghten is to be believed. In the Scotland Yard version of his paper, he wrote, 'No one ever saw the Whitechapel Murderer . . .' Macnaghten did not explain though how he could justify such a statement, if he did not know who the Ripper was, which in the next sentence of his memorandum he claimed to be the case. 'Many homicidal maniacs were suspected (of being the Ripper) but no shadow of proof could be thrown on anyone.' Macnaghten's assertion is therefore one which can be easily challenged. Was not the man seen with Annie Chapman by Mrs Long outside the entrance to No. 29 Hanbury Street the Ripper? Major Smith was convinced that Joseph Lawende, the Jewish traveller, saw the Ripper with Catherine Eddowes only minutes before her death. What of George Hutchinson's suspect? Was this man not the Ripper?

The police issued their first official description of the murderer after the Chapman killing:

Description of a man who entered the passage of a house where the murder was committed of a prostitute at 2 a.m. on September 8th. Age 37, height 5 feet seven inches. Rather dark beard and moustache; dress – dark jacket, dark vest and trousers, black felt hat. Spoke with a foreign accent.

The source of this description has never been discovered. In any case it appears to be irrelevant for Chapman was almost certainly not murdered until 5.30–6.00 a.m. She was certainly still alive at 2 a.m.

After Strides' death, the police released two descriptions:

At 12.35 a.m. September 30, with Elizabeth Stride found murdered on the same date in Berner's Street at 1 a.m., a man aged 28, height 5 feet 8 inches, complexion dark, small dark moustache; dress-black diagonal coat, hard felt hat, collar and tie, respectable appearance, carried a parcel wrapped in newspaper.

At 12.45 a.m., 30th with same woman in Berner's Street, a man, aged about 30, height 5 feet 5 inches; complexion fair, hair dark, small brown moustache, full face, broad shoulders; dress-dark jacket and trousers, black cap with peak.

At the Stride inquest, two witnesses gave detailed evidence about a man they saw with the victim on the night of her death. The first was William Marshall who saw a man, apparently middle-aged, talking to Stride in Berner Street at 11.45 p.m., over one hour before she was murdered:

Coroner: What sort of cap was he wearing?
Marshall: A round cap with a small peak to it something like what a sailor would wear.
Coroner: What height was he?

Marshall: About five feet six inches and he was stout. He was decently dressed, and I should say he worked at some light business and had more the appearance of a clerk than anything else.

Coroner: Did you see whether he had any whiskers?

Marshall: From what I saw of his face I do not think he had. He was not wearing gloves and he had no stick or anything in his hands.

Coroner: What sort of coat was it?

Marshall: A cutaway one.

Coroner: Are you sure this is the woman?

Marshall: Yes, I am. I did not take much notice of them. I was standing at my door and what attracted my attention first was her standing there some time and he kissing her. I heard the man say to the deceased, 'You would say anything but your prayers.' He was mild speaking and appeared to be an educated man. They went down the street.

The second witness, PC 452 H. William Smith, saw Stride in Berner Street at 12.30 a.m.:

Coroner: Did you see the man who was talking to her?

PC Smith: Yes, I noticed he had a newspaper parcel in his hand. It was about eighteen inches in length and six or seven inches in width. He was about five feet seven inches as near as I could say. He had on a dark felt deerstalker hat of dark colour and dark clothes.

Coroner: What kind of coat was it?

PC Smith: An overcoat. He wore dark trousers.

Coroner: Can you give any idea as to his age?

PC Smith: About twenty eight years.

Coroner: Can you give any idea as to what he was?

PC Smith: No sir, I cannot. He was of respectable appearance.

Clearly, the first of the descriptions issued by the police was based on the evidence of PC Smith. The second description seems to have come from Israel Schwartz, a Hungarian immigrant, who claimed that he saw a woman, whom he later identified as Stride, assaulted by a man in Berner Street around 12.45 on the morning of 30 September. Commenting on this statement, Chief Inspector Swanson said that he found it reliable, but doubted that that the man seen by Schwartz was in fact Stride's killer. Swanson was surely justified in this appraisal. It defies belief that the Ripper would have created such a public scene. Also, it should be noted that, according to Schwartz, the attacker pulled Stride away from Dutfield's Yard and not towards it.

The time of this incident must also be questioned. It will be recalled that James Brown saw Stride at 12.45 a.m. talking to a man in Berner Street. He did not see the man's face but noticed that he was about 5ft 7in tall and stoutish in build. He also wore an overcoat which almost reached his heels. This was a very prominent feature and one that does not at all tally with the simple 'dark jacket' seen by Schwartz. It will also be recalled that Mrs Mortimer, who lived only a few yards from Dutfield's Yard, stood outside her house between 12.30 and 1 a.m. She could hardly have missed this attack on Stride, yet she maintained that she saw nothing unusual.

It would appear then that Schwartz misjudged the time of the attack he witnessed and that this actually took place around 12.30, before Mrs Mortimer came to stand in the street and before PC Smith saw his suspect in the company of Stride. Schwartz was a newcomer to England who did not speak the language. Human nature being what it is, he would have been only too glad to tell the police what they wanted to hear, namely that he had seen Stride being attacked by a man only minutes before she was murdered, while in fact what he witnessed was Stride being robbed or simply beaten by a drunk or disgruntled client. Indeed it is worth speculating that the attacker was the man seen by Marshall and that after being assaulted by him, Stride met the man with the long coat, deerstalker hat and parcel described by PC Smith. It must also be remembered that Schwartz, like most witnesses in the Ripper case, would not have possessed a watch; this is why there are so many references in the case statements to the chiming of church clocks.

After Eddowes' murder, the City Police issued the following description:

> At 1.35 a.m., 30 September, with Catherine Eddowes, in Church Passage, leading to Mitre Square, where she was found murdered at 1.45 a.m., same date, a man, age 30, height 5 feet 7 inches, or 8 inches; complexion fair, moustache fair, medium build; dress: pepper and salt colour loose jacket, grey cloth cap with peak of same material, reddish neckerchief tied in knot; appearance of a sailor. Information respecting this man to be forwarded to Inspector McWilliams, 26 Old Jewry, London, E.C.

This information was based on the evidence of Joseph Lawende, who, as has been shown, saw a man and a woman together in a passageway leading to Mitre Square shortly before Eddowes was murdered. The woman was wearing a black jacket and a bonnet and Lawende saw her put her hand on the man's chest. Major Smith thought highly of the description. 'It was broad moonlight, almost as light as day, and (Lawende) saw them distinctly. This was, without doubt, the murderer and his victim.'

Is this an accurate assessment? Lawende pointed out at the inquest that he never saw Eddowes' face and that he identified her body only by her clothes, which were common enough. More importantly, he never claimed to have had a good look at the man he saw. When asked by Major Smith if he could easily recognise the man, he replied, 'Oh, no. I only had a short look at him.' This is confirmed by the official Metropolitan Police report on the Eddowes' murder written by Chief Inspector Swanson:

> . . . Mr. Lawende states that he could not identity the man; but as the man stood with his back to him, with her hand on the man's breast, he could not identify the body mutilated as it was, as that of the woman whose back he had seen, but to the best of his belief the clothing of the deceased, which was black, was similar to that worn by the woman whom he had seen, and that was the full extent of his identity.

George Hutchinson appears to be unique in that he is the only reliable witness to obtain a good facial view of a suspect. This is his extraordinary description of the man he saw with Kelly on the morning of her death:

> . . . age about 34 or 35, height 5ft 6, complexion pale. Dark eyes and eye lashes. Slight moustache curled up each end and hair dark. Very surly looking. Dress, long dark coat, collar and cuffs trimmed astrakhan and a dark jacket under, light waistcoat, dark trousers, dark felt hat turned down in the middle, button boots and gaiters with white buttons, wore a very thick gold chain white linen collar, black tie with horseshoe pin, respectable appearance, walked very sharp, Jewish appearance. Can be identified.

Abberline believed that Hutchinson was telling the truth and had his description disseminated to all stations. But was this man Jack the Ripper?

Hutchinson, it will be remembered, said that Kelly picked up this man at 2 a.m. and that he followed the couple to Miller's Court where he waited outside for about three quarters of an hour. It is fair to say then that he left his vigil at around 3 a.m. The medical evidence suggests that Kelly died after 2 a.m. Cries of murder were heard in Miller's Court between 3.30 and 4 a.m. This means that if the man Hutchinson saw was not the Ripper, then Kelly left her room sometime after 3 a.m., picked up another man and was murdered by him very soon afterwards. This is not impossible of course, but improbable. It is much more likely that Hutchinson's suspect was indeed the killer. If this conjecture is true, it follows that the Ripper, knowing that he had been seen with Kelly en route to her room, went to bed with her and murdered her in her sleep.

There is much to support this train of thought. Kelly's clothes were neatly folded on her chair, a clear sign that she had turned in for the night, or at least had gone to bed with a customer. Also, Dr Phillips, it will be recalled, testified that Kelly had been murdered while occupying the side of the bed closest to the partition, a strong indication that she was sharing her bed at the time of attack. In addition, Dr Bond, in his report on the murders, stated that 'the corner of the sheet to the right of the woman's head was much cut and saturated with blood, indicating that the face may have been covered with one sheet at the time of the attack.' If Bond is right, it follows naturally that Kelly was lying *underneath* the bedclothes when attacked, i.e. asleep or with a client.

To sum up, there are only three sightings worth serious consideration, those of Mrs Long, PC Smith, and Hutchinson. Mrs Long could offer no details of the man she saw with Annie Chapman other than that he looked over 40, seemed to be a foreigner, and wore a long coat. Smith placed his man's age at 28, while Hutchinson thought Kelly's client to be in his mid 30s. This discrepancy can be accounted for by the circumstances of the sightings; Hutchinson had a good look at his suspect's face in the light of a street lamp; PC Smith made his observations from a greater distance in a dark street; Mrs Long paid little attention to Chapman's companion.

However the other details given by Hutchinson and PC Smith are strikingly similar. They both saw a man about 5ft 6in to 5ft 8in tall, of respectable appearance with a moustache. They agreed that the man each saw carried a parcel in his hand, wore a dark felt hat and wore a long overcoat. With regard to this point, Dr Bond commented:

> I think (the killer) must be in the habit of wearing a cloak or overcoat or he could hardly have escaped notice in the streets if the blood on his hands or clothes were visible.

Smith and Hutchinson differ on the nature of the parcel they saw. Smith said that his suspect carried a 'newspaper parcel eighteen inches in length and six or eight inches in width.' Hutchinson's man had a 'kind of small parcel in his left hand with a kind of strap around it.' In an interview with *The Times*, he claimed that the parcel seemed to be about 8in long and covered in dark American cloth, which indicates that it was a type of bag or satchel after all. The two parcels do not seem then to be identical, although it must be remembered that the newspaper wrapping may have greatly altered the shape and size of the parcel seen by Smith. What is not in doubt though is that on two occasions a man likely to have been the Ripper was seen carrying a parcel. The purpose of the parcel must remain a matter of speculation, but in all probability it contained the Ripper's knife.

MODUS OPERANDI

Did the Ripper possess any medical knowledge? The doctors involved in the case were themselves deeply divided on this question and they have left behind a variety of statements which, taken selectively, could be used to support practically any point of view. However in the assessment of these statements, there is one factor which must not be lost sight of and that is the inability, or perhaps refusal, of Victorians to recognise the Whitechapel murders for what they were, namely sex crimes. As mentioned earlier, people at the time could not understand why anyone would want to rip a woman open unless it was for a tangible, material reason such as the sale of organs mentioned by Coroner Baxter at the Chapman inquest. To the contemporary mind then, only a doctor, or perhaps someone like a horse slaughterer, would have the motivation and, by natural extension, the skill to carry out the murders. This meant that the police doctors worked to some extent from a preconceived notion. They assumed medical knowledge on behalf of the killer and looked for evidence to support this view. This is not to say that they were necessarily wrong, but it is important to note how as the murders went on and their true nature became more apparent, professional opinion changed from favouring the medical knowledge theory to rejecting it outright.

Dr Llewellyn, who examined the body of the first victim, Mary Nichols, believed her killer had a degree of 'rough anatomical knowledge.' At the Chapman inquest, Dr Phillips went further, stating that the wounds inflicted on the victim were obviously the work of an 'expert – or one, at least, who had such knowledge of anatomical or pathological examination as to be enabled to secure the pelvic organs with one sweep of the knife.'

The double murder of 30 September showed beyond doubt that the Ripper was no ordinary murderer, driven by some sort of material gain. It is perhaps not surprising then that at the Eddowes inquest medical opinion was divided. Dr Brown, the City Police surgeon, held much the same view as Phillips had:

Coroner: Would you consider that the person who inflicted the wounds possessed great anatomical skill?
Dr Brown: A good deal of knowledge as to the position of the organs in the abdominal cavity and the way of removing them.

Coroner: You spoke of the extraction of the left kidney.
Would it require great skill and knowledge to remove it?

Dr Brown: It would require a great deal of knowledge as
to its position to remove it. It is easily overlooked. It is
covered by a membrane.

However two other doctors disagreed with Brown,
Dr Saunders, the first doctor to examine Eddowes in Mitre
Square, and Dr Sequeira, who also saw Eddowes as she was
left by her killer. Both men took part in the post-mortem and
they shared the opinion that the injuries showed, 'No evidence
of any anatomical knowledge other than that which could be
expected of a professional butcher.'

This range of views was reflected in the official Metropolitan
Police Report written by Chief Inspector Swanson:

The surgeon, Dr. Brown, called by the City Police, and
Dr. Phillips who had been called by the Metropolitan
Police in the cases of Hanbury Street and Berner Street,
having made a post mortem examination of the body
reported that there were missing the left kidney and the
uterus, and that the mutilation so far gave no evidence of
anatomical knowledge in the sense that it evidenced the
hand of a qualified surgeon, so that the police could
narrow their enquiries into certain classes of persons. On
the other hand as in the Metropolitan Police cases, the
medical evidence showed that the murder could have
been committed by a person who had been a hunter, a
butcher, a slaughterman, as well as a student in surgery
or a properly qualified surgeon.

Dr Thomas Bond wrote his report on the murders on
10 November, the day after Mary Kelly died. He based his
findings on the notes made by other doctors on the four
previous murders and on what he observed from examining

Kelly as she was found in her room, as well as on the results of her post-mortem. On the subject of whether or not the Ripper had any medical knowledge, his conclusions were unequivocal:

In each case the mutilation was inflicted by a person who had no scientific or anatomical knowledge. In my opinion he does not even possess the technical knowledge of a butcher or horse or horse slaughterman or any person accustomed to cut up dead animals.

It is perhaps no coincidence that in the same report, Bond postulated a sophisticated (indeed modern) theory of the Ripper's mental condition:

. . . He must in my opinion be a man subject to periodical attacks of Homicidal and Erotic mania. The character of the mutilations indicate (*sic*) that the man may be in a condition sexually, that may be called Satyriasis. It is of course possible that the Homicidal condition may have developed from a revengeful or brooding condition of the mind, or that religious mania may have been the original disease but I do not think either hypothesis is likely. The murderer in external appearance is quite likely to be a quiet inoffensive looking man probably middle-aged and neatly and respectably dressed . . .

In support of Bond, it is worth quoting the lay testimony of policeman Walter Dew who wrote with commendable common sense, 'I did not see all the murdered women, but I saw most of them, and all I can say is that if the wounds they sustained are representative of a doctor's skill with the knife, it is a very simple matter to become a surgeon.'

In April 1966, the eminent pathologist, Francis Camps, published a paper on material on the Ripper case which had been discovered in the basement of the London Hospital in

Whitechapel. This find included drawings of Eddowes' body as it was found in Mitre Square. From his study of these, Camps concluded that 'the cuts shown on the body could not have been done by an expert.' Several years later in his foreword to Daniel Farson's book, *Jack the Ripper*, he wrote that studying the pictures of the Ripper victims made him realise that 'far from being the work of a skilled surgeon, any surgeon who operated in this manner would have been struck off the medical register.'

Was the Ripper left-handed? The belief that he was has its origins in the evidence given at the Nichols' inquest by Dr Llewellyn who stated that the wounds on the victim had been inflicted by a left-handed person. However, Melville Macnaghten pointed out in his paper on the murders that other doctors did not agree with Llewellyn and it is worth speculating whether the Welsh doctor was influenced by the Tabram killing at the beginning of August in which the victim seems to have died under a frenzy of blows administered by a man wielding a knife (or bayonet) in each hand.

Certainly, most of the evidence suggests that the Ripper was right-handed. No doctor demurred from the conclusion that the Ripper forced his victims to the ground and then cut their throat from left to right. To do this, the Ripper must have knelt beside the head of the victim on her right side and cut her throat with his right hand, while at the same time holding her head steady by the chin with his left hand. There is also the testimony of Dr Brown at the Eddowes inquest to consider. He stated that as the Ripper's knife had divided the gristle of the ensiform cartilage, he could determine that the weapon had been used with the point 'towards the left side and the handle towards the right', an observation which clearly indicates that the weapon was held in the right hand.

There are two images in existence of Ripper victims as they were found, a drawing of Catherine Eddowes and the police photograph of Mary Kelly. The Eddowes drawing shows the right leg bent at an acute angle with the left leg in its natural position, running straight from the body. The Kelly photograph shows the right leg bent at a similar angle, with the flesh on the upper part sliced away right down to the thighbone.

It is reasonable to assume that the Ripper, in order to mutilate his victims, sat between their legs. To make room for himself and to give himself support he would naturally have pushed aside the leg of the victim opposite to the hand with which he was holding his knife. In other words he would have pushed aside the *right* leg of Eddowes and Kelly so that he could mutilate them with his *right* hand. The removal of the flesh from Kelly's thigh is a further sign of right-handedness on the part of the killer. Given the partitioned wall close to Kelly's right, it would have been very difficult for the Ripper to have committed this atrocity with his left hand.

And yet, evidence of ambidexterity can be found in the Kelly killing. Here is how Dr Bond envisaged the initial assault:

In the first four cases the murderer must have attacked from the right side of the victim. In the Dorset street case, he must have attacked from in front or from the left, as there would be no room for him between the wall and the part of the bed on which the woman was lying. Again the blood had flowed on the right side of the woman and spurted on to the wall.

This reconstruction, especially when taken in conjunction with Bond's already stated belief that when attacking Kelly, the killer pulled the bedsheet across her face, almost certainly means the Ripper struck the first, and probably fatal, blow with a knife held in his left hand.

The Kelly murder is unique in that the Ripper killed his victim with a direct and sudden knife attack to the throat. The evidence in the previous murders strongly suggests that the

Ripper first strangled his victims before placing them on the ground and then cutting their throats. This would explain why in the earlier killings there was so little spillage of blood. If a person's throat is cut while alive, a huge jet of blood would spurt out, as indeed happened in the Kelly murder. It would also explain, as Professor Camps points out in *The Investigation of Murder*, the obstruction to the victim's mouth mentioned in at least two cases and why there was 'no sign or sound of a struggle.' The Ripper's decision to kill Kelly with his knife instead of throttling her can probably be ascribed to the victim's physical condition. Unlike the other victims, Kelly was a young powerfully-built woman who would have been able to defend herself, for a while at least, against a male attacker. Doubtless it would have seemed to the Ripper far safer to resort to his knife. By all accounts though Kelly still managed to emit at least one cry of 'Murder'.

But how did the Ripper manage to strangle his victims so quietly? Disparity in strength cannot be the whole answer. Even the weakest woman can, if given a chance, scream very loudly, and this, as far as is known, did not happen in any of the murders. The answer would then seem to lie in the sort of sex the Ripper had, or set out to have, with his victims. Curiously, few writers have tackled this important aspect of the murders.

Colin Wilson has suggested that the Ripper had his victims fellate him. Wilson pointed out that 'Jack the Stripper', the man who murdered and left naked six London prostitutes in the mid-1960s, practised this form of sex with his victims. Semen was found in the throats of some of the bodies. Unfortunately, similar details are not available on the Ripper victims. It is simply not known if the doctors found, or even looked for, semen in the corpses of the Ripper's victims.

Wilson's theory is plausible. It would certainly explain the speed and relative silence of the murders. When the women bent, or knelt, down the Ripper's hands would naturally, and without arousing suspicion, have fallen onto the victim's shoulders, throat, or even face, making sudden strangulation a very simple operation. The pressure of the Ripper's fingers could have caused the bruising found on the victims. Nichols had on the right side of her face 'a recent and strongly marked bruise' while on the left she had 'a circular bruise which might have been produced by the pressure of the fingers.' Chapman had a bruise over her right temple with 'two distinct bruises each the size of the top of a man's thumb on the forepart of the top of her chest.' Stride had bruising over both her shoulders and beneath her collar bone. The top of her dress had been unfastened, possibly an arrangement to facilitate oral sex. Eddowes was so badly cut and mutilated that little, if any, mention of bruising was made in the medical reports. In fact, it is likely that the Ripper was in such an agitated state when he got her alone that he strangled her immediately without any pretence at having sex.

These details, although distasteful, are important for they shed a good deal of light on the sort of man the Ripper must have been and underline the basic, but often ignored, fact that sex murderers are obsessed with sex, as Dr Bond made clear in his report. In other words, Jack the Ripper was a man whose interest in sex had become such an irresistible passion that it could only be quenched, temporarily at least, by violence. *The Aberrations of Sexual Life* by Krafft-Ebing (edited by Dr Alexander Hartwich) provides a great deal of food for thought for anyone trying to understand the motive and mentality of Jack the Ripper. According to this, the victim is often strangled, after which her body is cut up, with particular emphasis placed by her killer on her internal genitalia which are occasionally taken away to form part of a collection. The men who commit such crimes, according to this account, often show such deviations as 'homosexuality, paedophilia and fetishism', and display a 'high degree of hypersexuality'.

A prime example of what this hypersexuality means in practice is afforded by the wife of the Boston Strangler, Albert de Salvo. After de Salvo's arrest, she told police that he was sexually insatiable and that she had long since given up trying to satisfy him. He used to have her four times a day, and at weekends even more. This was in addition to the other women he was constantly having. He was even in the habit of propositioning women in his wife's presence.

THE RIPPER CORRESPONDENCE

One of the most enduring and lively debates in the Ripper case was whether Jack the killer and Jack the author were one and the same man. At the very outset it must be said that some, indeed most, of the purported Ripper correspondence is bogus, being the work of imitators and practical jokers. For example, in October 1888, a young Bradford woman by the name of Maria Coroner sent two Ripper letters to the police and local press claiming that the murderer would come to Bradford 'to do a little business.' Coroner was identified and charged with causing a breach of the peace. In her defence, she said that she had sent the letters as a prank. The variety of the Ripper letters in style, content, and handwriting indicates that this young woman was not alone in imitating the first letters bearing the name by which the Whitechapel murderer is known to posterity.

What then of these missives, the original 'Dear Boss' letter dated 25 September 1888 and the postcard sent on 1 October after the double murder? They must have been the work of the same man, but was that man the Ripper? The police at the time were clearly willing to accept that he was, otherwise they would not have posted up the famous facsimiles of the letter and postcard around London in the hope that anyone recognising the handwriting would come forward. At some later stage however, they seem to have revised this opinion, for

Macnaghten and Anderson, in their respective memoirs, are at one in denouncing the missives as a hoax perpetrated by a newspaperman (although they disagree totally about the identity of the killer).

In his autobiography entitled *The Lighter Side of My Official Life*, which was published in 1910, Anderson said that the letters were 'the creation of an enterprising journalist'. He claimed that he knew the name of the journalist, but declined to divulge this information because 'no public benefit would result from such a course, and the traditions of my department would suffer.' In his *Days of My Years*, published in 1915, Macnaghten treated his readers to the same coy treatment:

In this ghastly production I have always thought I could discern the stained forefinger of the journalist – indeed a year later I had shrewd suspicions as to the actual author. But whoever did pen the gruesome stuff it is certain to my mind that it was not the mad miscreant who had committed the murders.

Walter Dew, a humble PC at the time of the murders, was of much the same opinion as his one-time superiors. In his memoirs, which were not published until 1938, he said that the letters did not deceive him and that he was ready to stake his reputation that they were faked.

On the whole though, the journalist-hoax theory has failed to impress writers on the Ripper murders. Daniel Farson describes the police case as 'far from certain'. Robin Odell suggests that the police accused a journalist of writing the letters because of the poor relations which then existed between them and the press. Odell adds that from what Macnaghten and Anderson said, it seemed 'that the police had no idea who wrote the letters, but that they put up a thin pretence of knowing.' Donald McCormick agrees with this, and asks, most pertinently, why the journalist, if he was known to the police, was not prosecuted as a public nuisance, and why, if the letters were fake, the police did not issue a statement to that effect in order to allay public fears.

However, as Tom Cullen points out, it is the contents of the missives themselves which cast most doubt on the hoax theory. In the 'Dear Boss' letter the author announced his intention 'to get to work right away' and to provide the police with the ears of his next victim. The killer did in fact strike again only a few days after the letter was received by the Central News Agency. It is true that he did not cut off the ears of either Stride or Eddowes, but *an apparent attempt was made to do so to the latter*.

Imagine the Ripper's state of mind after the Stride murder. Being forced by the arrival of Louis Diemschutz to leave Stride's body intact would have thrown the Ripper into a frenzy. Any thoughts of fulfilling his gruesome promise to the police would have been shoved to the back of his mind; his immediate aim would have been to calm the fury that was raging inside him and that could only be achieved by the full disembowelment of a woman as quickly as possible. Only after this had been done would the Ripper have turned to his victim's ear. However, as things turned out, the Ripper had only a few minutes to kill and mutilate Eddowes before the City PC returned to Mitre Square. It is entirely feasible then that as the Ripper cut through the lobe of Eddowes' ear in preparation for slicing it off, he heard the approaching footsteps of PC Watkins and fled. This reconstruction, though of necessity speculative, does show that the reason the author of the postcard gave for not fulfilling his promise – that he did not have time to do so – does have the ring of truth about it.

Some writers have scorned the postcard as a serious piece of evidence on the grounds that as it was postmarked 1 October, the day after the murders, everyone including the unidentified journalist, would have known about the 'double event' and not just the murderer himself. However it is difficult to credit that a hoaxer, having penned one letter, would on learning of the next two murders send another communication, this time taking the trouble to smear it in red ink (or perhaps real blood) and include the comment 'Number one squealed a bit', a gratuitous piece of information which, as far as a joker would know, the police might have been able to disprove (and there is no evidence that they ever did). It seems perverse to accept this explanation rather than that the killer posted the card himself, either on 1 October or late on 30 September. Indeed, it seems perverse to refuse to accept the conclusion that, in sending the original letters, the murderer sought to establish his credentials and make famous his chosen soubriquet. Otherwise why did the author ask for the 'Dear Boss' letter to be held back until he had struck again and at the same time announce his intention to provide the police with the ears of his next victim?

One essential point to make here is that it would have been in character for the Ripper to have written these letters. The Ripper's aim was to kill and mutilate prostitutes, but beyond that he was clearly intent on challenging, indeed terrorising, Victorian society as a whole. This attitude may explain why the original Jack the Ripper letters were sent to the Central News Agency and not Scotland Yard. The former would ensure publicity for them, while the latter might have suppressed them in the public interest. In any case, it seems that many serial murderers feel the need to write to the police. In British criminal history, Dr Neill Cream and Neville Heath spring to mind. In Germany, Peter Kurten, the Düsseldorf Ripper, consciously modelled himself on his Victorian predecessor and sent letters to the authorities who duly responded by making facsimiles of them in the hope of the handwriting identified.

If the Ripper did write the original letter and postcard, what can be inferred about him from them? The handwriting in the letter is clear and well rounded and both margins are extremely neat. This together with the vocabulary shows the author to have been an educated man. There is not one spelling error in the letter although there are a few relatively tricky words such as 'knife', 'squeal', and 'laughed'. There are certainly 'Americanisms' in the letter, most notably in the form of address, 'Dear Boss'; again this is more likely to indicate an educated, or travelled, man than a native American. It is difficult to imagine an American saying, except in jest, 'just for jolly wouldnt you'. As far as the contents of the missives are concerned there is very little which could throw any light on the background of the author. There are though two phrases worth commenting on. The first is, 'I want to get to work right away if I get a chance'. What, one may ask, was stopping him? Was he under some form of restraint? Did he live outside London and need to await the opportunity, or excuse, to travel there? The Ripper was, after all, a weekend killer, an indication that he was not a totally 'free' man in his movements. 'How can they catch me now?' is the other phrase of interest. This question can of course be easily dismissed as the ravings of a lunatic. But this would be to ignore the overall tone of the letter which is calculated and deliberate and not at all the work of a man who has totally lost his grip with reality. On the contrary, the author of the 'Dear Boss' letter seemed to have some reason to believe himself beyond earthly justice.

What of the package containing the 'From Hell' letter and kidney letter which was sent to Mr Lusk? Was that genuine? Major Smith, to whom Lusk forwarded the parcel, thought that it was, as he explained in his memoirs:

. . . I made over the kidney to the police surgeon, instructing him to consult with the most eminent men in the profession, and send me a report without delay. I give the substance of it. The renal artery is about three inches long. Two inches remained in the corpse, one inch was attached to the kidney. The kidney left in the corpse was in an advanced stage of Bright's Disease: the kidney sent me was in an exactly similar state. But what was of far more importance, Mr. Sutton, one of the senior surgeons of the London Hospital whom Gordon Brown asked to meet him and another practitioner in consultation, and who was one of the greatest authorities living on the kidney and its diseases, said he would pledge his reputation that the kidney submitted to them had been put in spirits within a few hours of its removal from the body – thus effectually disposing of all hoaxes in connection with it. The body of anyone done to death by violence is not taken direct to the dissecting-room, but must await an inquest, never held before the following day at the soonest.

So authoritative did Smith sound that Ripperologists once accepted his conclusions over such people as Dr Saunders, who examined Eddowes' body and in a letter to the press dismissed the package as a students' prank. However, the publication of the Metropolitan Police report on the kidney in Stephen Knight's 1976 book, *The Final Solution*, proves that Dr Saunders was correct to be sceptical for this showed that 'similar kidneys might and could be obtained from any dead person upon whom a post mortem had been made from any cause, by students or a dissecting room porter. . .'

That the kidney was a prank is hardly surprising in view of Lusk's prominence which made him a natural target for such treatment. After all, the kidney package was not the only purported package from the Ripper which came Lusk's way. Only a few days before the kidney arrived, Lusk had receiv the following postcard:

Say Boss – You seem rare frightened, guess I'd like to give you fits, but can't stop time enough to let you box of toys play copper games with me, but hope to see you when I don't hurry too much

bye-bye, Boss

What about the chalked message found above the discarded piece of Catherine Eddowes apron? Was this really done by the Ripper? Once again, opinion is deeply divided. A Metropolitan Police report states:

> To those police officers who saw the chalk writing, the handwriting of the now notorious letters to a newspaper agency bears no resemblance at all.

However, this conclusion was challenged by *The Times* on 9 October:

> . . . The witnesses who saw the writing however state that it was similar in character to the letters sent to the Central News Agency and signed 'Jack the Ripper' and though it would have been far better to have clearly demonstrated this by photography, there is now every reason to believe that the writer of the letter and postcard sent to the Central News Agency is the actual murderer.

Whichever view is correct, in the absence of a photograph any comparison between the Ripper letters and the chalk message could only have been made from memory, hardly the best method. In any case, to say that the handwriting in the two instances differs is not to say that the same man did not write both. A person's handwriting can change considerably under certain circumstances such as stress or fear.

A major problem with the message found after the Eddowes' killing lies with the second word, 'Juwes'. At the Inquest, Coroner Crawford went to great lengths to ascertain the correct spelling of the word:

Coroner: How do you spell Jews?
PC Long: J-E-W-S.
Coroner: Now was it not on the wall J-U-W-E-S. Is it not possible that you were wrong?
PC Long: It may be as to spelling.

After sending the constable to fetch his notebook, the Coroner continued with his questioning:

Coroner: This notebook contains the entry you made at the time as to the words written on the wall?
PC Long: Yes, it does. What I wrote down was 'The Jews are the men that will not be blamed for nothing'. The Inspector made the remark that on the wall the word was J-U-W-E-S. I entered in my book what I believed was an exact copy of the words.
Coroner: At all events there was a discrepancy between what you wrote down and what was actually written on the wall so far as regards the spelling of the word 'Jews'?
PC Long: The only remark the Inspector made was about the spelling of the word 'Jews'.

Crawford also queried Detective Sergeant Halse on the spelling:

Coroner: Would you read out to us the exact words you took down in your book at the time?
Det. Sgt. Halse: 'The Juwes are not the men that will not be blamed for nothing.'

Coroner: That is J-U-W-E-S?
Det. Sgt. Halse: Yes.

Several reports appeared in the press stating that 'Juwes'
was the Yiddish word for Jews. On 15 October, Warren said in
The Times that he had inquired into this claim and found it to
be untrue. Warren commented, somewhat evasively, on this
word in his report on the chalk message to the Home
Secretary. It should be noted that he did not actually give an
opinion as to the meaning or origin of the word:

> I may mention that so great was the feeling with regard
> to the Jews that on 13th ult., the Acting Chief Rabbi
> wrote to me on the subject of the spelling of the word
> 'Juwes' (*sic*) on account of a newspaper asserting that this
> was the Jewish spelling in the Yiddish dialect. He added:
> 'In the present state of excitement it is dangerous to the
> safety of the poor Jews in the East End to allow such an
> assertion to remain uncontradicted. My community
> keenly appreciate your humane and vigilant action during
> this critical time.'

In their book, *The Ripper File*, which was essentially the
script of an earlier BBC programme on the murders, authors
Elwyn Jones and John Lloyd argue that Warren was
intentionally vague about the word 'Juwes' because as a senior
Freemason, he recognised it as a reference to three figures
who feature prominently in Masonic ritual – Jubela, Jubelo,
Jubelum, the murderers of Hiram Abiff, the Masonic Grand
Master and builder of Solomon's temple.

When found after their murder of Hiram Abiff, the three
'Juwes' lamented their fate. Jones and Lloyd show that there
are noteworthy similarities between the laments of Jubela and
Jubelo and the Ripper killings:

Jubela: That my throat had been cut across, my tongue torn out, and my body buried in the rough sands of the sea at low water mark, where the tide ebbs and flows twice in twenty-four hours, ere I had been accessory to the death of so good a man as our Grand Master, Hiram Abiff!

Jubelo: That my left breast had been torn open and my heart and vitals taken from thence and thrown over the left shoulder . . . ere I had conspired the death of so good a man as our Grand Master, Hiram Abiff!

The throats of all the Ripper victims had been cut. Chapman and Eddowes had their intestines thrown over their shoulders. This was no casual action as the following cross-examination at the Eddowes' inquest shows:

Dr Brown: The abdomen was all exposed; the intestines were drawn out to a large extent and placed over the right shoulder; a piece of the intestine was quite detached from the body and placed between the left arm and the body.

Coroner: By 'placed' do you mean put there by design?

Dr Brown: Yes.

Coroner: Would that also apply to the intestines that were over the right shoulder.

Dr Brown: Yes.

What Jones and Lloyd have to say here is certainly worth noting. It is surprising therefore that they did not continue their line of thought and show the similarities that exist between the Kelly murder and the lament of the third Masonic murderer:

Jubelum: That my body had been severed in two in the midst, and divided to the north and south, my bowels burnt to ashes in the centre and the ashes scattered by the four winds of heaven. . . It was I who gave him the fatal blow; it was I that killed him outright!

Does this explain the mysteries which surround the Kelly murder? Could the burning and the ashes mentioned here account for the role played by the fire in Kelly's death? Were her bowels burned to ashes in the fire? Did the Ripper use the fire to heat his knife or some other instrument so that he could follow the lament literally and burn Kelly's bowels to ashes 'in the centre of her body'? These are questions which are clearly worth pursuing.

CONCLUSION

It would be too ambitious to expect firm answers to the problems tackled in this analysis. In the Ripper case, with its scant details and paucity of reliable evidence, there are few certainties. This though is not to say that the exercise has been in vain. If the above review cannot establish certainties, acceptable probabilities remain and the ability to put these forward is no small step towards the identification of the Ripper.

Given what has been said above, the likelihood is that the Ripper was *not* a medical man; that he *was* the author of the original 'Jack the Ripper' missives; and that he *was* the man seen by George Hutchinson. This is perhaps little by way of conclusion, but it does represent a firm foundation for any further investigation, establishing as it does a frame of reference, and a rough description, against which any suspect can be compared and evaluated. Who though are these suspects?

* * * * *

THE SUSPECTS

OFFICIAL VIEWS

Anyone looking to the official files on the Ripper murders or to the memoirs of the policemen involved in the case for a clue as to the killer's identity will be struck by the lack of material and the diversity of opinion. As far as can be established, Warren, Monro, and Abberline left no written opinion, for public or private use, on who the Ripper was. Henry Smith, Robert Anderson, and Melville Macnaghten did publish their memoirs and they all wrote about the Ripper's identity, but with a total lack of agreement. Anderson states as an 'ascertained fact' that the murderer was a Polish Jew. Smith, while claiming that there was 'no man living who knows as much about those murders' as himself, plainly admits that he had no idea who the Ripper was. He totally rejects Anderson's view though, denouncing it as a 'reckless accusation'. Macnaghten, who was the last of the three men to go into print, puts forward his conviction that the Ripper committed suicide immediately after the Kelly murder. Sir Melville makes it clear that his suspect, whom he does not name, is not identical to Anderson's Polish Jew.

In any study of official views on the identity of the Ripper, pride of place must go to Macnaghten, for he is the only policeman whose public views are reflected in a police document (which he himself wrote). This is the famous Macnaghten memorandum which was written in February 1894. Clearly, this must be scrutinised, but beforehand it will be instructive to say a little on Macnaghten's background.

Macnaghten was born into the Ulster branch of an ancient West of Scotland family in June 1853. His family had strong links with India and it was there that he went on leaving Eton in 1872. While looking after his estates in Bengal, he became acquainted with James Munro, then Inspector General of the Bengal Police. In 1884, Monro returned to London to become Head of the Metropolitan Police CID. Three years later in 1887, Macnaghten too came home, and took up residence in Chelsea with his wife, Dora, the eldest daughter of a Canon of Chichester. He looked to his friend, Monro, for a post at Scotland Yard, but trouble arose over this appointment with the Commissioner, Sir Charles Warren, and it was not until 1889, by which time Monro had succeeded Warren, that Macnaghten joined the police as a detective officer, with the rank of Assistant Chief Constable. Two years later, he became Chief Constable in charge of the CID. In 1903, he was promoted to Assistant Commissioner, a rank he held until his retirement ten years later. He died in 1921.

In February 1894, Macnaghten was given the task of writing a report to rebut allegations which had appeared in *The Sun* newspaper that one Thomas Cutbush was the Ripper. In his paper, Macnaghten effectively demolishes the case against Cutbush and in doing so mentions three men, 'any one of whom would have been more likely than Cutbush', to have been the Ripper. These men he lists as 'Kosminski, a Polish Jew' 'Michael Ostrog a "Russian doctor"' and 'Montague John Druitt, said to be a doctor'. To prevent misunderstanding, he precedes his comments on these suspects with the remark, 'many homicidal maniacs were suspected, but no shadow of proof could be thrown on any one'. He also shows that he was far from certain as to the killer's fate by suggesting that after the Kelly murder, the Ripper either committed suicide or was placed in an asylum by his relatives.

It would have been obvious to Macnaghten from the outset that his memorandum was an important one and that it would be read not just by his superiors at Scotland Yard, but by his political masters in the Home Office who required it as a briefing note to answer any Parliamentary questions which might arise from the newspaper allegations. Macnaghten, one presumes, should therefore have been very careful in what he wrote; he would have wished to be accurate, but he would also have sought to impress his readers, two aims which are not always easy to reconcile. Macnaghten's apparent attempt to do so may be reflected in the fact that two versions of his notes are known to exist.

One is the official version which Macnaghten thought fit to submit to his Commissioner and which is now to be found in the Public Record Office. The other version, which he kept in his possession, is almost certainly a rough draft which served as the basis for the finished product. After the death of Macnaghten and his wife, these private notes became the property of their eldest daughter, Julia, who in turn passed them to her son, Gerald Donner. He took them to India where he died in 1964. The notes vanished around this time and are now feared to be lost forever. Fortunately, Macnaghten's younger daughter, Lady Christabel Aberconway, made a copy of them, probably in the 1930s, and retained this for posterity.

In 1959, an allegation appeared in Donald McCormick's book, *The Identity of Jack the Ripper*, that Macnaghten had once admitted deliberately destroying proof of the Ripper's identity in order to protect the killer's family. Lady Aberconway denied this and claimed that if her father did make such a statement it would only have been to stop himself being pestered by people at his club, *The Garrick*, on the subject of the Ripper. In a letter to *The New Statesman* on 7 November 1959, she disclosed that she possessed her father's notes on the killings and that in them he identified three men whom he suspected and which one in his opinion was the actual murderer.

In the same year, Lady Aberconway, coincidentally, played host to Dan Farson, who was then preparing a television programme on the Whitechapel murders. On learning of his interest in this subject, she allowed Farson to examine her father's papers and use them, minus the suspects' names, in the television programme. In 1965, Tom Cullen published the private notes, names and all, for the first time in his book, *Autumn of Terror*. Dan Farson followed this up with his own book, *Jack the Ripper*, in 1972. This again mentioned Macnaghten's notes. However, the following year, the BBC, in another television series on the Ripper, made public the contents of Macnaghten's official paper. It was immediately apparent that there were important differences between the two versions.

These differences concern the three suspects named by Macnaghten. In his official version, Macnaghten describes them as follows:

(1) A *Mr. M.J. Druitt*, said to be a doctor and of good family, who disappeared at the time of the Miller's Court murder, and whose body (which was said to have been upwards of a month in the water) was found in the Thames on 31st Dec. – or about 7 weeks after that murder. He was sexually insane and from private info I have little but that his own family believed him to have been the murderer.

(2) *Kosminski*, a Polish Jew and resident in Whitechapel. This man became insane owing to many years indulgence in solitary vices. He had a great hatred of women, especially of the prostitute class, and had strong homicidal tendencies: he was removed to a lunatic asylum about March 1889. There were many circs connected with this man which made him a strong 'suspect'.

(3) *Michael Ostrog*, a Russian doctor, and a convict, who was subsequently detained in a lunatic asylum as a homicidal maniac. This man's antecedents were of the

worst possible type, and his whereabouts at the time of the murders could never be ascertained.

In his *private* notes, Macnaghten precedes his comments on the three suspects with the following preamble:

. . . I enumerate the case of three men against whom the police held very reasonable suspicion. Personally, and after much careful and deliberate consideration, I am inclined to exonerate the last two, but I have always held strong opinions regarding No 1 and the more I think the matter over, the stronger do these opinions become. The truth, however, will never be known, and did, indeed, at one time lie at the bottom of the Thames, if my conjections (*sic*) be correct.

On the suspects themselves, Macnaghten had this to say:

No. 1 *Mr. M.J. Druitt*, doctor of about 41 years of age and of fairly good family, who disappeared at the time of the Miller's Court murder, and whose body was found floating in the Thames on 31st December (*sic*), i.e. seven weeks after the said murder. The body was said to have been in the water for a month, or more – on it was found a season ticket between Blackheath and London. From private information I have little doubt but that his own family suspected this man of being the Whitechapel murderer; and it was alleged that he was sexually insane.

No. 2 *Kosminski*, a Polish Jew, who lived in the very heart of the district where the murders were committed. He had become insane owing to many years' indulgence in solitary vices. He had a great hatred of women with strong homicidal tendencies. He was (and I believe still is) detained in a lunatic asylum about March 1889. This man in appearance strongly resembled the individual seen by the City P.C. near Mitre Square.

No. 3 *Michael Ostrog*, a mad Russian doctor and a convict and unquestionably a homicidal maniac. This man was said to have been habitually cruel to women, and for a long time was known to have carried about with him surgical knives and other instruments; his antecedents were of the very worst and his whereabouts at the time of the Whitechapel murders could never be satisfactorily accounted for. He is still alive.

The first question that these extracts is likely to elicit is where Macnaghten got Druitt's name from. There is no reference to him elsewhere in the police files or in the memoirs of any other police officer. Macnaghten himself offers no clue other than to cite 'private information', not a police report or an official inquiry. In other words, Macnaghten heard about Druitt from someone he knew in his private life and he chose to credit what that person told him.

In fact the casual tone of Macnaghten's memorandum suggests that he did not rely for any of his comments on accurate, well documented police files. Despite the fact that Macnaghten was writing for the Home Office about a very serious matter, he did not appear to be entirely au fait with his subject. As might be expected, this is particularly noticeable in the private version. Druitt was 'alleged' to be sexually insane; Macnaghten 'believed' that Kosminski was still detained in an asylum; Ostrog was 'said' to have been habitually cruel to women. On a number of points, Macnaghten is simply wrong. For example, in his private notes, he says that Kosminski 'strongly resembles the individual seen by the City PC near Mitre Square.' Now, as has already been seen, there was no such figure in the Mitre Square case. Plainly, Macnaghten confused PC Smith, who saw Stride with a man shortly before her death, with the commercial traveller, Lawende, who saw Eddowes with a male companion near Mitre Square only minutes before she was found dead. Macnaghten seemed to realise his error for he dropped the reference to the PC in his final version. These inaccuracies are strange in view of what we know about Sir Melville's professional ability. In reporting his death, *The Times* stated on 13 May 1921:

> He was equipped for his duties with a marvellous memory, which his colleagues often tried vainly to catch tripping. He never forgot a face or a name connected with any of his duties, and he knew the characteristics and histories of practically every man in the department, which numbered some 700.

Especially noteworthy are the errors Macnaghten makes about Druitt, who was not a 41-year-old doctor, but a 31-year-old barrister/teacher. Nor did Druitt commit suicide 'at the time of the Miller's Court murder' on 9 November 1888, but in very early December of that year, during which time he continued to work and live as normal. Macnaghten's much vaunted 'private information' on his prime suspect was not, it seems, wholly reliable.

Macnaghten continued to regard Druitt as his prime suspect for the rest of his life, as can be seen in his memoirs, *Days of My Years* (1915), where he makes no mention at all of a Polish Jew or a Russian doctor but only to the Ripper as a suicide. Macnaghten does not, of course, name Druitt, or even mention how the killer might have disposed of himself, but in the opening paragraph of Chapter IV of his book, *Laying The Ghost of Jack The Ripper*, he writes:

> . . . Although, as I shall endeavour to show in this chapter, the Whitechapel murderer, in all probability, put an end to himself soon after the Dorset Street affair in

November 1888, certain facts, pointing to this conclusion, were not in possession of the police till some years after I became a detective officer.

In the concluding paragraph of this chapter, Macnaghten writes:

. . . I do not think that there was anything of religious mania about the real Simon Pure (i.e. the Ripper), nor do I believe that he had ever been detained in an asylum, nor lived in lodgings. I incline to the belief that the individual who held up London in terror resided with his own people; that he absented himself from home at certain times, and that he committed suicide on or about the 10th November 1888, after he had knocked out a Commissioner of police and very nearly settled the hash of one of her Majesty's principal Secretaries of State.

Of particular interest in Macnaghten's memoirs is his revelation that the police did not suspect Druitt until several years after the murders, which in practice means sometime between 1889 and 1894 when the Home Office memorandum was written. This raises an intriguing question. *Was Macnaghten saying here that his own memorandum was the first time that Druitt appeared in a police document as a Ripper suspect? Did his accusation of Druitt in that memorandum constitute the 'certain facts' pointing to the Ripper as a suicide?* The upshot of this train of thought is to place even greater emphasis upon Macnaghten's 'private information' for this, rather than some long-vanished police file, seems indeed to have been his most important source on the young barrister/teacher. Macnaghten's 'private information' was indeed very private.

As has been shown, the existence of Macnaghten's notes did not become public knowledge until the second half of the twentieth century. With the benefit of hindsight however, it can now be seen that they were published in a slightly altered form, in a book which appeared in 1898. This was *Mysteries of Police and Crime*, by Major Arthur Griffiths, an Inspector of Her Majesty's Prisons and a personal friend of Macnaghten. In his book, Griffiths refers to the Ripper killings and claims that the police 'held very plausible and reasonable grounds of suspicion' against three men, although he makes it clear that as 'far as actual knowledge goes' the identity of the Ripper was never uncovered. Griffiths mentions no names, but his wording leaves no doubt that he had access to Macnaghten's *private* notes:

. . . One was a Polish Jew, a known lunatic, who was at large in the district of Whitechapel at the time of the murders, and who, having afterwards developed homicidal tendencies, was confined in an asylum. This man was said to resemble the murderer by the one person who got a glimpse of him – the police constable in Mitre Court (*sic*). The second possible criminal was a Russian doctor, also insane who had been a convict both in England and Siberia. This man was in the habit of carrying about surgical knives and instruments in his pockets; and at the time of the Whitechapel murders he was in hiding, or, at least, his whereabouts were never exactly known. The third person was of the same type, but the suspicion in his case was stronger, and there was every reason to believe that his own friends entertained grave doubts about him. He was also a doctor in the prime of life, was believed to be insane or on the borderland of insanity, and he disappeared immediately after the last murder, that in Miller's Court, on the 9th November, 1888. On the last day of that year, seven weeks later, his body was found floating in the Thames, and was said to have been in the water for a month. The theory in this case was that after his last exploit, which was the most fiendish of all, his brain gave way, and he became furiously insane and committed suicide. It is at least a strong presumption that 'Jack the Ripper' died or was put under restraint after the Miller's Court affair, which ended this series of crimes. . .

The view of the Ripper as a suicide has been echoed over the years by a number of 'official' writers. In *The Story of Scotland Yard*, which was published in 1935, the author, Sir Basil Thomson, wrote that at the time of the Ripper murders CID officers believed the murders to be the handicraft of 'an insane Russian doctor' who 'escaped arrest by committing suicide at the end of 1888' (Thomson seems here to have confused Druitt and Ostrog). By way of explanation he adds that 'the only clue was the fact that the man who ripped women up with what must have been a surgical knife had probably been at some time a medical student.' Sir John Moylan, Assistant Under Secretary at the Home Office, states in his *Scotland Yard and the Metropolitan Police* (1929) that it was 'almost certain' that the Ripper escaped justice by committing suicide. What is essential to understand here though is that, as far as can be seen, Macnaghten is *the sole source of these claims*. This is why the above writers repeated Macnaghten's error by describing the suicide suspect as a doctor, rather than a barrister, a clear measure of how reliable their views are.

Most significantly, Macnaghten's colleague, Robert Anderson, had his own views on the subject of the Ripper. Indeed, he seems to have changed his mind at some point. In the Ripper files, he confesses in one document that the police had no clue at all as to the Ripper's identity. However, in his autobiography, *The Lighter Side of My Official Life*, published in 1910, he says:

One did not need to be a Sherlock Holmes to discover that the criminal was a sexual maniac of a virulent type; that he was living in the immediate vicinity of the scene of the murders; and that, if he was not living absolutely alone, his people knew of his guilt, and refused to give him up to justice. During my absence, the Police had made a house-to-house search for him, investigating the case of every man in the district whose circumstances were such that he could go and come and get rid of his bloodstains in secret. And the conclusion we came to was that he and his people were certain low class Jews; for it is a remarkable fact that people of that class in the East End will not give up their number to Gentile Justice.

And the results proved that our diagnosis was right on every point. For I may say at once that 'undiscovered murders' are rare in London and the 'Jack the Ripper' crimes are not within this category. . .

Having regard to the interest attached to this case, I am almost tempted to disclose the identity of the murderer. . . But no public benefit would result from such a course, and the traditions of my old department would suffer. I will merely add that the only person who ever had a good view of the murderer unhesitatingly identified the suspect the instant he was confronted with him; but he refused to give evidence against him.

In saying that he was a Polish Jew I am merely stating a definitely ascertained fact. And my words are meant to specify race, not religion. For it would outrage all religious sentiment to talk of the religion of a loathsome creature whose utterly unmentionable vices reduced him to a lower level than that of a brute.

A close inspection of Anderson's account shows that he is speaking not of the period after the Kelly murder on 9 November, but of after the Chapman killing on 8 September.

This in turn means that the Polish Jew he refers to is almost certainly John Pizer, the so-called Leather Apron who was arrested on suspicion of having killed Annie Chapman, but released when he provided the authorities with a cast-iron alibi. It is difficult to believe that a senior police officer would be so irresponsible as to accuse, even indirectly, a man who had been cleared of guilt, but given the similarities between Anderson's story and the Pizer case, no other conclusion is possible (unless it is that the police released a man they *knew* to be the Ripper, thereby allowing him to kill again!). Pizer's arrest was a major event in the Ripper case. It attracted great publicity and led briefly to the belief that the killer had been caught. In addition, a witness did come forward to identify Pizer and did later retract his evidence, but not for the reason suggested by Anderson. As has already been shown, this 'witness' was Emanuel Violenia whose evidence, according to *The Times*, was 'wholly distrusted' by the police. Doubtless, Violenia was only too glad to change his original statement when faced with the prospect of being charged with wasting police time.

Conclusive proof that Anderson's account should not be taken seriously lies in the fact that no support for it can be found in the official files or in any of the other police memoirs. Indeed, Sir Henry Smith, Commissioner of the City Police, attacks Anderson most forcefully in his own autobiography:

Sir Robert does not tell us how many of 'his people' sheltered the murderer, but whether they were two dozen in number, or two hundred, or two thousand, he accuses them of being accessories to these crimes before and after their committal. Surely Sir Robert cannot believe that while the Jews, as he asserts, were entering into this conspiracy to defeat the ends of justice, there was no one among them with sufficient knowledge of the criminal law to warn them of the risks they were running.

Sir Robert talks of the 'Lighter Side' of his 'Official Life'. There is nothing 'light' here; a heavier indictment could not be framed against a class whose conduct contrasts most favourably with that of the Gentile population of the Metropolis. . .

(All of the above renders quite incomprehensible the so-called 'Swanson Marginalia', pencilled notes purportedly made by Chief Inspector Donald Swanson in a copy of Anderson's memoirs, naming Kosminski as Anderson's suspect. Perhaps a serious forensic examination of these notes, which came to light shortly before the Centenary of the Ripper murders in 1988, could shed some valuable light on this mystery.)

Inspector Abberline, who did not publish his memoirs, is reported to have believed that the poisoner, George Chapman, and the Ripper were one and the same. When Chapman was arrested on 25 October 1902, Abberline is said to have told the arresting officer, 'You've got Jack the Ripper at last!'

Some support for the Chapman theory comes from Detective Sergeant Leeson in his Lost London (1934) where he describes it as the only theory to have 'the slightest foundation in fact'. However, Leeson, who was only a constable during the Ripper murders, does not endorse the theory. He admits that he does not know the Ripper's identity and claims that the mystery will never be solved. He does however have his suspicions in the form of a certain (unnamed) doctor 'who was never far away when the crimes were committed. . .'

Walter Dew, also a constable during the Ripper murders, dismisses the doctor theory in his autobiography, *I Caught Crippen*, where he states that 'not even the rudiments of surgical skill were needed to cause the mutilations I saw.' He also saw no good reason to believe that George Chapman was, in fact, the Ripper. As for his own opinion on the killer's identity, Dew confesses that, despite being closely involved in the Ripper case from start to finish, 'I am as mystified now as I was then by the man's amazing elusiveness'.

The only reasonable conclusion that can be reached here is that the police had no firm idea who the Ripper was and that each officer, when he came to write his memoirs, was forced to rely on his own 'private information' and recollections of his own role in the case. A certain amount of embellishment and exaggeration is to be expected. The Ripper memoirs, after all, were written to make money and therefore had to attract buyers. Consequently, Sir Henry Smith, having no suspect to name, wrote at length about a subject he knew something about, namely the kidney which was sent to Mr Lusk and forwarded by that gentleman to the City Police. Macnaghten turned to his memorandum, and in particular the private version of it, for material to include in his autobiography. Leeson and Dew, very junior officers at the time of the murders, concentrated on local colour and atmosphere.

It may have been vanity as well as pecuniary interest which led Anderson to relate his discredited story about the Polish Jew 'positively identified' as the Ripper. Being Head of the CID during the murders, Anderson could not, presumably, bring himself to admit publicly that he was as much in the dark as everyone else about who the killer was. But whatever Anderson's motivation, the important point to make here, is that when given the chance to state his views to the world, the former Irish barrister could find a no more convincing suspect than John Pizer, a man whose innocence was established before the double murder of 30 September.

If the police memoirs are disappointing, the official Ripper files are even more so. Given the interest generated by the murders and the impact they had on Victorian society, one would expect the files to be crammed with detailed reports and investigations which reach at least a tentative conclusion as to the Ripper's identity. This however is simply not the case. Macnaghten's memorandum is in fact the only document which comes close to listing anyone as a serious suspect and, as has already been shown, he obtained Druitt's name from 'private information'. The other names in the file are of men who simply cropped up during enquiries or were brought to the attention of the police. One example is 'Mary', a male barber despite his name, who was believed by the German police to have been in the habit of sticking sharp objects into women's breasts, but who was found to have been in prison during the murders. Another is a former soldier called Dick Austen who was reputedly a woman hater who had threatened to 'kill every whore and cut her insides out', but who could not be traced by Abberline. There are in fact a good number of such cases in the files, men who 'could have been' the Ripper but who, as far as is known, were not investigated to the point where they could be eliminated from suspicion.

As far as the Ripper's identity is concerned however, it is improbable that the files ever contained anything more important than Macnaghten's memorandum, otherwise the diversity of opinion between the senior police officers involved in the case would surely not have occurred and Arthur Griffiths, writing in 1898, would not have quoted Macnaghten's private notes. Also, if such a document had existed, would it have vanished without trace? Would not a copy have been kept by its author or another police officer? And given the interest in the subject, would that person, or his descendants, have resisted the urge to publish it?

There is one more scenario to consider. This is that some people in authority knew very well who the Ripper was and that, to protect his identity, they ensured that his name was never committed to the files. Support for this viewpoint can be found in the claim mentioned earlier that Macnaghten had deliberately destroyed documentary proof of the Ripper's identity. This allegation was originally made by Hargrave L.

Adam, a noted criminologist, who said that Macnaghten had once made this startling confession to him. 'An unprecedented thing, surely, for a police official to do', Adam commented. In fact, Macnaghten in an article in the *Daily Mail* in 1913 stated that he had indeed destroyed all his documents on the Ripper case and that 'there is now no record of the secret information which came into my possession at one time or another'. That is, surely, an unprecedented thing for a police official to say.

More will be said about Adam's allegations later, but it is worth recording here that Macnaghten himself seems to have indulged in removing items from the Ripper files himself. In fact, it seems that Macnaghten appropriated nothing less than the original 'Dear Boss' letter. In his review of Dan Farson's book on the Ripper in the *Guardian* on 7 October, Philip Loftus related that his active interest in the subject went back to 1950 when he was staying with Gerald Donner, Macnaghten's grandson. In Donner's home Loftus saw a Jack the Ripper letter, written in red ink, framed and hanging on the wall. Loftus thought this to be a copy and said so to Donner. 'Copy be damned,' said Donner, 'that's the original.' As proof, Donner produced his grandfather's handwritten notes (which as mentioned earlier disappeared after Donner's death in India).

So much then for the 'official' views on the Ripper's identity. It remains to be seen what the 'amateur' sleuths have had to say over the years about this mystery.

UNOFFICIAL VIEWS

The purpose of this section is not to give an exhaustive account of all the published theories on the Ripper's identity. It is instead to get straight to the heart of the matter and consider which suspects match the picture of the sort of man experience and common sense suggest the Ripper to have been, and which tally broadly with the conclusions reached in the section concerning evidence. That picture is summed up here as follows:

> Jack the Ripper was male; he was a sex maniac who acted out of hatred for the female sex; he worked alone; he was, as George Hutchinson believed, in his thirties; he was an Englishman; and soon after the last murder he either committed suicide or was placed under some form of detention.

At a stroke then any theory of the 'Jill the Ripper' variety can be dismissed out of hand. True, there is no absolute physical proof that the Ripper was male; as far as is known, the doctors who inspected the Ripper's victims found no semen or any sign that the women had had intercourse with the murderer. But why would a prostitute go to a secluded spot late at night with another woman? And it is simply too much to accept that a woman could inflict on a member of her own sex, or the other sex for that matter, the sort of injuries suffered by Mary Kelly. This is not to take a starry-eyed view of the so called gentler sex, but merely to record that while there have been many brutal female murderers, none have been known to mutilate a victim *for the sake of mutilation*. The drive to do this, it can be confidently stated, is the preserve of the male sex murderer.

The man who cut Mary Kelly to ribbons was clearly on the brink of obvious insanity and could not long have remained undetected in normal society. In any case, such was the murderer's taste for blood at that stage, that he would not have stopped killing unless he was forced to do so. It follows then that any theory naming a suspect who lived as a free man for many years after 1888 must be treated with real scepticism. Many suspects fall at this hurdle, including Dr Roslyn D'Onston Stephenson, a colourful adventurer who lived a peaceful, if eccentric, existence until well into the twentieth century when he simply disappeared and Dr Tumblety, an American collector of female body parts, who did not die until 1903. Down too goes Walter Sickert, the painter, who lasted – almost incredibly – until 1942. Another casualty here is James Kelly who was incarcerated in Broadmoor Criminal Lunatic Asylum in 1883 for murdering his wife, and who escaped from that institution in early 1888. Kelly's antecedents and his mental condition certainly make him an eligible candidate for the role of a serial killer. However, the problem here is that Kelly remained at large until 1927 when he returned to Broadmoor Asylum and gave himself up. It defies belief that he murdered five women in 1888 and then went into 'retirement' for the next thirty-odd years.

The Ripper's age is another obstacle which many suspects fail to clear. The Ripper was almost certainly under 40 years of age, which means (to choose but one example) that James Maybrick, the Liverpool merchant at the centre of the 'Ripper Diary' controversy, who was 50 at the time of the killings, can be confidently removed from the list of suspects.

The fact that the Ripper was a sex maniac rules out a whole host of suspects, including the above mentioned Dr Tumblety; Stephen Knight's 'political assassin', Sir William Gull; and the convicted murderers, George Chapman, Dr Neill Cream, Frederick Deeming and William Bury. Chapman and Cream were both poisoners and there is no evidence that they ever changed their modus operandi. Cream in any case was in an American prison at the time of the Ripper murders. Deeming too, who murdered two wives and his four children, had an alibi in the form of an English prison. Moreover, all three men lived apparently rational lives well after 1888. Cream and Deeming were both hanged in 1892 and Chapman in 1903. It is true that William Bury, a sawdust merchant, brutally murdered his wife in Scotland in 1889, but he did so for personal reasons, not due to a hatred of women.

The Ripper's ability to speak and write English is a mighty obstacle in the path of any theory which sees the Ripper as anything other than an Englishman, or at least a native speaker of English. The man seen by George Hutchinson in the company of Mary Jane Kelly shortly before she was murdered was almost certainly the Ripper. Hutchinson heard this man and Kelly conduct a conversation, but did not detect a foreign accent. It is true that Hutchinson said that the man had a Jewish appearance, but he almost certainly meant an integrated Jew, someone who in terms of education and background was to all intents and purposes, an Englishman. He clearly did not mean a low class, newly-arrived Jewish immigrant who would have stood out as an obvious foreigner. Indeed it is highly unlikely that Whitechapel prostitutes would have gone with such a man at the height of the Ripper scare. In short, the Ripper was clearly a man who was capable of winning the confidence of the women he approached.

All of these points tell heavily against the theory that a foreigner like Aaron Kosminski was the Ripper. It is impossible to believe that Kosminski, a recently arrived Polish hairdresser, was the man who so charmed Mary Kelly with the flourish of his red handkerchief. At the time of the Ripper murders, Kosminski was a complete down and out who was suffering from hallucinations. When he was finally placed in Colney Hatch Lunatic Asylum in March 1891 (and the fact that he had remained a free man for so long after the last Ripper murder is itself a reason for rejecting him as a suspect), he was described as a person who wandered the streets, eating food which he found in the gutter. Kosminski remained in the asylum until his death in 1919. As far as can be seen, asylum records contain no suggestion that he was the Ripper.

It is not even at all certain that this Aaron Kosminski is identical to the Kosminski mentioned by Macnaghten in his memorandum and this doubt underlines the fact that some of the Ripper suspects cannot be positively identified. Indeed, two of the early suspects, the 'Dr Stanley' mentioned by Matters in his *Mystery of Jack the Ripper* and Donald McCormick's 'Dr Pedachenko', cannot be proven to have ever existed.

This ruthless pruning of the Ripper suspects has left only one standing – Macnaghten's prime suspect, Montague John Druitt. He must now be scrutinised.

MONTAGUE JOHN DRUITT
AN EXERCISE IN DEDUCTIVE REASONING

Montague John Druitt was born in Wimborne, Dorset, on 15 August 1857, the second son of William Druitt, a prominent local surgeon, and his wife, Ann. He attended Winchester College, one of the leading public schools in the country, where he displayed skill at debating, and then read Classics at New College, Oxford. On graduating with a disappointing Third, he took up a post as a teacher at a boys' boarding school in Blackheath, to the south east of London, where, in pursuit of his life-long passion for cricket, he joined the local sports club. Still teaching, he joined the Inner Temple in 1882 and was called to the Bar in 1885. At the end of November 1888 he got into 'serious trouble' at his school and was dismissed, shortly after which he apparently travelled by rail to Hammersmith in north-west London and drowned himself in the River Thames. His body was pulled from the river at neighbouring Chiswick on the last day of the year. The inquest into his death, at which his elder brother, William, gave evidence, concluded that he had committed suicide 'whilst of unsound mind'.

These are the salient facts of the short, tragic life of Montague John Druitt, the 'sexually insane' prime suspect of Melville Macnaghten. The purpose here is not to delve deeply into the minutiae of Druitt's life, but to analyse the existing evidence so that we can better assess Macnaghten's accusation.

The *starting point* is this author's discovery (see pages 250–1) that when the nineteen-year-old Druitt arrived at Oxford from Winchester in the autumn of 1876, he was refused membership of the Oxford Union, the most famous debating society in the world. This *Rosetta Stone*-like find tells us something at long last about Druitt's *character* and what his peers thought of his moral standing, which, obviously, was not very much. That Druitt, *a former treasurer of the Winchester Debating Society whose two brothers had been elected to the Union*, should himself be barred from it strongly suggests that when he entered Oxford he was already displaying signs of the 'sexual insanity' ascribed to him by Macnaghten.

The *London Gazette* for 25 January 1881 recorded that the newly graduated Druitt had passed the Preliminary Civil Service Examination. Druitt failed, though, to secure a post with the Civil Service, which is not surprising given his poor degree. However what is relevant for our purposes is the identity of *two* of the men who sat that examination with him, and what those men signal about Druitt.

One was Evelyn Ruggles Brise (1857–1935), an Old Etonian who, with a First from Balliol College, Oxford, did obtain a Civil Service post. He was attached to the Home Office, where he rose rapidly, becoming the Private Secretary to Henry Matthews, the Home Secretary at the time of the Ripper murders. In 1892 Ruggles Brise became Commissioner of Prisons and in 1895 Chairman of the Prison Commission, a post he held until 1921.

Cricket records show that in June 1876 Ruggles Brise and Druitt played against each other in the *Winchester vs Eton* match. A few months later the two men went up to Oxford, where they spent *four years* studying and playing cricket. As

Private Secretary to the Home Secretary, Ruggles Brise would have worked closely with senior police officers, in which capacity he stood administratively, if not operationally, at the heart of the Ripper investigation, as the official files attest.

Ruggles Brise must therefore be considered Macnaghten's main source on Druitt. At Oxford, Ruggles Brise would have learned why Druitt was blackballed by the Union, a shock which probably caused quite a stir. He was also in a position to hear about Druitt's suicide soon after the last Ripper murder and of any rumours which circulated about him. It is totally credible, therefore, that when Macnaghten was tasked with writing his paper on the Ripper case in 1894, he drew on material supplied to him by his fellow Old Etonian and one-time Home Office liaison, Ruggles Brise.

Part of that material can be deduced from the fact that at Oxford Ruggles Brise was a member of Vincent's Club, the university club for Blues and sportsmen, along with *Thomas Seymour Tuke*, whose family ran the Manor House Asylum in Chiswick, close to where Druitt's body was dragged from the Thames and where Druitt's mother died in 1890. *In short, Ruggles Brise told Macnaghten that Dr Tuke had declared Druitt 'sexually insane' and why he had done so.*

This would clear up another matter, namely how Arthur Griffiths got permission to use Macnaghten's notes in his 1898 book *Mysteries of Police and Crime*. The answer appears to be that Griffiths, an Inspector of Prisons, approached his superior, Evelyn Ruggles Brise, Chairman of the Prison Commission, *who had helped Macnaghten compile his notes and who had known the prime suspect personally.*

There is yet more. Macnaghten wrote his report for his political masters, which in 1894 meant Prime Minister William Gladstone and Home Secretary Herbert Asquith, *both of whom had served as president of the Oxford Union.*

That implies that Asquith – a near-contemporary of Druitt at Oxford and, like him, a London barrister – knew about this 'sexually insane' suspect long before Macnaghten put pen to paper, which in turn suggests that the factual inaccuracies in Macnaghten's notes, so baffling up to now, were actually official disinformation designed to protect not just Druitt's pupils (see pages 251–2), but also the policeman's own highly placed sources.

The second examination candidate of relevance here is Charles Kains Jackson (1857–1933), who, like Druitt, also failed to obtain a Civil Service post. There is reason to believe that he and Druitt had much more than this failure in common.

A lawyer, poet and journalist, Charles Kains Jackson was, by Victorian standards, an outspoken advocate of the '*Greek ideal*' of boy-love. He was a 'friend' of Lord Alfred 'Bosie' Douglas (1870–1945), the most famous lover of Oscar Wilde. Bosie Douglas went to Winchester, the same school as Druitt, and was an active pursuer of boys before he met Wilde in 1891. As shall be seen, Oscar Wilde, who was at Oxford with both Montague Druitt and his brother William, was, like Montague, barred from the Union. Given the tragedy which was to engulf Wilde, there can be little doubt as to the exact nature of his problem with that august body.

It is against this background that we must ask why Druitt accepted a teaching post at the Blackheath school in early 1881. Did he do so simply to support himself? If so, why did he stay there after he had begun his legal work?

The likeliest explanation *by far* is that he went to (and remained at) the school because he found boys sexually attractive. At a boarding school, he would have been in close contact with boys, *day and night*, and would have been able to watch them bathe, probably naked, in the school's swimming pool.

In considering the nature of the 'serious trouble' which led to Druitt's dismissal from his school at the end of November 1888, we must remember exactly what happened, which was that, shortly after being sacked, Druitt simply *vanished*. Nobody *knew* what had become of him until his body was pulled from the Thames on the last day of 1888.

However, thanks to an important, but curiously neglected, source, we know what his friends *thought* had happened to him. During the month of December 1888, the committee of Druitt's Blackheath sports club held a meeting, the minutes of which recorded that Druitt, 'having gone abroad', was to be relieved of his post as honorary secretary and treasurer.

Those three words – *having gone abroad* – shine like a beacon straight to the heart of the Druitt mystery. Druitt's sporting friends would have known why he had been dismissed from his school and the fact that they *believed* that he had left the country is crucial to our understanding of Druitt and, therefore, the Ripper case. What Druitt's friends almost certainly meant was that he had *fled* the country to avoid prosecution under the Criminal Law Amendment of 1885, as Lord Arthur Somerset did the following year in the wake of the Cleveland Street Scandal, and as Oscar Wilde should have done when he was forced to drop his libel case against the Marquis of Queensberry in 1895.

Where Druitt went after being sacked can be deduced via simple logic: *a 'sexually insane' man sought help from an asylum.* Next to Hammersmith is Chiswick, where stood in 1888 the Manor House Asylum in Chiswick Lane, a very short distance from Thornycroft's Wharf, where Druitt's body was pulled out of the river. This asylum, *where Druitt's mother died in 1890*, was run by Thomas Seymour Tuke, *an Oxford contemporary of both Montague Druitt and his brother, William, a member of the same Oxford Masonic lodge as Oscar Wilde, and of the same Oxford sports club as Evelyn Ruggles Brise. Voilà!*

The logic is that, on being sacked, Druitt went to Tuke in the hope of receiving 'protection' against criminal prosecution and *only* when he saw that this was not possible did he decide to end his torment, which is why he had bought a return

1. George Francis 'Frank' Miles (1852–91), artist and onetime companion of Oscar Wilde. His relationship with Oscar Wilde helped inspire Wilde's only novel, *The Picture of Dorian Gray*, the story of a privileged man whose life of vice in the East End of London turns him into a murderer. For the significance of the above border, see page 262.

2. An impression of a man seen with the last victim, Mary Jane Kelly, shortly before she was murdered. (*Illustrated Police News*)

3. Lily Langtry, the society beauty made famous by Frank Miles in drawings such as this. In 1881, she gave birth to a daughter who had been sired by a member of the Royal Family. To support herself, she became an actress. Note that Miles signed his picture with his initials, 'FM.' These letters appear on the wall beside the corpse of Mary Kelly (see illustration 8).

4. Oscar Wilde stayed with Frank Miles as his 'boarder' at 1 Tite Street from 1880 until late 1881. In 1885, Wilde moved into 16 Tite Street with his wife, Constance. Wilde dropped apparent hints about the Ripper murders in several of his works, most notably *The Picture of Dorian Gray*. Wilde joined Oxford's Apollo Masonic Lodge in February 1875, along with Thomas Tuke, who ran the Chiswick asylum close to where Druitt's body was recovered. (*Neil Bartlett Collection*)

THE outbreak of the mysterious salmon disease in the Tweed is the more to be regretted, as the season which has just closed has been the best for many years, and there seemed every prospect that this famous river would regain its old reputation. The disease was very prevalent in the spring of 1879, but now it has come at a worse season, and just when the river is swarming with fish. A company in Berwick, who farm the net-fishings, have this year declared a dividend of 2½ per cent.; last year they were obliged to expend £2,500 of their reserve fund, in order to pay expenses.

HOSPITAL CHRISTMAS.

How happily will sleep that night
  Each little girl and boy,
Their tiny arms with fond delight
  Clasped round a brand new toy;
To them it is a joy supreme
  Such pretty things to see,
And if at midnight hour they dream,
  Of pain it will not be!

SURELY the climax of teetotal festivity has at length been reached. *Vide* the following advertisement:—

The Temperance Christmas Hamper contains an assortment of pure, non-intoxicating drinks for the dinner-table, banquets, festive gatherings, &c., including Sparkling Hygeia, Sparkling Phosphade, Aquatheim, &c.

THE Stereoscopic Company have again brought out their well-known "Guinea Box." This year's box contains a phantascope, which produces a series of grotesque apparitions, a little printing press, a "prolific top," and three or four other amusing novelties, and it will probably prove as attractive as its predecessors.

SCRUTATOR.

MRS. LANGTRY.

I WAS just about to write my impressions of Mrs. Langtry as an actress, when the following letter from a lady in London to a friend in the country, upon the function at the Haymarket Theatre last Thursday, fell in my way, so I publish it in order to save myself trouble:—

MY DEAR MARY,—It was such fun on Thursday at the Haymarket, and I was so sorry, dear, you could not get a ticket. We had such trouble in getting ours. Mitchell said that the theatre people had kept them all for themselves, and the theatre people said that Mitchell had taken them all. I don't know what was the real story, or what Jack paid for our stalls, for he has not yet told me.

You know, dear, one was obliged to go to this thing, for I never should have heard the end of it from *her* if I had not been there. Well, everybody was there who could get in. The Prince and Princess had the Royal box, and the Tecks and the Lornes were, I heard, stuffed away somewhere, though I did not see them. Only fancy, dear, *her* going on the stage, and attacking an art. The play was called "She Stoops to Conquer." It is very funny. I suppose it is written by Byron or Burnand, because it is funny, and I think it is intended to represent our grandfathers and grandmothers, for the actors wore powder, and were dressed like footmen. Not a bad idea, don't you think so? *She* came on in the first act, in a lovely dress, dear. I knew at once it was by that horrid Mason, who never will, say what I can, make my waist as small as *hers*, although you know it is really smaller when neither of us squeeze in. Her stays must have been awfully tight. It was a lemon-coloured satin brocade, with large bunches of roses, and I mean to get one like it, for I am sure it would suit my style. *She* had not much paint on, and I suppose *she* thinks *she* does not require it. We all clapped *her* when *she* came on. Poor thing, *she* did look so dreadfully nervous that I quite pitied *her*. But *she* soon got over it, and then went on quite like a real actress. I expected *her* every moment to break down, and was so glad that *she* didn't. You know that you and I have always said that *she* is a fool, but it really seems that *she* isn't, for I heard someone behind me, who looked like one of those horrid men who write for newspapers, say: "She's got some stuff in her." In the next act *she* came on in another dress. It was a cream-coloured white Indian muslin, made with a sash, and *she* had on a large hat and feathers. You know, dear, people say that *her* head is classical, and I think classical heads look better without large hats on them. *She* had not much to do in this act, and when someone asked the newspaper-man behind me, he said, "This isn't her great scene; you'll see her as a barmaid in the next one." As a barmaid! only think. I wonder what next *she* will do? Well, *she* really did come dressed up as a barmaid. Oh, it was such fun. Do you know, I quite envied *her*. Between you and me, *she* did look quite too nice. *She* had a short grey dress, and *her* waist looked still smaller than before. How does *she* manage it? You know, dear, that *her* feet will not go in your shoes or mine. But they didn't look large at all. Poor thing, how *she* must have pinched them in. *She* bobbed and curtsied just as I suppose all barmaids do. How I should like to be a barmaid! What fun it would be. The young man, whom *she* was to end by marrying, seemed to like her better as a barmaid than as a fine lady, for he got quite familiar, and I thought at one time that he was going to kiss *her*. But *she* stopped him, and said something about a horse's teeth—I forget what it was—but it made us laugh so, and gave *her* a good opportunity to show *her* own teeth, which *she* likes, you know. When *she* had done being a barmaid, the newspaper man said, "She'll do; she only wants a little more experience, and to learn to keep her hands quiet, to be a capital actress." In the last act *she* was still dressed as a barmaid, and everybody seemed somehow to marry everybody, except a gentleman in a red coat, who calls a lady about as old as himself his mamma. They applauded very much at the end, and when the curtain was taken up again a lot of bouquets were thrown to *her*. One was thrown from the Royal box, one came from the Duchess of Manchester, one from Lady Londesborough, one—a huge one—from a gentleman sitting in a box opposite the Royal box, and I threw *her* the one that Jack had given me. *She* picked them all up, and stood bowing and smiling until the curtain fell. Jack, you know dear, is very clever, and I would back his opinion against anyone else's upon anything in the world. He had not said a word whilst the play was going on, but when it was over, I asked him to give me his true opinion about *her*. He said "she's ripping," and for Jack to say this *she* must be very good. All the newspapers praise *her*, and it must be delightful to have whole columns written about one's face, and one's eyes, and one's acting, and have hundreds and hundreds of people looking at one through opera-glasses, instead of staying at some dull country house; and when one goes to a horrid county ball, only having it said in a little paragraph that one is dressed in blue, or red, or yellow. *She* says that *she's* engaged at the Haymarket to act in another piece. I do hope that she will not fail in it, don't you, dear? How I should like to be an actress—it seems so easy! My eyes are as good as hers, in fact, better; my feet are smaller, and so is my waist. All my friends say I am clever, and Jack says my voice is better than *hers*. Tell me truly what you think of it. I saw Miss Neilson act Juliet once a long time ago. I am sure I could do it like her. But then, if I do play Juliet, could I wear in one of the acts a barmaid's dress? It really is quite too pretty. Write at once, and say what you think. What awful weather, dear!
          Always yours affectionately,

5. From *Truth* magazine of 22 December 1881, a satirical article on Lily Langtry's stage debut which was attended by the Prince of Wales. This article contains the line, 'He said, "she's ripping," and for Jack to say this *she* must be very good.'

MR. OSCAR WILDE is going to the United States at the end of this week in the *Arizona*, having made arrangements to bring out his Republican play "Vera" there, and during his stay he will deliver a series of lectures on modern life in its romantic aspect. The Americans are far more curious than we are to gaze at all those whose names, from one cause or another, have become household words, and in this I think that they are wiser than we are, for it is difficult to realise the personality of anyone, without having seen him. Mr. Wilde—say what one may of him—has a distinct individuality, and, therefore, I should fancy that his lectures will attract many who will listen and look.

DEAR TRUTH,—Will you give me some advice? I am tormented by the organ nuisance. The police are very civil and do all in their power to keep it down. I don't mind being abused or sworn at, and day by day leave my work, or my luncheon, or my dinner, to make the itinerant musician "move on." It is troublesome, but what can I do? There seems no law to allow you to give a nuisance in charge if, after due warning, he comes again. It is a perpetual coming on the nuisance's part—a rushing out on mine—and a "moving on." Then I have a disagreeable neighbour who says she "likes music," writes to me impertinent, anonymous letters; encourages or allows her servants to shriek at me and make uncomplimentary remarks about my religion, which happens to be Roman Catholic, all because I ask the organ-grinder to "move on." More than that, she gets the smaller organs inside her area gate (the piano ones, happily, she cannot manage, and there I score), and then I and the police are helpless. Can I summon this musical woman for making her area a public nuisance? If not, what can I do?　　　　　　　　　　　　　　　P. K. Q.

I HEAR of two *mots* of Lady Borthwick, who has much of the readiness of her uncle, Charles Villiers:

"Quel age a cette femme?" said a beau of eighty, looking at a pretty woman. Lady B.: "L'age que vous voyez!—une femme n'a pas d'age!" Old Beau: "Ni un homme non plus!" Lady B.: "Un homme n'a pas d'age, s'il sait plaire." Exit old Beau in doubt. Orleanish Frenchman (bitterly): "L'Angleterre a très mal agie. Elle ne s'est jamais montrée notre amie. Elle nous a beaucoup pris et rien donné." Lady B.: "C'est vrai, Monsieur, nous avons été les plus heureux, car c'est notre rôle de recevoir les éxilés que la France nous donne!"

MEMBERS of the Raleigh may call to mind a man of somewhat remarkable appearance, striking shirt-cuffs, and resplendent jewellery, whose luck at écarté was the all-absorbing topic some four or five years ago. No stakes were too high for this gentleman, and one after another vainly essayed to vanquish him. His high play and success were not confined to London, but the Curragh Camp, Aldershot, and other military centres shuddered at the name of Donald Shaw, of the 86th. Luck, however, seems to have deserted him. At the last session of the Central Criminal Court, he pleaded guilty, and was sentenced to eighteen months' imprisonment with hard labour for forging the name of a friend.

A CONTEMPORARY expresses surprise at the enthusiasm with which Dickens wrote about Mrs. Carlyle. "None of the writing women come near her at all." This was in the lifetime of George Eliot — but, then, Dickens knew Mrs. Carlyle well, and that was enough to account for any amount of eulogy; for that all his geese were swans, his correspondence affords abundant evidence. It is melancholy and also ludicrous to note the prodigious

estimation in which he held a great number of the contributors to *Household Words* and *All the Year Round*, and the inordinate trouble he took to coach them, and the time he spent in giving them advice; for it cannot be said that the majority of those of whom he predicted such great things have become distinguished in literature.

I HEAR with pleasure that a cheap edition of Dickens's "Letters" will be published in the course of next year. The three volumes will be rigorously revised, and many of the shorter and more private letters will be cut out. There are undoubtedly a great number which, although of the deepest interest to the "Gad's" circle, and to Dickens's friends, are yet *caviare* to the multitude, as they are full of hints and inuendoes which an ordinary reader cannot appreciate, and most of those relating to the readings should be expunged. The volume lately published contains some of the very best letters Dickens ever wrote.

IN the second volume of Mr. Morley's admirable life of Cobden, there is an opportune extract from a letter written by Cobden in 1857, which may be commended to the notice of those who are so absurdly clamouring against the idea of a radical alteration in the rules of the House of Commons, and denouncing all proposals in this direction as sinister and revolutionary :—

I wish there could be some Bessemer's power invented for shortening the time of speaking in the House. My belief, after a long experience, is, that a man may say all that he ought to utter at one "standing" in an hour, excepting a Budget speech or a Government explanation, when documents are read. The Sermon on the Mount may be read in twenty minutes, the Lord's Prayer takes one minute to repeat; Franklin and Washington never spoke more than ten minutes at a time.

THE Corporation of London have not exhibited much consideration for the interests of their old tenants at the condemned Leadenhall Market, for they gave them notice to quit their holdings this week, which means their losing the most lucrative week in the whole year. I don't suppose the authorities desired wantonly to cause serious loss to the salesmen and inconvenience to the public, but it certainly seems to be what Dickens would have denounced as a very "jolter-headed" proceeding.

THE following letter from a friend of mine in Aberdeenshire deals with Sir Bartle Frere, who seems to have indulged at once in reckless assertions and reckless conclusions, when writing upon the Aberdeenshire farmers. It is perhaps as well that Sir Bartle should have treated home matters in this fashion, as it enables us to estimate the amount of confidence to be attached to his facts and opinions in regard to South Africa. Knowing nothing about Aberdeenshire, why should he write about it? Surely, even to Sir Bartle Frere, it would have been easy not to write about Aberdeenshire :—

I cannot refer you to anything whatever justifying Sir Bartle Frere in saying that the tenants of Aberdeenshire "are talking seriously and systematically of withholding their rents." I have no hesitation in declaring it to be a pure and unfounded slander; not in the least creditable to the man who uttered it, though it may enable one to understand his own policy as an administrator more clearly.

Sir Bartle Frere's assertion betrays in the first place total ignorance of the character of the Aberdeenshire tenant farmers—an ignorance easily enough accounted for, and, in a sense, excusable; but, in the second place, it betrays an ignorance of the facts, certainly not excusable in anyone assuming the responsibility of writing as he has done in an influential organ.

In course of the farmers' meetings, perhaps one or two expres-

6. From the same edition of *Truth* magazine, a report on Oscar Wilde's trip to America where he planned to stage his play, *Vera*. A character in this play is believed to be the model for the Michael Ostrog described by Melville Macnaghten as a Ripper suspect.

7. The Ripper's last victim, Mary Jane Kelly who was murdered on 9 November, the birthday of the Prince of Wales. She is buried under the Frenchified name, *Marie Jeannette* Kelly, strikingly similar to that of Lily Langtry's daughter, *Jeanne Marie*. (*Illustrated Police News*)

8. The body of Mary Jane Kelly as it was discovered on 9 November 1888. *A Rebours*, the French work which 'poisoned' Dorian Gray in Wilde's novel, contains a passage which reads like a blueprint for her murder. The letters 'FM,' the initials of Frank Miles, appear on the wall beside Kelly's torso.

9. The cover of *The Lodger*, the most famous book ever written on Jack the Ripper. Its author, Marie Belloc Lowndes, was a childhood friend of Oscar Wilde who often visited him at his marital home in Tite Street.

10. Melville Leslie Macnaghten, the senior police officer who lived at 9 Tite Street at the time of the Ripper murders. Quoting 'private information', he named Montague John Druitt as his prime suspect in an official file.

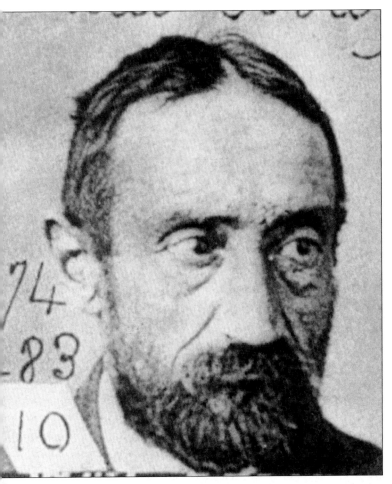

11. Michael Ostrog, the petty thief named by Melville Macnaghten as a minor Ripper suspect. Ostrog, who bears a strong resemblance to a character in Wilde's play, *Vera*, once stole property from a Fellow of New College Oxford, where Montague John Druitt studied.

12. Montague John Druitt, the prime suspect of Melville Macnaghten. Montague and Oscar Wilde were both at Oxford University between 1876 and 1878. Montague's death closely mirrors that of a character in Wilde's short story, *Lord Arthur Savile's Crime*. For the author's analysis of Druitt, see page 150. (*Provost and Fellows of Winchester College*)

13. William Harvey Druitt, Montague's elder brother. He and Oscar Wilde entered Oxford University in October 1874 and served together as probationary members of the Oxford Union. William Druitt was elected; Oscar Wilde was not. (*The Red House Musuem*)

Date.	Name of Stranger.	Name of Member.
Ap.12.	J. S. Hall	Chas Poole Ch. Ch.
12.	R. Whittam	P. S. Fisher Ch. Ch.
— 12	J. de W. Green	Wm.[?] Willetts Lewis M. :
	Mr. J. Druitt	B. H. Druitt Triu. Coll. :
12.	F. R. Smith	
	E. ? Chapman }	A. Robertson. Triu. Coll.
13	L. G. Bridson Triu. Coll. Cam.	F. Phillips Ball Coll
13	Rev.[?] R. H. Barlow Triu. Coll. Cam.	

14. An entry from the *Stranger's Book* (File 022/12/A4/1) in the Archives of the Oxford Union showing that Montague Druitt, then still a schoolboy at Winchester, was signed into the Union on 12 April 1875 by his elder brother, William. (*Reproduced by kind permission of the Oxford Union*)

15. Oscar Wilde's signed entry in the Probational Members Subscription (sic) (File 022/8/F2/1) in the Archives of the Oxford Union. The absence of the letter 'E' in the margin means that Wilde failed to win election to the Union, almost certainly because he led what was perceived to be an 'evil life'. (*Reproduced by kind permission of the Oxford Union*)

16. The signature of Montague John Druitt in the Probational Members Subscription File with its absent 'E' in the margin shows that Druitt, like his Oxford contemporary Oscar Wilde, was blackballed by the Oxford Union. Druitt was described by Melville Macnaghten as 'sexually insane'. (*Reproduced by kind permission of the Oxford Union*)

17. Prime Minister Herbert Asquith, Home Secretary when Macnaghten wrote his report in 1894. As a former President of the Oxford Union, from which Druitt was blackballed, Asquith had probably already heard of this 'sexually insane' suspect. (*National Portrait Gallery, London*)

18. Evelyn Ruggles Brise, the senior Home Office civil servant who must be considered Macnaghten's prime source on Druitt. He was at Oxford with Druitt *and* Thomas Tuke, the Chiswick asylum owner and very likely the doctor who declared Druitt 'sexually insane.' (*National Portrait Gallery, London*)

19. Thorneycroft Wharf in Chiswick, where Druitt's body was recovered from the Thames. Before drowning himself, Druitt probably visited the nearby asylum run by Thomas Tuke, his Oxford contemporary. Tuke attended Brasenose College with Audley Miles, Frank's cousin. Was Frank Miles brought to Tuke's asylum on the night of the last Ripper murder? (*Courtesy of the VT Group*)

railway ticket. That Tuke had known about Druitt's carnal proclivities *since their time at Oxford together* is discernible from Macnaghten's confident description of Druitt as 'sexually insane', a term the policeman would not have used in his note unless he was quoting professional medical opinion, *namely that of Dr Tuke, either directly or indirectly, via such sources as Ruggles Brise or Oscar Wilde.*

The recovery of Druitt's body from the Thames made necessary an inquest into his death, the main concern of which was apparently to contain the scandal in order to shield Druitt's family and his school. That is why Druitt's brother, William, was *not* asked to elaborate on his statement that Montague had been dismissed from his school after getting into 'serious trouble' there, and why nobody from the school gave evidence. This would also explain the reference to the insanity of Druitt's mother, which, in all probability, was a smokescreen designed to conceal the real reason for Druitt's suicide: *sexual misconduct towards his pupils.*

There is another reason to believe that the inquest was less than totally dedicated to revealing the whole truth about Druitt. Local embarrassment caused by the revelation that Druitt knew Thomas Tuke would not have ended there, for Tuke had close links to the prominent Sich family, which possessed several substantial houses on Chiswick Mall, the esplanade on the riverbank adjacent to the spot where Druitt's body was brought ashore. The Sichs were also the owners of the local Lamb Brewery, *which meant that they owned the Lamb Tap pub, the very place where the inquest into Druitt's death was held.*

This analysis seriously weakens the case that Druitt was the Ripper, for it *appears* that Druitt killed himself following a sex scandal at his school and not because he was a serial killer. Perhaps the allegations against him simply stemmed from the disgust Victorian gentlemen such as Ruggles Brise and (future prime minister) Herbert Asquith felt at the behaviour of a child molester. On the other hand, there is Macnaghten's assertion that, according to 'private information', Druitt's own family suspected him of being the Ripper. *Who, we must still ask, supplied him with this 'private information'?*

That question aside, the analysis highlights what was almost certainly the underlying cause of the Ripper murders, *namely the corrupting power of vice.* Oscar Wilde wrote about this from his prison cell when, in 1896, he petitioned the Home Secretary for a reduction of his two-year sentence and *for the sort of medical treatment which Druitt had probably received from Wilde's Masonic brother, Thomas Tuke.* In this appeal, Wilde described the passions which had led to his imprisonment as 'sexual insanity', *the same phrase Macnaghten used to label Druitt.* Elaborating, Wilde wrote that vices '. . . make their dwelling house in him who by horrible mischance has become their victim: they are embedded in his flesh: they spread over him like a leprosy: they feed on him like a strange disease: at the end they become an essential part of the man . . .'

Here a 'Lord of Language' issued a vivid reminder of the dangers we run when we unleash the sexual beast within us. Wilde lost two years of his freedom, his brilliant career and his family. Druitt lost his life. As for the Ripper, he would have undergone a similar transformation, a degeneration which claimed not just him for a victim, but also at least five women in the East End of London.

All of which leads to the conclusion that, if the Ripper was not Druitt, he was another member of the vice rings then operating in London.

* * * * *

THE QUEST

PART ONE

Frank Miles is a figure of mystery and tragedy. Like many people before and since, he was summoned to the great hall of fame only to falter on the way. For a few brief years around 1880, he was one of the leading society artists in the country, with no shortage of commissioned works from leading members of the establishment including the Prince of Wales. His pencilled drawings of pretty female faces and heads were reproduced cheaply and sold in great numbers. In this way, he, more than any other artist, made Lily Langtry, that late nineteenth-century phenomenon, famous and successful. A regular exhibitor at the Royal Academy, he was a personal friend of the dominant literary figures of the day. Such was his brief prominence that in December 1877, in a burlesque on the opening of the Grosvenor Gallery, he was parodied in a work entitled, *The Grasshopper* along with James McNeil Whistler and Oscar Wilde.

At this time, Miles appeared to be set for a lucrative career and perhaps, via his landscapes which are considered by experts to be his best works, a permanent, if minor, place in the history of British art. But it was not to be. His popularity dried up and he himself dropped out of society. His plight was doubtless exacerbated by syphilis which he was unable to remove from his system and which forced him to terminate an engagement to be married. He was reportedly removed to Brislington asylum near Bristol on 27 December 1887 where he died on 15 July 1891 of general paralysis of the insane.

Today Miles is virtually unknown. He has a brief entry in the *Dictionary of National Biography* and has minor mentions in most reference works on late Victorian art. The press in Nottinghamshire, his home county, have honoured him over the years with a few articles on his works. Other than this, he is a mere footnote, a useful name to pad out a paragraph, illustrate a point or construct atmosphere. So obscure is he that he is often confused with John Everett Millais (for example, the authoritative Benezit attributes *The Widow's Mite* and *Ophelia* to Frank Miles). The exception to this is Lily Langtry, who wrote sympathetically and at length on Miles, presumably out of a sense of debt. Their mutual friend, Oscar Wilde, who had a great deal to thank Miles for himself, acted in a very different way.

Soon after leaving Oxford in 1878, Wilde went on to live with Miles, first in Salisbury Street off the Strand and later at No. 1 Tite Street, Chelsea in a house which Miles had specially built. In this relationship, Miles, two years older than Wilde, was, in the material sense, by far the dominant partner. With a generous allowance from his wealthy father and the royalties from his drawings, Miles was able to keep his friend in style. This simple fact can be discerned from both the Court Directory in the *Post Office London Directory* for 1881, which lists Miles as the occupant of No. 1 Tite Street, but makes no mention of Wilde; and from the 1881 Census, which names Miles as the head of the household, but describes Wilde as merely a 'boarder'.

Freed from the vulgar need to earn a living, and with his friend's extensive social connections at his disposal, Wilde could fruitfully devote his time to making himself 'famous or notorious'. He achieved this in part through the 'aesthetic movement' in which the worship of flowers played an important part. During this period, Wilde was rumoured to be in the habit of walking through London in outlandish garb, with a large flower in his hand. This interest in flowers was, as Lily Langtry records, inspired by Miles:

Frank Miles was a gardener first and an artist afterwards ... He was the pioneer in the revival of the herbaceous border and also in bringing flowers within the means of the general public. Through him Oscar Wilde became a flower worshipper and popularised the daffodil and daisy, but Frank had won a reputation as a cultivator and hybridiser of beautiful lilies and narcissi before Oscar ever thought of pinning his love to them.

After his quarrel with Miles, Wilde kept strangely silent about his artist friend. Robert Ross, who met Wilde in 1886, believed himself to be the playwright's first male lover. Lord Alfred Douglas only learned of Miles on a visit to Oxford in 1892, after he had become Wilde's favourite. Douglas though failed to persuade Wilde to talk of Miles, who was by then dead. Robert Sherard seemed to have been luckier. He told Hesketh Pearson that Wilde had once described how he had saved Miles's bacon but never referred to him again. It is not surprising then that Pearson concluded:

The few accounts of Miles vary so greatly that it is impossible to separate fact from fiction.

The purpose of what follows is twofold. It is to prove Pearson wrong and give as full and accurate an account of Miles's life and career as the meagre sources allow. And secondly, to put forward an explanation for the mystery which has come to surround the popular artist and the silence which Wilde maintained about him. The solution offered here is that Miles was Jack the Ripper; that he was motivated by his break with Wilde and the resentment he felt at his failure in life; that Wilde came to learn that his friend was the Whitechapel murderer and dropped hints about it in several of his works, most notably, *The Picture of Dorian Gray*; that Miles, by then hopelessly insane, was not formally prosecuted in order to prevent an embarrassing affair concerning the Royal family from becoming public knowledge; and that Macnaghten was somehow influenced by Wilde in the writing of his memorandum to the Home Office on the identity of Jack the Ripper.

George Hutchinson reported that the man he saw with Kelly only hours before her death sported 'a slight moustache curled up (at) each end' and was about 34 or 35 years old. Miles was 36 at the time of the murders and did indeed have a moustache. There is a definite resemblance between the artist's impression of Hutchinson's suspect and the photograph of Miles reproduced here. Moreover, Miles was also an amateur actor; on 24 May 1881, he took part in an amateur production of *Herne the Hunted* by William Yardley and Robert Reece. This was a hobby which could well explain the flamboyant dress of Hutchinson's suspect who wore an astrakhan coat and button boots with gaiters. Miles could therefore have been the man seen by Hutchinson, but so could any number of men. Clearly, any theory hoping to establish Miles as the Ripper must be far more detailed. This theory will be revealed in due course. First though, Miles himself must be described.

George Francis 'Frank' Miles came from a wealthy Bristol family which had made its name in the West Indian trade. The family was a traditionally large one. His grandfather, Philip John Miles, who represented Bristol in Parliament, had eight sons, all of whom were educated at Eton. His father, the Reverend Robert Henry William, had ten children, six sons, of whom Frank was the youngest, and four daughters. A member of the High Church Tractarian Movement, Revd Miles was an extensive landowner in Cardiganshire where the family home was the priory. He was also a prebendary of Lincoln Cathedral and, after 1844, the Rector of Bingham Priory near Nottingham. Robert Lowe, who became

Chancellor of the Exchequer under Gladstone, was born here, as, on 22 April 1852, was Frank Miles.

Both Revd Miles and his wife, Mary, the daughter of Revd J.J. Cleaver, afterwards Peach, were talented artists. They allowed Frank to study art at home and on the continent, and gave him the opportunity to practice what he learned by decorating the walls and windows of Bingham Priory. Frank seems to have grown up in largely female company, amid his sisters and his mother, a dominant woman who exercised a particularly strong influence over him. John Ruskin, the Victorian art critic, is said to have commented that Frank Miles had to get on because of his ability to paint clouds and his love for his mother.

As a young man he spent a lot of time in the south of Wales where, with such pieces as *The Salmon Leap, Cenarth Falls, Cardiganshire*, he did what was probably his best work. Remarkable as it may seem, he was, like two of his brothers, colour blind, and it was probably this disability which led him to give up art and study architecture. For a year he worked under A.W. Bloomfield, but his heart lay elsewhere and following persuasion from his friends, Millais and Leighton, returned to his original choice of career. What he learned here enabled him to help in the restoration of the priory in 1873. In 1874, he exhibited at the Royal Academy for the first time with *A Study of Reflections*. Around the same time he began in earnest his output of female portraits.

Some of Miles's drawings still survive in Nottingham. These possess such names as *I've Been Roaming, The Gardener's Daughter, My Little Lady* and *A Little Queen*. These drawings show that Miles often liked to attach a piece of poetry to his studies. *The Gardener's Daughter* was apparently drawn to illustrate some lines from Tennyson which are attached beneath. Below *A Greek Maiden* (dated 1873) is a verse from Longfellow's *Beware* which sounds entirely inappropriate:

> She has two eyes so soft and brown
> Take care! Take care!
> She gives a side glance and looks down
> Beware! Beware!
> Trust her not
> She's fooling thee.

Although despised by the art establishment, these drawings became extremely popular and appeared in nearly every stationer's shop and high class magazine in the country, most notably *Life* whose circulation soared as a result, securing for Miles the post in the journal of artist-in-chief. Understandably, the owner of *Life*, Heinrich Felberman, held very positive views on the quality of Miles' drawings, as he records in his autobiography, *The Memoirs of a Cosmopolitan*:

> . . . No one could bring out better than he the points of a face, idealising where there was charm, concealing where there was harshness in expression. And yet his drawings retained a perfect likeness.
>
> It soon became the rage among society beauties to be 'done' by Frank Miles and be published in Life. Among the first to appear were the Countess Grosvenor, the Countess of Lonsdale, Viscountess Castereargh, the Marchioness of Ormonde, Mrs. Cornwallis West, Lady Carvagh, the Countess of Dudley, the Marchioness of Londonderry, the Marchioness of Waterford, the Countess of Ilchester, Miss Laurie Craigie Halkett, who was considered the most perfect type of beauty to be found in England at that time, and Lily Langtry, then at the height of her phenomenal success in London society.

Many, if not most, of Miles's models came from 'the humbler walks of life' as the euphemism goes. The only one of these women known to posterity is Sally Higgs whom Miles first saw selling flowers outside Victoria Station. He was so struck by her beauty that on the spot he persuaded her mother to let him take her back to his studio as a model. She also worked as a live-in servant and in due course assumed the position of informal hostess at the gatherings which Miles and Wilde held. She quickly became one of the most sought after models in London and sat for Leighton, Marcus Stone, and W.E.F. Britten. Sally took this dramatic change in lifestyle in her stride. Frank Harris, who met her in Tite Street, thought her a 'born Bohemian' who was 'not troubled with any so called moral scruples'. E.A. Ward, who maintained an interest in her after she left Miles, states in his *Recollections of a Savage* that she married a young man just down from Eton. According to Ward, the young man's father separated the couple by sending the boy to America and ensuring that Sally had no more than £2 a week to live on. Ward added that Sally later married a man called Ernest who had inherited a large fortune. He finally left her but agreed to provide her with £500 per annum.

Popular as Sally was, she could never hope to compete with Miles's most famous model, Lily Langtry. It would be wrong to say that Miles 'found' Langtry. After all, she sat for many artists and it was Millais who gave her the name by which she is best remembered, 'The Jersey Lily'. Miles though would not have agreed. He told Frank Harris that he had 'discovered and immortalised' her. On another occasion, he exclaimed, 'I with my pencil, Oscar with his pen, will make her the Joconde and Laura of this century'. Langtry did not appear to discourage Miles in believing that a special relationship existed between them. She clearly enjoyed his company and attention and was shrewd enough to realise his value to her. She acknowledged Miles's role in her career by selecting as the frontispiece for her memoirs a study of her in which her face is seen from three angles, in the same manner as Van Dyck's famous portrait of Charles I. In these memoirs, she speaks of her visits to Miles's studio and of the celebrities she met there, 'all thoroughly enjoying the Bohemian atmosphere.'

Miles seems to have fallen for Langtry at his first sighting of her, which is believed to have been at a party given by Lady Sebright in May 1876. Miles was so enraptured that he immediately made two sketches of her and handed one to her as a demonstration of his feelings. One reason why they got on so well may have been their common background, for Langtry, like Miles, was the child of a Church of England Rector. It is perhaps not surprising then that Langtry once visited Bingham Priory, staying for a week. Miles, at some stage, decorated the walls of the priory with two female heads as part of a series designed to illustrate the *Fruits of the Spirit*. From this arose the local legend that one of the models was Langtry herself. In September 1930, the *Nottingham Journal* printed this as a fact and was promptly rebuked by Miles's two surviving sisters. A local historian, a Mr S. Race, put the record straight in a later article where he points out that the portrait bears no resemblance to Lily Langtry and quotes his sisters to the effect that Frank 'would never have introduced anything into their father's church which would have been out of keeping with its atmosphere'.

Miles was greatly helped in his own career by his friendship with Lord Ronald Gower, the son of the Duke of Sutherland and brother of the Duchess of Westminster. Gower was also a close friend of the Marquis of Lorne, husband of Princess Louise, the youngest daughter of Queen Victoria. Princess Louise was a respected sculptress in her own right, and through Gower, himself a sculptor, got to know Miles. Her brother, Leopold, Victoria's youngest son, also became a regular visitor to Miles's studio. He was present one day when Miles completed a profile study of Lily Langtry. He bought it on the spot and took it home to hang over his bed in Buckingham Palace. According to Langtry, the Queen visited his bedroom one day when he was ill and spotted the drawing on the wall. She was not amused by what she saw and, pulling up a chair, took the portrait down then and there.

The Prince of Wales, who had taken Langtry as his first publicly-acknowledged mistress, did however approve of Miles's work. In November 1880, *Life* magazine quoted him as saying, 'The most charming pictures I have seen of ladies are those issued by *Life*. They are the only pictures that do them justice.' The Prince purchased one of Miles's Academy works, *The Flower Girl*, and commissioned him to do portraits of his wife, the future Queen Alexandra, and other members of his family, including presumably his eldest son, the future Duke of Clarence. This Royal patronage proved of immense value to Miles, but it seems to have caused resentment in some circles, as his obituary in *The Magazine of Art* implies:

. . . Although essentially a 'shop window' artist, and fashionable, it was unkindly stated at the time, through having been successful in the presentation of a picture to the Prince of Wales, he was more graceful in taste and more artistic in spirit that his photographed drawings give any idea of.

Ambitious and fleetingly successful though Miles might have been, gardening, and not work, remained his first love. Lily Langtry always found a new flower awaiting her every time she sat for Miles. She also records that Miles unsuccessfully proposed a 'naive scheme for planting the London parks with bulbs, and obtaining permission from the authorities to allow the children to pick the blooms.' Miles's entry in the *Dictionary of National Biography* identifies his as 'a devoted student of Japanese art and also of botany, which led him to study the flowers depicted by Japanese artists, and, by ascertaining the places from which they came, to introduce many for the first time into England.' In a speech at the reopening of Bingham Priory after its extensive renovation in

1873, Miles called for churchyards to be restored with flowers and carefully tended. His father's churchyard at least enjoyed such treatment. Miles planted there a ginkgo tree, which is still standing, and a large number of rare and exotic plants. The scene in all its splendour was captured in *The Garden of Bingham Rectory* which Miles exhibited at the Royal Academy.

It is not known when Miles and Wilde first met, but it appears to have been before the summer of 1876, for on 4 June of that year, Gower recorded in his diary, 'By early train to Oxford with F. Miles. . . There I made the acquaintance of young Oscar Wilde, a friend of Miles. A pleasant cheery fellow, but his long haired head full of nonsense regarding the Church of Rome. His room filled with photographs of the Pope and of Cardinal Manning.'

Gower and Wilde took an instant liking to each other and within weeks were planning to go, with Miles, on a pilgrimage to Rome. At the last moment however, Gower decided that he could not spare the time. 'We would have been a great Trinity', bemoaned Wilde to his Oxford friend, William Ward. In December that year, Wilde visited Gower at his Windsor home which he later described as one of the most beautiful he had ever seen.

In mid-July, Miles and his two friends spent several days at Bingham. Wilde, relaxing after his examination in Classical Moderations for which he was awarded a First, thoroughly enjoyed the break as he confessed in a letter to another friend, Reginald Harding, where he maintained the place would be Paradise, but for the absence of 'serpents or apples'. Wilde found the four Miles sisters 'very pretty' and the church paintings done by Frank and his mother 'simply beautiful'. He took the opportunity to debate religion with Miles's father, whom he described as 'a great friend of Newman, Pusey and Manning at Oxford and a very advanced Anglican'.

In August, Wilde returned the favour and brought Miles to Ireland on a fishing and shooting holiday. They stayed at

Moytura House which had been built overlooking Lough Corrib by Wilde's father, Sir William Wilde, and later at Illaunroe Lodge in Connemara. Here they spent a relaxing time, enjoying the sporting pleasures of the countryside. This was a new experience for Miles who, with initial reservations, received instruction from Wilde on how to catch salmon and shoot grouse. Towards the end of the holidays, Wilde wrote from the lodge bemoaning the fact that he had had little success with either, although, by way of compensation, he had caught plenty sea-trout and many hares. He added, 'I have Frank Miles with me. He is delighted with all.'

Nearly a century later, while researching his book, *The Unrecorded Life of Oscar Wilde*, Rupert Croft-Cooke visited Illaunroe Lodge and there found evidence of Miles's delight in the form of a mural which the artist had painted on the entrance hall of the building. Reminiscent of the paintings with which Miles had decorated the walls of Bingham Priory, the work consists of two cherubs fishing. One has caught a salmon and is jubilant; the other has nothing and is sad. Beneath them is the title, *Tight Lines*.[1]

Before returning to Oxford, Wilde arranged in September to go with Miles to Bristol and visit the St Raphael church, which had been financed by the Revd Miles and which had an almshouse for seamen attached to it. He remained close to Miles during his remaining two years at university and after the announcement of his first class degree in Greats on 19 July 1878 rowed with him to Pangbourne in a birchbark canoe. He took the Rudiments of Religion examination on 22 November and six days later graduated as a Bachelor of Arts. By the second half of the following year, he and Miles were living together in London.

Miles, his income now swelling, had hired the distinguished architect, Edward Godwin, to build him a house in fashionable Tite Street, Chelsea. Godwin had earlier built the 'White House' for Whistler in this street (when the American was forced to vacate this house following his ruinous law suit with Ruskin, he wrote above the front door, 'Except the Lord built the house, they labour in vain that build it. E.W. Godwin F.S.A. built this one.'). The Whistler design had run into trouble with the Metropolitan Board of Works, and Miles's design met similar opposition when it came before the Board in the summer of 1878. Part of the problem was apparently the large flower balconies which Miles wished for the front part of the house. A modified plan was however accepted and work on the house eventually got underway. The final design was of interlocking triangles with red and yellow brickwork and a roof covered in green slates.

In the meantime, Miles and Wilde moved into temporary accommodation in what Lily Langtry recalled as 'a curious old-world house looking over the Thames at the corner of Salisbury Street, Strand, London. It was a very ghostly mansion with antique staircase, twisting passages, broken down furniture, and dim corners.' Here the two men began their brief, but hectic, social life together. An early event to celebrate was the award to Miles of a special Turner medal for a study he had made of an ocean coast. This medal was awarded in addition to the annual Turner Gold Medal. On Christmas Eve 1879, a tea was held to give Miles the chance to display his prize. Guests included Wilde's mother, who had moved to London after the death of her husband, Walter Sickert and his sister Helena,[2] the Countess of Lonsdale, and, of course, Lily Langtry.

This socialising probably intensified when the two men moved to Miles's new home in August 1880. Wilde liked it but found the address 'horrid'. Fortunately, his poetic mind quickly solved that particular problem. The site of Miles's house had been occupied by a dwelling owned by a 'Miss Skeates'. Inspired by this, and perhaps also by the presence nearby of a house owned by a descendant of Shelley, Wilde talked his friend into calling his new home, 'Keats House'.

Of all the eminent figures Wilde and Miles entertained during their life together, none was more favoured than Lily Langtry. Wilde first met her in Miles's studio while still an undergraduate. She found him physically repulsive, but thought his voice to be one of 'the most alluring' she had ever heard, 'round and soft, and full of variety and expression.' Wilde, for his part, was enchanted by her looks and resolved to assist his friend in making her famous. In the summer of 1879, his most famous poem about her, *The New Helen*, appeared in the London magazine, *Time*. It was reprinted in his *Poems* in 1881.

The move to London gave Wilde the opportunity to devote much more of his time to glorifying 'the Lily'. Helpful as this was to her, Langtry did find some of his behaviour embarrassing. On one occasion, he fell asleep outside her door, and Mr Langtry, coming home late (and probably under the influence), fell over him. On another occasion, she spoke sharply to Wilde in order to get rid of him. Later in the theatre, she noticed a commotion in the stalls and looking across, saw Wilde being led away in tears by Miles.

Wilde's attention though did have its constructive side. He tried to fill in the gaps in her education by instructing her in the classics and teaching her Latin. Langtry mentions that he took her to lectures in the British Museum on Greek Art by Sir Charles Newton and that the students, delighted by this spectacle, used to stand and cheer. She also turned to Wilde for advice on other matters, as the following letter shows:

Of course I'm longing to learn more Latin but we stay here till Wednesday night so I shan't be able to see my kind tutor before Thursday. Do come and see me on that afternoon about six if you can.

I called at Salisbury Street about an hour before you left. I wanted to ask you how I should go to a fancy dress ball here, but I chose a soft black Greek dress with a fringe of silver crescents and stars, and diamond ones in my hair and in my back, and called it Queen of Night. I made it myself.

I want to write more but this horrid paper and pen prevent me so when we meet I will tell you more (only don't tell Frank).

Clearly then, Miles and Wilde invested a great deal of time and effort in Lily Langtry. Miles in particular seemed to believe that his destiny was linked to her and that he would ride high in the wake of her success as a socialite. However any hopes he had for making her the 'Joconde and Laura' of the century were shattered by a crisis which hit Langtry in the second half of 1880. To the world at large it was the bankruptcy of her husband in October 1880 which brought about her abrupt change of circumstances and career. This bankruptcy was obviously a serious and damaging development; all her husband's possessions had to be sold off to pay his debts. However, the real extent of her problems at this time was known only to a very few. This was that her affair with Prince Louis of Battenberg, who had replaced the Prince of Wales as her royal lover, had resulted in a pregnancy.

Naturally, there was no question of marriage. Prince Louis was sent on a long voyage. (Three years later he married the Queen's granddaughter, Princess Victoria, becoming in due course the father of Earl Mountbatten of Burma and grandfather to the present Duke of Edinburgh, husband of Queen Elizabeth II) Discreet arrangements were made for Langtry to travel to Paris where in March 1881 she gave birth to a daughter. Shortly afterwards, Langtry handed the child over to her mother in Jersey for upbringing and then returned to London to pick up the pieces of her life. The girl was told that Langtry, whom she saw from to time, was her aunt and did not learn the truth about her until she was 14. She did not learn the real identity of her father until she was 21.

Despite the extreme sensitivity of this scandal, Wilde used it as the basis for his first successful play, *Lady Windermere's Fan* (1891). Needless to say, Langtry makes no mention of her illegitimate daughter in her memoirs. She does admit though that Wilde wrote the play for her and has the temerity to state the following:

. . . Why he ever supposed that it would have been at the time a suitable play for me, I cannot imagine, and I had never contemplated him as a possible dramatist. Besides, knowing him as well as I did, and listening by the hour to his rather affected, amusing chatter, was not an effective prelude to taking him seriously, nor had he even hinted that he was engaged on any work. He called one afternoon, with an important air and a roll of manuscript, placed it on the table, pointed with a sweeping gesture, and said:

'There is a play which I have written for you.'

'What is my part?' I asked, not at all sure if he was joking or not.

'A woman,' he replied, 'with a grown up illegitimate daughter.'

'My dear Oscar,' I remonstrated, 'am I old enough to have a grown-up daughter of any description? Don't open the manuscript–don't attempt to read it. Put it away for twenty years.' And in spite of his entreaties I refused to hear the play.

On her return to London after the birth of her daughter, Langtry sought advice from her close friends on how she could support herself, and, indirectly, her child. Typically, Miles proposed that she become a market gardener. Wilde was horrified at this suggestion and asked, 'Would you compel the Lily to tramp the fields in muddy boots?' He thought that Langtry should take up acting and introduced her to Henriette

Labouchere, the wife of Henri Labouchere MP, the editor of *Truth* magazine (and the man largely responsible for the law which sent Wilde to prison in 1895). Mrs Labouchere had been a professional actress and agreed to give Langtry drama lessons. Such was the student's talent, and doubtless reputation too, that within months, Mrs Labouchere had persuaded the lessees of the Haymarket theatre, Mr and Mrs Bancroft, to let Langtry play the part of Kate Hardcastle in a production of *She Stoops to Conquer*. The premier took place on the afternoon of Thursday 15 December 1881 in the presence of the Prince and Princess of Wales. It was a grand success, as the review in *The Times* makes clear:

> . . . When we say that yesterday's representation was eminently successful, we are playing the highest compliment to the performers who principally contributed to this result. Foremost amongst these was Mrs. Langtry who, it would be affectation to conceal, was the grand attraction of the piece – the attraction which brought together one of the most distinguished audiences that have recently assembled in a theatre. The house overflowed with rank, fashion and celebrity . . .
>
> The audience came prepared to make every possible allowance, but none whatever was required, so far as she was concerned. The oldest playgoers who had seen half a dozen Miss Hardcastles were astonished at the ease with which she glided into the part, the accuracy of the conception, and the felicity of the execution throughout. She was good in all, but the test scene is the one in which she plays the barmaid, and here she assumed the pert tone and the required degree of flippancy without once approximating to vulgarity.
>
> . . . As it was understood that her success or failure in this performance was to decide whether she would or would not adopt the stage as a profession, it was

confidently assumed that the die was cast, and speculations are already afloat as to the next part she should play . . .

With this performance of Kate Hardcastle, Langtry earned herself a new career, one that was to stand her in good stead for the rest of her life. Unfortunately, the two men who had done so much to help her were not to celebrate with her together; if indeed celebrate was what Miles wanted to do. While she was preparing for the role, Miles and Wilde quarrelled and split up. A few days after her great debut, Wilde sailed for America on the lecture tour which was to spread his fame to the New World and beyond.

The split between Miles and Wilde has never been satisfactorily explained. Langtry, who should have been a prime source, is strangely silent on this subject. Rupert Croft-Cooke suggests that the two men may not have quarrelled at all and that Wilde simply left Keats House to go on his tour. To say this though is to ignore the fact that, as far as is known, during his year long tour, Wilde never wrote to Miles or made any mention of his name. In mid-January 1882, he arranged from America to have newspaper articles on his trip sent to a list of people in the British Isles. This list includes his mother and Whistler, but not Miles. The following month, Whistler and others sent a congratulatory telegram to Wilde which began, 'Oscar! We of Tite Street and Beaufort Gardens joy in your triumphs and rejoice in your success . . .' Miles, the man who brought Wilde to Tite Street, was not a signatory.

Quarrel then the two men did. E.A. Ward in his *Recollections of a Savage* gives a detailed account of this argument and its causes (which Frank Harris repeats in his memoirs). According to Ward, the source of the trouble was the publication in 1881 of Wilde's *Poems*, some of which so offended Miles's father that he more or less ordered his son to evict Wilde and have no more to do with him. Citing Sally

Higgs, the model cum servant girl, as his informant, he describes what happened when Miles told a furious Wilde that he had to move out:

> 'Very well, then,' said Wilde, 'I will leave you. I will go now and I will never speak to you again as long as I live.'
>
> He tore upstairs, flung his few belongings into a great travelling trunk, and without waiting for the servant to carry it downstairs, tipped it over the banisters, whence it crashed down a valuable antique table in the hall below, smashing it into splinters. Hailing a passing cab he swept out of the house, speechless with passion, slamming a door he was never to darken again.

Some biographers of Wilde have treated this story with scorn, arguing that it does not tally with the characters of Wilde and Miles and their circumstances. However, Professor Richard Ellmann found documentary evidence to support Ward's account in the form of letters written by Revd Miles to his son and Wilde urging them to separate. These letters, which are in the possession of the William Andrews Clark Library in the University of California, are quoted by Ellmann in his very detailed biography of Wilde. These extracts show that while Revd Miles found several elements of Wilde's poetry disturbing, there was one poem in particular which angered the Rector and which his wife had in fact excised from their copy of Wilde's book. In a letter to Wilde on 21 August asking him to leave his son, Miles's father described this poem, which is probably *Charmides*, as licentious and harmful.[3]

There is however, a problem with Ellmann's interpretation. If Miles obeyed his father so readily, why did Wilde not leave Keats House immediately? The Revd Miles wrote to Miles and Wilde during the summer of 1881, yet Wilde's correspondence shows that he remained at Keats House until much later in the year. There would seem therefore to be another factor involved here. It is suggested that this was Wilde's decision to go to America on a tour.

On 30 September 1881, the theatrical producer, Richard D'Oyly Carte, sent the following cable to Wilde from New York:

Responsible agent asks me to inquire if you will consider offer he makes by letter for fifty readings beginning November first. This is confidential. Answer.

This offer apparently came out of the blue. Nevertheless, Wilde reacted quickly. The following day, 1 October, he cabled back, 'Yes, if offer good. Chelsea, Tite Street.' *It is important to note that Wilde did not anticipate a change of address.*

The arrangements were not quite to Wilde's satisfaction and negotiations with the Americans continued over the following weeks. One reason for Wilde not wishing to leave England on 1 November, was to see the production of his first play, *Vera or the Nihilists*, which was scheduled for a single performance at the Adelphi Theatre on the afternoon of 17 November 1881.

The trouble with *Vera* was that, unlike Wilde's later plays, it was no light-hearted comedy, but a serious political drama about Russian revolutionaries who murder the Tsar and attempt to kill his son. This would have been controversial enough for the Victorian stage at any time, but 1881 was a singularly inopportune time in view of the assassination in March that year of Tsar Alexander II by political malcontents. Wilde initially resisted pressure to drop the play, but in late November he finally succumbed and agreed to cancel the Adelphi Theatre production.

Both of Wilde's major biographers, Ellmann and H. Montgomery Hyde, say that this enforced abandonment of a treasured project made the proposed trip to America all the more important to Wilde who saw the New World as the home of free political expression and the country which would stage his play. To an unidentified recipient in America he wrote from Tite Street offering to send him a 'new and original drama on Russia', which, he asserted, could not be performed in London because its '"passion" was democratic.'[4]

Bolstered with this new incentive, Wilde completed his preparations for his American tour and sailed for New York aboard the SS *Arizona* on Christmas Eve 1881.

There are strong grounds therefore for arguing that it was Wilde's decision to go to America and stage his play *Vera*, which finally caused the split between Miles and Wilde. If the story attributed to Sally Higgs is accurate, and if Miles did in fact force his friend to leave, this eviction could only have taken place after Wilde had declared his resolve to take his treasured play across the Atlantic. It is possible then that Miles resented his friend's sudden thirst for independence. Perhaps Miles felt that the younger man, described in the 1881 Census as his 'boarder', was being ungrateful and that after having received so much from their friendship, Wilde had no right to go off on his own.

The exact nature of that friendship will be examined later. It is sufficient to say now that their quarrel does indeed have the appearance of a lovers' tiff which the partners regretted soon afterwards but were unwilling to end for reasons of injured pride. For example, if the two men did part forever on such bad terms, why did Miles continue to call his home Keats House? And why did Wilde, following his marriage in 1884, move into a Godwin-designed house at No. 16 Tite Street, only a few doors from his former friend? There is no firm evidence that the two men ever spoke to each other after their quarrel in 1881, but they surely saw one another in the street, and, through mutual acquaintances, kept up to date with each other's affairs. In what might be called a Freudian slip, Wilde on at least two occasions (in 1885 & 1886) in letters from his marital home, gave Keats House as his address.[5]

If sources differ over the cause of the rift between Wilde and Miles, they do not over the artist's fate after 1881. All agree that while Wilde and Langtry went on to achieve lasting fame, he faded rapidly into oblivion. His drawings stopped selling. His parents both died in 1884. And he fell prey to an illness which he could not conquer. Frank Harris writes that Miles's popularity declined almost at once and that he became something of a recluse. Ward offers more detail:

. . . Dame Fortune ceased to smile on Miles or his work, which clever, dainty and novel, was lacking in vigour and adaptability. Gradually it failed to retain its hold on a fickle public. He was a kindly, sociable fellow, more devoted to his garden than to the laborious work of his profession, with the result that he was soon forgotten. Whether his heart was broken by disappointment will never be known, but the sad fact remains that he lost his reason, and the spoilt darling of London drawing-rooms ended his days in a home for the insane.

Miles' personal feelings on his change of fortune can be discerned from a letter he wrote to *The Times* in December 1885 on, of all things, The Irish Question. He was staying at this time in Kelsterton, Flintshire, close to the family home of the Gladstone's. At church one morning, he met the son of the great statesman and put to him some proposals on how to handle the Parliamentary tactics of the Irish nationalist, Charles Stuart Parnell. Correspondence on these proposals passed between the two men and on 12 December Miles published this in *The Times* along with a covering letter which began:

Sir, Allow me for a moment to emerge from the obscurity in which I am enveloped . . .

Three days later, unhappy with the treatment given to his suggestions, he again wrote to *The Times*, explaining that the young Gladstone had misinterpreted his meaning and that when he had referred to some people as being prescient, he did not mean himself, but the 'great philosophical historians of the past, the seers of the future.' Miles admitted that his motive in this affair had been to register 'a sly hit at Mr. Chamberlain's button-hole', but doubted whether he had achieved anything. 'I guess (Chamberlain) will feel it as little as the witty Dean said he and the Chapter would feel if you scratched the dome of St. Paul's.'

Although Miles's drawings slumped in popularity, he continued to exhibit at the Royal Academy throughout the 1880s. He had two portraits in 1883, a study entitled *Sea Dreams* in 1884, *Awakened Memories* in 1885 and two portraits in 1886. He exhibited twice in 1887, one a portrait of Mr Charles Rome and the second, his last, the prophetically entitled *The Unknown Land*.

On 19 February 1887, Miles had another letter published in *The Times*, this time on the proper use of the Crystal Palace. He asked the manager to 'put himself in the place of the British public and look at the Palace from afar'. He called for the improvement in the standard of the food at the Palace, and in its library service, and for its opening hours to be extended. He also suggested that the Palace should run a series of lectures three nights a week 'addressed to the populace, on scientific subjects or on matters deeply interesting to them.' The letter is somewhat long and meandering, but lucid enough. Nevertheless, by the end of that year, according to the *Dictionary of National Biography*, Miles's health had deteriorated to the point where his admission to Brislington asylum was considered necessary.

In March 1888, *The Magazine of Art* recorded the death of Frank Miles, describing him simply as 'the well known painter of pretty heads.' *The Nottingham Evening Post* on 1 and 2 March 1888 also carried notices of his death. These were fuller, complete obituaries in fact, calling Miles 'an artist of undoubted merit and high repute' and his demise a serious loss to the world of art. These reports were however premature. Miles actually lived on until July 1891, with accounts of his death and funeral appearing in Bristol newspapers. The following month, *The Magazine of Art* carried a second, and fuller, report of his death. This said that Miles had 'for some years lived in retirement owing to a complete breakdown of health.' It dismissed his drawings of pretty heads as 'weak' and named his landscapes as his most serious studies.

Miles is buried in the churchyard of St Mary's Parish Church, Almondsbury near Bristol. His gravestone states that he died on 15 July 1891 aged 39. This date is confirmed by his Death Certificate which gives the cause of death as 'General Paralysis of the Insane, 4 Years' and his address as 'Tite Street, Chelsea.'

People who knew Miles generally state that he was kindly, amusing and charming. The final obituary in the *Magazine of Art* speaks of his popularity with his friends. The prominent Nottinghamshire cricketer, Richard Daft, says in his *Kings of Cricket* that the hours he spent with Miles chatting, gardening, playing tennis and sitting for portraits, were among the happiest in his life. There was though another side to Miles, one that the world did not see and that his family presumably wished to conceal. S. Race, a Nottingham historian who wrote articles on Miles for the local press in the 1930s, clearly heard stories about his subject. In the original draft of one of his articles, which now forms part of the S. Race collection in the Nottinghamshire Archives Office, he wrote a revealing sentence which does not appear in the final version. 'Frank Miles', he wrote, 'was the "bad boy" of his family, but a much loved one.' This remark begs the all-important question. *How 'bad' a boy was Frank Miles?*

In her memoirs, Lily Langtry gives an account of Miles's end which is so bizarre that it must be seen as a parable rather than the literal truth. She says that her brother, a member of the Indian Civil Service, accidentally shot a sacred peacock while out hunting. A few months later he was mauled by a tiger and later died of blood poisoning. Langtry held the peacock responsible for her brother's death and resolved to get rid of another stuffed peacock which had come into her possession. At first she did not know what to do with the bird but soon hit on the idea of giving it to Wilde with whom she had had an argument over some trivial matter. Consequently, she had the bird delivered to Keats House. The plan went awry. Wilde was not at home when the 'gift' arrived and:

> . . . Miles, thinking it impossible that I could intend to bestow such a valuable gift on Oscar after my recent tiff, and, believing it must, therefore, be meant to embellish his studio, took possession of it, and he, too, became a man of sorrow. His father died soon after, and, though Frank was about to marry a charming girl, the engagement was interrupted by an illness, from which he never recovered.
>
> I should have felt some responsibility for these further tragedies had I not explained to Frank Miles the direful propensities of the bird.

The last paragraph is especially enigmatic. It is not clear if 'these further tragedies' are the events mentioned immediately above or others which Langtry chose not to elaborate upon.

She does though seem to be saying that Wilde narrowly missed a fate which befell Miles. This may well concern the illness to which she refers, which was of course syphilis, as Miles's Death Certificate confirms in the form of 'General Paralysis of the Insane'. Both Richard Ellmann and Montgomery Hyde record that Wilde contracted syphilis while at Oxford or shortly afterwards and that he was cured with a course of mercury treatment which turned his teeth black, but which enabled him, after an obligatory two year wait, to marry in 1884 and sire two children. Both biographers assert though that Wilde was heterosexual in his youth and that he caught the disease from a (female) prostitute. Montgomery Hyde goes so far as to suggest that it was the recurrence of the disease in his system which forced Wilde to break off marital relations with his wife and resort to homosexuality.

However, other writers, such as Rupert Croft-Cooke in his *The Unrecorded Life of Oscar Wilde* and more recently Neil McKenna in his *The Secret Life of Oscar Wilde*, maintain that Wilde was a practising homosexual throughout his entire adult life. Rupert Croft-Cooke sees 'no ambiguity at all' in Wilde's friendship with Miles and describes the artist as 'one of those sophisticated queers' who like to 'camp outrageously' in high society. For Neil McKenna, the friendship between Wilde and Miles was one which gave both men 'emotional and sexual expression' as well as the freedom to have carnal relationships with other men.

In an attempt to establish which argument is correct, this author has carried out research into Wilde's time at Oxford and in particular his relationship with the Oxford Union Society. This body was founded in 1823 by twenty five undergraduates of Oxford University as the 'Oxford Union Debating Society'. It changed its name to its present title two years later and rapidly won recognition as the most famous debating society in the world, a distinction it holds to the present day.

In the late nineteenth century, students who wished to join the prestigious Oxford Union and who could afford the subscription were required to serve a Probationary period, apparently their first term at university, during which time they would be assessed for their suitability as members. In the Union Archives, which are now housed in the Oxfordshire

Record Office, there is a file entitled *Probational Members Subscriptions* (*sic*) for the period 1862–90 (022/8/F2/1). Among the entries for the Michaelmas (i.e. autumn) Term for 1874, there is listed one 'Oscar F. Wills Wilde' of Magdalen College as having paid his subscription of £1 2*s*. What is missing though in the left-hand margin of this entry is the letter 'E' which was pencilled in beside the names of those Probationers who were actually elected to the Union.

This means that Oscar Wilde, one of the leading figures of nineteenth-century literature, was denied entry to the Oxford Union, a fact confirmed by the Society's 'Index of Members' for 1873–90 (022/8/A2/1) which does not contain Wilde's name.

The Union files give no reason for Wilde's rejection, which placed him in a very small minority. In Wilde's intake of Probationers, roughly 128 were accepted, while some 23 – including Wilde himself – were refused entry. However, a later incident with the Union provides a convincing explanation for Wilde's 'blackballing'.

In October 1881, Wilde sent a copy of his *Poems* to the Union (the same volume which apparently caused trouble with Frank Miles's father). The copy had been solicited by the Union's secretary, but despite this the Union held a debate on the suitability of Wilde's work for inclusion in its library and by a vote of 188 to 180 decided to return the *Poems* to Wilde, which the secretary duly did with an apology. The reason advanced in the debate for this astonishing rejection – apparently the only time in the history of the Oxford Union when a work was sent back to its author – was plagiarism, a charge which is difficult to credit. However, the *Oxford and Cambridge Undergraduate's Journal* for 17 November 1881 clearly implied that the crucial issue in this affair was not Wilde's standing as a writer, but his character:

> . . . if a man leads an evil life in the University, even though he may not suffer for his acts at the time, yet his

character will not have escaped the notice of his colleagues, who afterwards will have it in their power to call his remembrance to the past . . .

In short, the real reason for the rejection of Wilde's *Poems* – and by extension of Wilde himself several years earlier – was the 'evil life' he led while at university, one that was absolute anathema to the 'muscular Christianity' of the Oxford (indeed Victorian) Establishment. That is to say, Wilde's homosexual activities during his Probationary period 'did not escape the notice of his colleagues' or of the University Establishment and that knowledge was sufficient to deny him membership of the Oxford Union, a fact which has not been revealed until now.

A further source on Wilde's university activities is no less a figure than George Curzon, the Viceroy of India. A contemporary of Wilde at Oxford, Curzon became President of the Union and actually participated in the above debate on Wilde's *Poems*. In July 1891, Curzon opposed Wilde's proposed membership of the literary Crabbet Club and made a speech in Wilde's presence, attacking the writer's character. An observer, William Scawen Blunt, wrote in his diary that Curzon, having known Wilde at Oxford, was familiar with 'all his little weaknesses and did not spare him, playing with astonishing audacity and skill upon his reputation for sodomy and his treatment of the subject in *Dorian Gray*', a reference to Wilde's recently published novel, *The Picture of Dorian Gray*, of which much more will be said later.

That Oscar Wilde was an active homosexual as a student can be discerned from the character of one friend in particular, Lord Ronald Gower, with whom Wilde spent much time while at Oxford and who led what the 'muscular Christians' would undoubtedly have seen as a very 'evil life'. Gower was the son of a Scottish Duke and an accomplished sculptor, but he was also a promiscuous homosexual who was in the habit of cruising the seedy areas of London in search of willing young men whom he pursued with a sensuality which shocked even his intimates. Despite this however, he never ran foul of the law, unlike that other bastion of the gay Victorian underworld, Lord Arthur Somerset, who had to flee the country when the Cleveland Street scandal erupted. It appears though that when Wilde was imprisoned for homosexual offences in 1895, Gower discreetly moved to the south of France for a while.

It is *inconceivable* that Wilde and Miles could have consorted with Gower without realising the sort of man he was, or even without themselves indulging in the very practices the aristocrat enjoyed so much. Wilde's own relationship with Gower alone suggests that they were from an early stage part of a homosexual ring. When Wilde went to visit Gower in his magnificent Windsor home in December 1876, only a few months after first meeting, he took with him a young artist by the name of Arthur May. In letters to friends, Wilde admitted that he had 'taken a fancy' to May and that the two had 'rushed into friendship'. (Wilde might have regretted taking May to see Gower; the young man seems to have dropped out of Wilde's life after this. Perhaps, as Croft-Cooke suggests, he fell under the influence of the wealthy and more experienced Gower.)

The argument put forward above, based on the author's original research, is clearly a powerful one. It now seems virtually certain that Oscar Wilde was a practising homosexual, the leader of an 'evil life', from his early student days. This in turn means that he and Miles were physical lovers, which raises the strong possibility that, as Lily Langtry seems to imply, one man caught syphilis from the other. However, the important fact here is that while Wilde recovered from the disease, Miles did not.

Miles's interest though was not restricted to men; he was apparently a very active bisexual. According to Robert

Sherard, who once persuaded Wilde to talk about Miles, the artist 'could have shaken hands on a common taste with Victor Hugo'. By this Sherard presumably meant that, like the great Frenchman, Miles was sexually insatiable.[6] In his biography of Hugo, Samuel Edwards describes his subject's sex life as 'little short of astonishing'. According to Edwards, it was not uncommon for Hugo to have sex with several women – including prostitutes and courtesans – during the day and then go home to a night of love-making with the woman he regarded as his principal partner.[7]

If Sherard is to be believed, Miles was particularly fond of exposing himself to young girls. As he told Hesketh Pearson, 'Miles had a predilection for exhibition natural enough in a struggling artist but reprehensible, parait-il, where only small girls in single spies are invited to contemplation. Wilde told me how he had saved Miles' bacon but never referred to him again.'

The incident alluded to is apparently, but not definitely, that described by Sherard in *The Real Oscar Wilde* and repeated by Hesketh Pearson in his own biography of Wilde. In this Wilde came back to Keats House one day to find Miles packing his bags in a state of great distress. When asked the reason for this, Miles admitted having committed an offence, adding, 'I am sure the parents have laid an information and that I am liable to be arrested at any moment. I am trying to get away before the police come.' At that moment the police did arrive, demanding entry. Wilde told his friend to escape across the rooftop while he held the police back. He did this by throwing his considerable weight against the door. By the time the police finally managed to force entry, Miles was long gone. The officers were furious but Wilde, using his famous charm, appeased them by saying that he thought the whole thing to be a hoax as his friend had left for the continent that morning.

There is another case in print where Miles had his bacon saved by Wilde. This is to be found in an anonymous contribution to *The Great Reign*. On this occasion, Miles was being blackmailed by a woman who had persuaded him to 'commit an act of extreme folly' by 'pretending that certain things were so that were not so in truth', which presumably means that Miles had sex with an underage girl. On learning of his friend's plight, Wilde packed him off and invited the blackmailer round for a meeting. At that meeting, Wilde listened sympathetically to the woman and expressed interest in supporting her case. But he explained that before he could do so, he had to see the evidence which the woman possessed. Deceived by Wilde's acting, the woman produced the incriminating document and handed it to him. Wilde read it carefully and asked the woman if she had taken a copy. On learning that she had not, Wilde turned and threw the document into the fire. Furious, the woman called up her male accomplice from the street, but he found Wilde's bulk too imposing and he departed with the woman to be heard of no more.

This then was Frank Miles; a man brought up by a dominant mother, along with four sisters, in a strong religious atmosphere; a man who was a slave of his sex drive to the point of child molestation; a man who knew the ways of prostitutes and was in the habit of picking them up; a man whose promising career was snatched from him; a man who watched his friends realise their dreams while he faded into obscurity; a man whose health was destroyed by promiscuity with, it appears, both sexes and who died a syphilitic lunatic. Without doubt, he was a man with good cause to bear a grudge against the world and against women in particular. This grudge, in all probability, would have intensified during the 1880s when Miles, his life in ruins, had the time to brood in obscurity and reflect on how things had gone wrong and who was to blame.

There are two points worthy of special notice. The first is Miles's sexual nature, a condition which was shared by the Boston Strangler, and which brings to mind the comments of Dr Bond in his paper on the Ripper murders where he wrote that the killer, in his opinion was 'subject to periodical attacks of Homicidal and Erotic mania' and might have been 'in a condition sexually, that may be called Satyriasis'. The second point is the date when Wilde decided to go to America and leave his friend. Wilde received this offer on 30 September and accepted the following day. 30 September and 1 October. *The dates of the double event and the sending of the Ripper postcard.*

* * * * *

PART TWO

In the theory that Frank Miles was Jack the Ripper, the starting point must be the date on which the *Dictionary of National Biography* says he was admitted to Brislington asylum in Somerset. That any person should be admitted to an asylum during Christmas week is an indication of a sudden, unexpected event, rather than a simple deterioration in the person's condition. Miles was admitted to Brislington asylum on 27 December 1887, *the day after the woman known only as 'Fairy Fay' was reportedly murdered.*[8] *(Christmas may have held bad memories for Miles; it will be recalled that Wilde sailed for America on Christmas Eve 1881.)*

As has already been mentioned, Miles was announced dead the following March by *The Magazine of Art* and *The Nottingham Evening Post*. What is important to note about these reports is not just that they were made, but that, as far as can be seen, *they were never retracted.* This means that during the Ripper murders, when sex criminals and known sexual deviants would have been questioned by the police as a matter of routine, Miles, a known child molester, was, to the world at large, *no longer alive*. ('How can they catch me now?' the author of the Jack the Ripper letter asked, as if he believed himself beyond mortal reach.)

What then lay behind these false obituaries? One possibility is of course that they appeared as part of a scheme to remove Miles from the asylum so that he could live out the remaining years of his life in more comfortable surroundings. The second obituary in *The Magazine of Art*, in August 1891, certainly indicates by its wording that Miles had not been in formal confinement. Miles, according to this notice, had 'for some years lived in retirement owing to a complete breakdown of health.' It is important to note that Brislington asylum seems to have been more a hospital for well-to-do patients, rather than a secure prison-like institution.

Unfortunately there does not seem to be any documentary evidence which could shed any light on Miles's stay at Brislington. The records of the asylum have long since been destroyed. The Public Record Office possesses what could be termed the Lunatic Register, which logs the movement of lunatics throughout the country and their fate; namely improvement, if any, and date of release or death. *The Private Patients in County Asylums and Hospitals* is the part of this register which should contain the relevant information on Miles. It should, but it does not. As far as this researcher can see, *there is no mention in this volume of a George Francis Miles entering an asylum in 1887 or of anyone by that name dying in an asylum in 1891, which would mean that Miles was never formally certified insane.*[9]

Given this set of circumstances, it follows that if Miles was the Ripper, he was a man 'on the loose'; a man who had slipped free from some form of restraint and had gone on the rampage; a man who during his liberty would have moved into lodgings or temporary accommodation, in order to avoid arrest not just from the police but also from his family and friends, anxious to return him to his original place of detention. As has been shown, Forbes Winslow, the amateur detective, believed the Ripper to be an escaped or recently released inmate of an asylum. Moreover, it must be said that the *rate* at which the Ripper killed – five women in ten weeks despite the increasing likelihood of capture – indicates that he was driven not just by a great hatred of women, but also by the knowledge that his time was limited. These though are general points. More specific evidence is required here, material which without question can be used to implicate Miles. Two separate strands of such evidence are offered below. Each strand is impressive on its own; taken together they are compelling.

The first submission is to be found in the writings of another of Melville Macnaghten's friends, the journalist George Sims. As mentioned earlier, Macnaghten 'leaked' his suspicion of Druitt to Arthur Griffiths. There is no doubt that Sims too was allowed to be 'in the know' about Druitt. In his memoirs, he stated that the Ripper's body 'was found in the Thames after it had been in the river for nearly a month . . .' In 1903, he wrote in the magazine, *The Referee*:

Jack the Ripper committed suicide after the last murder – a murder so maniacal that it was accepted at once as the deed of a furious madman. It is perfectly well known at Scotland Yard who Jack was, and the reasons for the police conclusions were given in the report to the Home Office, which was considered by the authorities to be final and conclusive . . .

However in *The Mysteries of London* (1906), Sims shows that he had heard another version of events, one that clearly concerned someone other than Druitt. In this book, Sims writes of the Ripper as an outwardly normal man travelling through London without arousing the least suspicion. Sims seems to have been given detailed information on this man for he claims that the Ripper used tramcars and omnibuses and 'travelled to Whitechapel by the underground railway, often late at night.' This information is hardly likely to have been elicited from a suicide. However, what is particularly important here is Sims's description of the Ripper:

> . . . He was a man of birth and education, and had sufficient means to keep himself without work. For a whole year at least he was a free man, exercising all the privileges of freedom. And yet he was a homicidal maniac of the most diabolical kind.

A free man for a whole year at least. Sims is obviously saying here that the Ripper had been released or allowed to escape from an asylum. Miles was certainly 'a man of birth and education' and he was financially independent. Note too the length of time which Sims claims the Ripper was free. If Miles was removed from the asylum around the time of the false obituaries in late February/early March 1888 and not returned there until after the murder of Mary Kelly, he would have been at liberty for practically the whole of 1888, *very close to the year quoted by Sims.* Did Sims base his description on information provided by Macnaghten? Was this information identical to that which Hargrave Adam accused Macnaghten of destroying? These are not idle questions for, as shall be shown, Macnaghten was in the position, quite literally, to know about Miles.

The second strand of evidence concerns Oscar Wilde himself. It is suggested here that Wilde learned the truth about Miles and divulged this to a close friend who, some years after Wilde's death, used this knowledge in a veiled, but nevertheless very public, way. What is there to support this contention?

The Magazine of Art, which carried the false obituary on Miles, was published by Cassell and Company Ltd from its offices in La Belle Sauvage, No. 66 Ludgate Hill (i.e. Fleet Street). Between November 1887 and October 1889, Wilde edited another Cassell publication, *The Woman's World*, from these very same offices. He was also at this time on close terms with Edwin Bale, who ran Cassell's art department, and W.E. Henley who until 1886 had been the editor of *The Magazine of Art* and was still a Cassell's employee. Wilde therefore would surely have read the false obituary on his old friend and neighbour. But did he know the obituary to be false? And did he later learn what became of his former lover?

Evidence that he did indeed is to be found in that most famous of all books on the Ripper, *The Lodger*, by Marie Belloc Lowndes, who on the title page of her book quoted the 88th Psalm:

> Lover and friend has thou put from me
> and mine acquaintance into darkness.

It is at first sight curious that a woman with the refined background of Marie Belloc Lowndes should write a book on Jack the Ripper. In her *Diaries and Letters*, she attributes the inspiration for her novel to a guest at a dinner party who claimed that his mother's butler and cook, who were husband and wife, took in lodgers and believed that they had once let a room to Jack the Ripper.

This however may not have been the whole truth, for in the introduction to this book she reveals that her mother's friendship in Dublin with Sir William and Lady Wilde in the 1860s created 'a very real link between myself and their Oscar' and that in later years she took to visiting Wilde and his wife, Constance, in their Chelsea home. So fond were her memories of Wilde that she thought it only natural that people would be 'drawn to *No. 16 Tite Street* by the host's brilliance and exuberant grace and charm.' (Author's emphasis)

Marie Belloc Lowndes visited Wilde at No. 16 Tite Street, where he was the head of the household. However, Wilde, who had once lived at No. 1 Tite Street with his 'Lover and Friend', was named in the 1881 Census as Miles's 'boarder', a synonym for 'lodger'. *Did this onetime relationship between Miles and Wilde inspire the title, indeed the very construction, of her classic Ripper novel?*

It has already been pointed out that if Miles was the Ripper, he had almost been released from some sort of restraint. The Ripper, as described by George Sims in his 1906 book quoted above, was clearly an escaped inmate of an asylum. *This was the solution accepted by Marie Belloc Lowndes, who, as shall be shown later, actually refers to George Sims in a veiled form in her novel.* Here is the explanation given in *The Lodger* by the Commissioner of the Metropolitan Police on how the murderer came to be at large:

I have just been informed that a month ago this criminal lunatic, as we must of course regard him, made his escape from the asylum where he was confined. He arranged the whole thing with extraordinary cunning and intelligence, and we should probably have caught him long ago, were it not that he managed, when on his way out of the place, to annex a considerable sum of money in gold, with which the wages of the asylum staff were about to be paid. *It is owing to that fact that his escape was, very wrongly, concealed.* (Author's emphasis)

In fact, Mrs Belloc Lowndes went out of her way at the outset to make it clear that her escaped lunatic was from a privileged background, as Frank Miles was. Here is her account of the man's arrival at the home of the landlady, Mrs Bunting, who had at one time been a lady's maid:

On the top of the three steps which led up to the door, there stood the long, lanky figure of a man clad in an

Inverness cape and an old fashioned top hat. He waited for a few seconds blinking at her, perhaps dazzled by the light of the gas in the passage. Mrs. Bunting's trained perception told her at once that this man, odd as he looked, *was a gentleman, belonging by birth to the class with whom her former employment had brought her in contact.* (Author's emphasis)

The stranger, who is carrying a narrow bag in his left hand, 'a new bag made of strong, black leather', asks about a room. Here is Mrs Bunting's immediate reaction:

> . . . It seemed too good to be true, this sudden coming of a possible lodger, and of a lodger who spoke in the pleasant courteous way which recalled to the poor woman her happy far-off days of youth and of security.

There are even stronger grounds for believing that Mrs Belloc Lowndes was thinking of Miles when she created Mr Sleuth, the lodger/murderer in the novel. When Mrs Bunting shows Mr Sleuth her best rooms, she is surprised by his reaction:

> On the dark green walls hung a series of eight engravings, portraits of early Victorian belles, clad in lace and tarlatan ball dresses, clipped from an old book of beauty . . .

Mr Sleuth at first turns this room down, but eventually accepts it. From here he asks Mrs Bunting to bring a Bible to him along with his meal:

> But a great surprise awaited her; in fact, when Mr. Sleuth's landlady opened the door of the drawing room she very nearly dropped the tray. She actually did drop the Bible, and it fell with a heavy thud to the ground.

The new lodger had turned all those nice framed engravings of the early Victorian beauties, of which Mrs. Bunting had been so proud, with their faces to the wall!

Seeing Mrs Bunting's astonishment, Sleuth offers an explanation for his action:

Mr. Sleuth got up. 'I – I have taken the liberty to arrange the room as I should wish it to be,' he said awkwardly. 'You see, Mrs.-er- Bunting, I felt as I sat here that these women's eyes followed me about. It was a most unpleasant sensation, and gave me quite an eerie feeling.'

Later he adds:

'I prefer bare walls, Mrs. Bunting,' he spoke with some agitation. 'As a matter of fact, I have been used to seeing bare walls about me for a long time.'

Afterwards, Mrs Bunting recalls a similar incident from her youth when she looked after an old lady. Staying with this lady was her favourite nephew, Algernon, 'a bright, jolly young gentleman, who was learning to paint animals in Paris.' Early one morning Mrs Bunting, who was then known as Ellen Green, entered the dining room to find that Algernon 'had the impudence to turn to the wall six beautiful engravings of paintings done by the famous Mr. Landseer!' On being asked the reason for this, he replied, 'How can I draw ordinary animals when I see *these half-human monsters* staring at me all the time I am having my breakfast, my lunch and my dinner?' (Algernon calls the maid 'fair Helen', the name Wilde gave to Lily Langtry in his most famous poem about her.)

The fact that Marie Belloc Lowndes placed so much emphasis on exactly the type of drawings in which Frank Miles specialised is a clear indication that she was in fact writing about him. However, the strongest sign of all that Belloc Lowndes had Miles in mind when she wrote *The Lodger* is to be found in her *Diaries and Letters* where she states that when her novel was first serialised in the press, by which time Wilde was long dead, she received letters of praise, including a postcard from '*my old friend Robert Sherard, who had written interesting and revealing books concerning Oscar Wilde.*' (Author's emphasis)

Robert Sherard, the intimate friend and biographer of Oscar Wilde! The one man to whom Wilde is known to have spoken to about the sexual proclivities of Frank Miles. The man who is quoted as saying, 'Wilde told me how he saved Miles's bacon, but never referred to him again.'

Why should this man have felt the need to write to Belloc Lowndes after the publication of *The Lodger*? In the light of all that has been said above, surely a convincing answer is that *Sherard, like Belloc Lowndes herself, knew Miles to be the Ripper, and that he wrote to her praising what he recognised as a cleverly composed and well disguised account of the truth.*

In *The Lodger*, the murderer does not call himself Jack the Ripper, but 'The Avenger'. This would be, of course, a perfect soubriquet for Miles if he were the Ripper. However, the real significance of this name is to be found in a hitherto ignored letter in the police files on the Ripper where the author actually calls himself 'the Avenger'. This letter, which is printed – not written – in red crayon, reads as follows:

> To the Occupier of This House
> Fool? Asst Cod? Duffer? Woman???
> Beware? the Avenger is on your track, and you had
> better make tracks for America if you want to save
> your bacon. Shall pay you a visit soon
> so beware???
>
> Jack the Ripper

Note the points of similarity here. The author, that is Jack the Ripper/the Avenger, urges the 'occupier' of the house to 'make tracks for America' as Wilde did when he left Miles in late 1881. Also, as mentioned above, Wilde has been quoted as claiming to have saved Miles' bacon. Unfortunately the address of the house is not given on the file, nor is there any explanation provided as to how the letter found its way into the hands of the police. There is though one important detail that is relevant here, and that is the date of the letter marked on the file by the police themselves. *This is 16 October – Oscar Wilde's birthday.*

If Miles did send the above letter to Wilde in a personal capacity, it follows that he might have sent the original 'Dear Boss' letter to him in his erstwhile professional capacity as a Fleet Street editor. The Americanisms in the letter would too be a reference to the rift between the two men and the proud boast, 'How can they catch me now?' a tease that the police were looking for a 'dead man', partly as a result of a false obituary in a Fleet Street magazine. There is further evidence to consider, evidence that the very name 'Jack the Ripper' was a far from arbitrary selection and that it had its origins in the painful and unhappy separation which Miles and Wilde experienced in late 1881. In other words it might well have been the original 'Dear Boss' letter which alerted Wilde to the fact that his former friend, lover and neighbour was the Whitechapel murderer.

It will be recalled that following the birth of her illegitimate daughter in early 1881, Lily Langtry turned to her friends for advice and help in the choice of a career, and that Wilde arranged for her to take drama lessons from the wife of Henry Labouchere, the editor of *Truth* magazine, who in turn secured for her the part of Kate Hardcastle in a production of *She Stoops to Conquer*. Not surprisingly, Labouchere's *Truth* carried an article on Langtry's performance. Entitled simply 'Mrs. Langtry', it appeared in the Scrutator column in the issue dated 22 December 1881, only days before Wilde left for America. It is satirical in nature and takes the form of a letter from a woman to a friend by the name of Mary.

The letter begins with the authoress snidely pointing out that she managed to obtain tickets for the show while her friend did not. 'Well, everybody was there who could get in. The Prince and the Princess had the Royal Box, and the Tecks and the Lornes were there, I heard stuffed away somewhere, although I did not see them.' Langtry is not mentioned in the letter by name, but simply by the female pronouns. The emphasis is the original.

'Only fancy dear, *her* going on the stage and attacking an art.'; 'We all clapped *her* when *she* came on. Poor thing, *she* did look so nervous that I quite pitied *her*. But *she* soon got over it, and then went on quite like a real actress . . .' 'They applauded very much at the end, and when the curtain was taken up again a lot of bouquets were thrown to *her*. One was thrown from the Royal box . . . and I threw *her* the one that Jack had given me. *She* picked them all up, and stood bowing and smiling until the curtain fell.'

'Jack' is Mary's husband or companion and about him she goes on to say:

Jack, you know dear, is very clever and I would back his opinion against anyone else in the world. He had not said a word while the play was going on, but when it was over, I asked him to give his true opinion. *He said 'she's ripping' and for Jack to say this **she** must be very good. (author's emphasis)*

Now the Jack mentioned here is most probably modelled on Wilde himself. Around that time it was the height of literary fashion to poke fun at him and his mannerisms (hence the description of him as being 'very clever'.) This had been done recently on stage in *Where's the Cab?* by James Albery, *The Colonel* by Frank Burnard and, most notably, in *Patience* by Gilbert and Sullivan which was in fact still then running in the West End. Throughout 1881, the artist, George du Maurier, had parodied Wilde in the pages of *Punch*, giving him such names as 'Ossian Wildeness', while Miles was labelled 'Drawit Milde'. Wilde was certainly on the mind of the editor of *Truth*, for the *very same edition* of that magazine carries an article on Wilde's forthcoming trip to America which begins:

Mr. Oscar Wilde is going to the United States at the end of this week on the *Arizona*, having made arrangements to bring out his Republican play 'Vera' there . . .

It is hardly fanciful therefore to suggest that the above edition of *Truth* article, *with its references to both Lily Langtry and to Wilde's play* Vera *being staged in America*, stuck in Miles's mind and that the name 'Jack' came to have a special significance for him which he was to use to chilling effect years later. After all the events of late 1881 would have left an indelible impression on him. He surely had cause to resent the success of his former friend both in his search for fame and in his attempts to cure himself of syphilis. His own career plummeted after the split with Wilde and his failure to defeat the syphilis in his system denied him the social acceptability which marriage would have given him. He had cause too to resent the actions of his great 'discovery', Lily Langtry. If she had not become pregnant by a Prince, his plans for her might have come to fruition. As it was, she was forced to become an actress, as Wilde had suggested. Miles had not wanted this; he thought that she should become a market gardener. The depth of his feelings on this is not known, but it is by no means unlikely that he was deeply disturbed at the thought of his female idol becoming involved in a profession which was then believed by many to be only one step away from prostitution. Perhaps during the 1880s, as he brooded on the wreck his life had become, he developed an obsession with his former friends and came to see them as one reason for his problems. The 'Dear Boss' and 'Avenger' letters have already been explained in this way. The responsibility Langtry expresses in her memoirs for 'these further tragedies' concerning Miles can also be explained by this train of thought.

There is another question to consider here. Was Mary Kelly, the last Ripper victim, one of Frank Miles's models? In effect another Sally Higgs? She was after all an attractive woman, and Miles was certainly in the habit of picking up women of her class. Kelly grew up in Carmarthen, not far from Cardiganshire where Miles' father was a major landowner, and where Miles did most of his serious work. If Miles did know Kelly in Wales then it is more than likely that he was the West End figure to whom she turned on moving to London in the early 1880s. On whether there is any truth in this part of the Kelly legend, *The Scotsman* had this to say on 12 November 1888:

Some statements have appeared respecting the deceased's antecedents. It is said that she formerly lived for some time in a fashionable house of resort in the West End. There is reason to believe that not only are these statements well founded, but that she maintained some sort of connection with companions of her more prosperous days. Seeing that it was contrary to Kelly's custom to take strangers to her room, it is believed that her destroyer offered her some exceptional inducement.

George Hutchinson's statement surely supports the view that Kelly knew the man he saw her pick up. After all, Kelly laughed readily on meeting the man and promptly accepted his proposition, which, it is worth considering, may have involved something as well as sex, or even other than sex. 'You will be alright for what I have told you.' was what Hutchinson heard the man say. Perhaps the man wished to draw Kelly. There was, it should be remembered, a cheap print found in Kelly's room entitled *The Fisherman's Widow*, from which, according to some sources, the Ripper draped pieces of her flesh. (Unfortunately a picture of this name cannot be traced). It is indeed strange that someone as hard up as Kelly should have kept even this modest adornment in her tiny room unless she had very good reason to do so, for example that she had sat as the model.

The aim in establishing a link between Kelly and Miles is to draw attention to the Frenchified Christian names which Kelly adopted and which she was buried under. If Miles was the West End figure who took her to Paris, it is reasonable to postulate that it was he who persuaded her to call herself Marie Jeannette. The significance of this is obvious. *Lily Langtry's illegitimate daughter was christened Jeanne-Marie.*

Here then is a plausible explanation for the abrupt termination of the Kelly inquest and the suppression of evidence referred to by the Coroner. If Miles was identified as the murderer shortly after the Kelly murder, then the government would naturally have felt that the less there was said about Kelly's background the better. There would have been no question of Miles being placed on trial or even of his being identified in official documents as the Ripper. Such a course of action would have led inevitably to the disclosure of the Lily Langtry connection and with it the existence of her Royal offspring. *Indeed, the fact that the Kelly murder took place on the birthday of the Prince of Wales, Langtry's onetime lover, could alone explain why the authorities wanted to say as little as possible about the killing.*

Miles would simply have been (re)placed in an asylum where within a short time the syphilitic germs in his system would have rendered him incapable of harming or incriminating anyone. *The fact that several months before Miles had been reported dead would obviously have helped here.* Meanwhile the government would maintain the public pretence that the Ripper was still at large and continue to draft men into Whitechapel in anticipation of further murders. The police files show that this policy went on until March 1891, only a few months before Miles's actual death, and the month before Oscar Wilde's only novel, *The Picture of Dorian Gray*, was published in volume form.

* * * * *

Oscar Wilde was a highly autobiographical writer. In the preface to *The Picture of Dorian Gray*, he wrote that 'The highest, as the lowest, form of criticism is a mode of autobiography.' Wilde clearly modelled the plot of his first successful play, *Lady Windermere's Fan*, on Langtry's affair with Prince Louis Battenberg. As it is alleged here that this suppressed scandal became closely linked to the Ripper case, a basic test of the theory under discussion is to ascertain whether Wilde dropped any hints or clues in his writing about the identity of the most sensational murderer of his day.

There is no question that the forename 'Jack' held a special significance for Wilde. In his most famous play, *The Importance of Being Earnest*, he named the leading character Jack Worthing. When discussing his misplaced cigarette case Jack announces, 'I have been writing frantic letters to Scotland Yard about it. I was very nearly offering a large reward.' As anyone familiar with this play will know, the name Jack Worthing is itself a pseudonym, the young man's real name being Ernest Moncrieff. ('Ernest in town and Jack in the country.') Algernon, *the same name used by Marie Belloc Lowndes for the nephew in 'The Lodger'*, is his brother, although that fact is not revealed until the end of the play.

Greater weight can be attached to a study Wilde produced, only a few months after the Ripper murders, of Thomas Griffiths Wainewright, *the early nineteenth century artist, mass murderer and user of pseudonyms*. As Wilde writes, Wainewright:

. . . though of an extremely artistic temperament, followed many masters other than art, being not merely a poet and a painter, an art critic, an antiquarian and a writer of prose, an amateur of beautiful things and a dilettante of things delightful, but also a forger of no mean or ordinary capabilities, and as a subtle and secret poisoner almost without rival in this or any other age.

Of Wainewright's pseudonyms, Wilde had this to say:

Scott, the editor of the London magazine, struck by the young man's genius . . . invited him to write a series of articles on artistic subjects, and under a series of fanciful pseudonyms he began to contribute to the literature of his day. *Janus Weathercock, Egemot Bonmet, and Van Winkvooms, were some of the grotesque masks under which he chose to hide his seriousness or to reveal his levity. A mask tells us more than a face. These disguises intensified his personality.*

Wilde later adds:

. . . Modern journalism may be said to owe almost as much to him as to any man of the early part of this century. He was the pioneer of Asiatic prose, and delighted in pictorial epithets and pompous exaggerations. To have a style so gorgeous that it conceals the subject is one of the highest achievements of an important and much admired school of *Fleet Street leader writers*, and this school Janus Weathercock may be said to have invented.

In attempting to explain the apparent contradictions in the man's character, Wilde says:

His crimes seemed to have an important effect on his art. They gave a strong personality to his style, a quality that his early work certainly lacked. In a note to the life of Dickens, Forster mentions that in 1847 Lady Blesington received from her brother, Major Powell, who held a military appointment at Hobart Town, an oil portrait of a young lady from his clever brush; and it is said that 'he had contrived to put the expression of his own wickedness into the portrait of a nice kind hearted girl.'

M. Zola, in one of his novels, tells us of a young man who, having committed a murder, takes to art, and paints greenish impressionist portraits of perfectly respectable people, all of which bear a curious resemblance to his victim. The development of Mr. Wainewright's style seems to me far more subtle and suggestive. One can fancy an intense personality being created out of sin.

With regard to his eccentric behaviour, Wilde says:

Like Disraeli he determined to startle the town as a dandy, and his beautiful rings, his antique cameo breast pin, and his lemon coloured kid gloves were well known. . .

The man seen with Mary Kelly by George Hutchinson shortly before her death wore a '*horse shoe-pin*'. And in the statements to the press, Hutchinson said that the man he saw was carrying a pair of brown kid gloves.

All of the above quotes can surely be used to support the contention that Wilde had Miles, alias Jack the Ripper, in mind when he wrote this study of Thomas Wainewright. What is particularly striking though is the title Wilde chose for his work, *'Pen, Pencil and Poison'*, a phrase which is strongly reminiscent of the exclamation attributed to Miles about Lily Langtry, 'I with my pencil, Oscar with his pen, will make her the Joconde and Laura of this century.'

In the 'Dear Boss' letter, the author announced that he would not 'quit ripping' whores until he got 'buckled'. This last word means of course caught or arrested, but it has another meaning, namely married. It will be remembered that according to Lily Langtry, Miles was forced to break off his engagement because of 'an illness from which he never recovered' (i.e. syphilis). Wilde was more fortunate; he managed to eradicate the syphilis from his system and was able to marry, bringing his wife to live in Tite Street only a few doors from his former friend. The word 'buckled' may then have been another reference, like the name 'Jack the Ripper' itself, to the break-up of Wilde and Miles in 1881. To support this view, attention must now turn to Wilde's only novel. *The Picture of Dorian Gray*, the central event of which is the termination of Dorian's engagement to the young, and illegitimate, actress, Sybil Vane, who had been fathered by a 'highly connected' figure.

Wilde began writing *The Picture of Dorian Gray* in late 1889, about a year after the Ripper murders. The work first appeared in *Lippincott*'s monthly magazine for July 1890. The volume edition was published in April 1891. This version contained six new chapters, many revisions and a preface which consisted of a list of epigrams, including the warning:

All art is at once surface and symbol. Those who go beneath the surface do so at their peril. Those who read the symbol do so at their peril.

The appearance of *Dorian Gray*, sometimes referred to as the first French novel in the English language, caused a storm of protest from the established press which condemned the work as decadent and immoral. 'Dullness and dirt are the chief features of Lippincott's this month', said *The Daily Chronicle*. *The St James Gazette* sought to protect its readers. 'Not being curious in ordure, and not wishing to offend the nostrils of decent persons, we do not propose to analyse "The Picture of Dorian Gray" . . . Whether the Treasury or the Vigilance Society will think it worthwhile to prosecute Mr. Oscar Wilde or Messrs Ward, Lock & Co, we do not know: but on the whole we hope they will not.' *The Scots Observer* apparently did not share this leniency. 'The story – which deals with matters only fitted for the Criminal Investigation Department or a hearing in camera – is discreditable alike to author and editor. Mr. Wilde has brains, and art and style; but if he can write for none but outlawed noblemen and perverted telegraph boys, the sooner he takes to tailoring (or some other decent trade) the better for his own reputation and the public morals.'[10]

Wilde defended himself vigorously, pointing out that his aim in writing the novel had been misunderstood. On one occasion he admitted that the public, on hearing his book described as wicked, would rush out to read it, but warned that 'they will find it is a story with a moral . . . a terrible moral . . . which the prurient will not be able to find in it, but which will be revealed to all those whose minds are healthy.'

Like *Dr Jekyll and Mr Hyde*, *The Picture of Dorian Gray* is a study of light and dark, good and evil. *Dorian Gray* differs from Stevenson's work though in that the contrast is made not by two men occupying the same body, but by two separate characters, Basil Hallward, the painter, and Dorian Gray, his handsome young friend. The third main character in the novel, the cynical and world-weary Lord Henry Wotton, acts as the counterbalance to Hallward and becomes the pernicious influence who leads Dorian towards his downward spiral into degeneracy and crime. As Wotton says to Dorian, 'I should like to know someone who has committed a real murder.'

The plot is well known. At the beginning of the novel, Hallward and Dorian are good friends. The artist has just finished a portrait of the beautiful young man and presents it to him. On seeing himself thus, Dorian wishes that he could remain looking so young and that the painting would age in his stead. He learns later that, by some supernatural means, his wish has been granted. He also discovers that the picture reflects not just his physical appearance, but his moral character as well. 'It is the face of my soul', as he describes the transformation. He conceals the painting from everyone, including Hallward, with whom he quarrels, and, seemingly freed from the consequences of his actions, falls prey to temptation and sinks into a life of indulgence and vice. He is helped in this by Wotton who lends him a 'poisonous' book. After years of this behaviour, Hallward confronts Dorian in a climatic scene and urges him to change his ways.

Dorian will not listen, but in an attempt to explain his actions he finally agrees to let Hallward see the painting. The artist is appalled at what he sees. 'You have done enough evil in your life. My God! Don't you see that accursed thing leering at us?' This is too much for Dorian. He seizes a knife and kills Hallward. Although he manages to dispose of the body without detection and make it appear that the artist had simply vanished, he can never put the murder behind him. Finally he attacks the painting with the same knife he used to kill Hallward, but succeeds only in killing himself. On entering the room, his servants find on the wall 'a splendid portrait of their master as they had last seen him, in all the wonder of his exquisite youth and beauty'. On the floor lay a dead man who had been stabbed through the heart. 'He was withered, wrinkled and loathsome of visage. It was not until they had examined the rings that they recognised who it was.'

Wilde hit on the idea of the painting while sitting for a young Canadian artist by the name of Frances Richards. On seeing the completed work for the first time, Wilde remarked,

'What a tragic thing it is! The portrait will never grow older, and I shall. If only it was the other way!' However, the inspiration for the story of Dorian Gray has never been satisfactorily identified. It is suggested here that Wilde based the story of Dorian Gray on his experience with Frank Miles – on their life together, their quarrel and their separation, and Miles's subsequent transformation into a murderer. The first step in this argument is to name the real-life models of the characters in the novel.

The disguise covering Lord Henry Wotton was so thin that he was recognised on publication as Lord Ronald Gower. This was a verdict which has not been challenged over the years. The identities of the real life Dorian Gray and Basil Hallward though have remained very much a matter of speculation. Wilde's son, Vyvian, quoting Hesketh Pearson, claimed that Hallward was based on an artist by the name of Basil Ward. The problem with this story is that, as far as can be seen, no such artist ever existed. Several other names have been put forward over the years, but none convincingly. It is argued here the model was the logical choice, the man who with Gower and Wilde made up the 'great Trinity' of which Wilde wrote while at Oxford – *Frank Miles*.

The evidence for this begins in the first paragraph of the novel which in describing Hallward's studio brings to mind Miles' reputation as a gardener:

The studio was filled with the rich odour of roses, and when the light summer wind stirred amidst the trees of the garden, there came through the open door the heavy scent of lilac, or the more delicate perfume of the pink flowering thorn.

On the same page, reference is made to Miles's interest in Japanese botany and art. Here Wotton, on a visit to Hallward's studio notices that 'now and then the fantastic shadows of birds in flight flitted across the long tussore-silk curtains that were stretched in front of the huge window, producing a kind of momentary Japanese effect, and making him think of those pallid jade faced painters of Tokio, who, through the medium of an art that is necessarily immobile, seek to convey the sense of swiftness and motion.' At the bottom of the same page there is the disclosure that Hallward went to Oxford, where Miles and Wilde did indeed spend a good deal of time. Later in the same chapter, Hallward reminds Wotton of a landscape he had done and which he refused to sell despite a tempting offer. 'It is one of the best things I have ever done'. As already mentioned, art authorities agree that Miles was at his best doing landscapes.

There is reason to believe that Dorian's great *beauty* was modelled on that of a young man called John Gray with whom Wilde had become infatuated shortly before he started writing the novel in 1889. However, Dorian's *character* is another matter. It is suggested here that Dorian the man, like Basil Hallward the painter, was based on Frank Miles; that is to say on the man Miles became and not the one with whom Wilde spent several years of his life. As Dorian reminds Hallward in the novel, 'Each of us has Heaven and Hell in him, Basil'. In this respect the quarrel between Hallward and Dorian is of prime importance. During the quarrel in 1881, Wilde is quoted as telling Miles, 'I will leave you. I will go now and *I will never speak to you again as long as I live*'. In the argument in the novel, Dorian warns Hallward, '. . . on my word of honour I will never speak to you again as long as I live'. (Author's emphasis) When Wilde took Miles to his family hunting lodge in Ireland in 1876, Miles expressed a lack of interest in shooting animals. In the novel, Dorian and Henry Wotton attend a bird shoot on a country estate where a man is accidentally shot. Wotton believes the shooting should be stopped for the day. Dorian, *by this time already a murderer*, replies bitterly, 'I wish it were stopped for ever, Harry. The whole thing is hideous and cruel . . .' When discussing the disappearance of Hallward later in the novel, Wotton remarks to Dorian, 'When you and he ceased to be great friends, he ceased to be a great artist.' This is surely a reference to the decline in Miles's career after his break with Wilde.

The literary link between the novel and the separation of Miles and Wilde must also be considered. It will be recalled that the poem which prompted Canon Miles to urge his son to evict Wilde was, according to Professor Ellmann, *Charmides*. Ellmann also says that the theme of Dorian Gray, 'the relation of passion to art, goes back to Charmides' fevered night with Athena's bronze nakedness in Wilde's poem. Charmides' violation of art by life was a sacrilege like Dorian's attempt to substitute one for the other.' Early in the novel, Dorian complains to Hallward, 'You like your art better than your friends. I am no more to you than a bronze figure. Hardly as much I dare say.'

There would appear then to be more than meets the eye in the explanation given by Hallward to Wotton at the beginning of the novel as to why he refused to exhibit his new picture of Dorian:

> 'Harry', said Basil Hallward looking him straight in the face, 'every portrait that is painted with feeling is a portrait of the artist, not of the sitter. The sitter is merely the accident, the occasion. It is not he who is revealed by the painter; it is rather the painter who on the coloured canvas reveals himself. The reason I will not exhibit this picture is that I am afraid that I have shown in it the secret of my soul.'

As mentioned earlier, Miles and Dorian Gray had one experience in common: they were both forced to terminate an engagement. It is time now to study in detail Dorian's romance with Sybil Vane and the consequences of his decision not to marry her. In Part Four of the novel, Dorian describes to Wotton how he came to meet her:

As I lounged in the park, or strolled down Piccadilly, I used to look at everyone who passed me, and wonder, with a mad curiosity, what sort of lives they led. Some of them fascinated me. Others filled me with terror. There was an exquisite poison in the air. I had a passion for sensations . . . Well one evening about seven o'clock I determined to go out in search of some adventure. I felt that this grey, monstrous London of ours, with its myriad of people, its sordid sinners, and its splendid sins, as you once phrased it, must have something in store for me. I fancied a thousand things. The mere danger gave me a sense of delight. . . I don't know what I expected, but I went out and wandered eastwards, soon losing my way in a labyrinth of grimy streets and black grassless squares. About half past eight I passed by an absurd little theatre, with great flaring gas jets and gaudy play bills.

Here Dorian found the 'romance of his life', Sybil Vane, who was playing the female lead in *Romeo and Juliet*. She was the 'loveliest thing' Dorian had ever seen, 'a girl hardly seventeen years of age with a flower like face, a small Greek with plaited coils of dark brown hair, eyes that were violet wells of passion, lips that were like the petals of a rose.' Dorian fell for her instantly and in Part Four gushes out his feelings of ecstasy to Wotton who in turn pokes mild fun at his companion, a reaction which the young man does not appreciate:

'I wish now I had not told you about Sybil Vane.'
   'You could not have helped telling me Dorian, all through your life you will tell me everything you do.'
   'Yes, Harry, I believe that is true. I cannot help telling you things. You have a curious influence over me. *If I ever*

did a crime, I would come and confess it to you. You would understand me.'

Dorian's engagement quickly follows and one night he invites Wotton and Hallward to the dingy theatre where the actress is appearing. The evening is however a disaster. Sybil's performance is embarrassingly bad and Dorian's friends leave early. After the play, Dorian rushes to Sybil's dressing room for an explanation. She says that her love for him means more to her than acting and that she wished to leave the stage and devote her life to him. Dorian is furious. 'You have killed my love.' he tells her, adding, 'You used to stir my imagination. Now you don't even stir my curiosity. You simply produce no effect. . .' The girl begs forgiveness, but despite her entreaties, Dorian leaves telling her that he will never see her again.

Stunned by this experience, Dorian walks home in a daze *through the very East End slums the Ripper stalked*:

Where he went he hardly knew. He remembered walking through dimly lit streets, past gaunt black shadowed archways and evil looking houses. Women with hoarse voices and harsh laughter had called after him. Drunkards had reeled by cursing and chattering to themselves like monstrous apes. He had seen grotesque children upon door-steps, and heard shrieks and oaths from gloomy courts.

Later that night while alone, Dorian realises for the first time the supernatural powers of his picture. He notices with a shock 'the touch of cruelty in the mouth' of his image. He thinks at first that this could not be:

No, it was merely an illusion wrought on the troubled senses. The horrible night he had passed had left

213

phantoms behind it. Suddenly there had fallen upon his brain that tiny speck that makes men mad. The picture had not changed. It was folly to think so.

However, Dorian forces himself to see the truth and resolves to return to the young actress. He is however overtaken by events for Wotton calls on him the following morning and tells him that Sybil Vane has committed suicide in her dressing room. Dorian's reaction is of the utmost significance:

'*So I have murdered Sybil Vane*', said Dorian Gray, half to himself – '*murdered her just as surely as if I had cut her little throat with a knife*. Yet the roses are not less lovely for all that. The birds sing just as happily in the garden. And tonight I am to dine with you, and then go on to the Opera, and sup somewhere, I suppose, afterwards. How extraordinarily dramatic life is . . .'

Wotton encourages Dorian in this misogyny:

I am afraid that women appreciate cruelty, downright cruelty, more than anything else. They have wonderfully primitive instincts. We have emancipated them, but they remain slaves looking for their masters, all the same. They love being dominated. I am sure you were splendid . . .

Basil Hallward, who calls later, is appalled by Dorian's new attitude. '*Why, man, there are horrors in store for that little white body of hers!*' he exclaims. Dorian though remains unrepentant. Basil asks to see his painting but Dorian, mindful of the changes in it, refuses to allow this, despite the artist's unashamed declaration of love for him. He also refuses to sit again for Hallward. The artist departs, saddened by this. 'You spoilt my life as an artist by refusing Dorian. No man came across two ideal things. Few come across one.'

The rift with Hallward brings Dorian even further under the malicious influence of Wotton who gives the young man a 'poisonous' book. The effect of this book on Dorian is enormous:

For years Dorian could not free himself from the influence of this book. Or perhaps it would be more accurate to say that he never sought to free himself from it. He procured from Paris no less than nine copies of the first edition, and had them bound in different colours, so that they might suit his various moods and the changing fancies of a nature over which he seemed, at times, to have almost entirely lost control. The hero, the wonderful Parisian, in whom the romantic and scientific temperaments were so strangely blended, became to him a kind of prefiguring type of himself. And, indeed, the whole book seemed to him to contain the story of his own life, written before he had lived it.

The book gradually comes to obsess Dorian until there are 'moments when he looked on evil simply as a mode through which he could realise his conception of the beautiful.'

Needless to say, the changes in Dorian's character which result from all of this are most marked. This is particularly noteworthy in respect of his behaviour in the East End of London, of which there are several references in the novel. At the beginning of the book, Dorian is involved in social work in the East End. These are the first words spoken between Dorian and Wotton when they are introduced:

'You have not spoiled my pleasure in you, Mr. Gray,' said Henry, stepping forward and extending his hand. 'My aunt has spoken to me often about you. You are one of her favourites and, I am afraid, one of her victims also.'

'I am in Lady Agatha's black books at present,' answered Dorian, with a funny look of penitence. *I promised to go to a club in Whitechapel with her last Tuesday, and I really forgot all about it.* We were to have played a duet together-three duets, I believe. . .'

At a dinner party, Lady Agatha reproves her nephew, Lord Henry Wotton, for trying to dissuade Dorian from doing social work in the East End. 'They would love his playing,' she points out. 'I want him to play to me,' Wotton replies. This sparks off a conversation around the table.

'But they are so unhappy in Whitechapel,' continued Lady Agatha.

'I can sympathise with everything, except suffering,' said Lord Henry, shrugging his shoulders. 'I cannot sympathise with that. It is too ugly, too horrible, too distressing. There is something terribly morbid in the modern sympathy with pain. One should sympathise with the colour, the beauty, the joy of life. The less said about life's sores the better.'

'Still, the East End is a very serious problem,' remarked Sir Thomas, with a grave shake of the head.

'Quite so,' answered the young lord. 'It is the problem of slavery, and we try to solve it by amusing the slaves.'

The politician looked at him keenly. 'What change do you propose, then?' he asked.

Lord Henry laughed. 'I don't desire to change anything in England except the weather,' he answered. . .

Under the influence of Lord Wotton, Dorian does indeed give up social work, but not his travels to the East End:

There were moments, indeed, at night, when lying sleepless in his own delicately scented chamber, or in the sordid room of the ill famed tavern near the docks which, under an assumed name, and in disguise, it was his habit to frequent, he would think of the ruin he had brought down upon his soul, with a pity that was all the more poignant because it was purely selfish.

. . . Then, suddenly some night he would creep out of the house, go down to dreadful places near Blue Gate Fields, and stay there, day after day, until he was driven away.

. . . Curious stories became current about him after he had passed his twenty fifth year. It was rumoured that he had been seen brawling with foreign sailors in a low den in the distant parts of Whitechapel and that he consorted with thieves and coiners and knew the mysteries of their trade. . .

Long after the death of Sybil Vane, Dorian is spotted leaving an East End vice den by her brother, James. Having sworn to avenge her, he rushes after Dorian and threatens to shoot him. To save his life, Dorian points to his youthful features, claiming that he could not possibly be the man who had wronged Sybil. James Vane apologises but learns a few moments later from a prostitute that he has been tricked:

'Why didn't you kill him?' she hissed out, putting her haggard face quite close to his. 'I knew you were following him when you rushed out from (the den). You fool! You should have killed him. He has lots of money, and he's as bad as bad.'

'He is not the man I am looking for,' he answered, 'and I want no man's money. I want a man's life. The man whose life I want must be nearly forty now. This one is little more than a boy. Thank God, I have not got his blood upon my hands.'

The woman gave a bitter laugh. 'Little more than a boy!' she sneered. 'Why, man, it's nigh on eighteen years since Prince Charming made me what I am.'

'You lie!' cried James Vane.

She raised her hands up to heaven. 'Before God I am telling the truth,' she cried.

'Before God?'

'Strike me dumb if it ain't so. He is the worst one that comes here. They say that he has sold his soul to the devil for a pretty face. It's nigh on eighteen years since I met him. He hasn't changed much since then. I have though,' she said with a sickly leer.

'You swear this?'

'I swear it,' came in hoarse echo from her flat mouth. 'But don't give me away to him,' she whined, 'I am afraid of him. Let me have some money for my night's lodging.'

He broke from her with an oath, and rushed to the corner of the street, but Dorian Gray had disappeared. When he looked back, the woman had vanished also.

It is remarkable that although writing about the East End *the year after the Ripper murders*, Wilde made no reference in his novel to the killings which had caused such a sensation. An open reference that is, for it is argued here that Wilde wrote *The Picture of Dorian Gray* with the Whitechapel murders very much in mind. Indeed, the whole point, so to speak, of the novel – its wit, its decadence, its depiction of encroaching evil – can be encapsulated in Dorian's reproach to Lord Wotton, '*You cut life to pieces with your epigrams.*'

Apart from Dorian's death itself, there are two acts of violence in the novel involving the use of a knife. The first takes place shortly after Dorian sees the painting of himself for the first time. Hallward is so upset by the effect the picture has on his young friend that he decides to destroy it:

Dorian Gray lifted his golden head from the pillow, and with pallid face and tear stained eyes looked at Hallward as he walked over to the deal painting table that was set beneath the high curtained window. What was he doing there? His fingers were straying among the litter of tin tubes and dry brushes, seeking for something. Yes, it was for the long palette-knife, with its thin blade of lithe steel. He had found it at last. He was going to rip up the canvas.

With a stifled sob the lad leaped up from the couch, and, rushing over to Hallward, tore the knife out of his hand, and flung it to the end of the studio. *'Don't, Basil, don't!' he cried. 'It would be murder!'*

Murder does occur in the second instance of violence. This takes place one night when, after years of silence, Hallward comes to see his former friend and remonstrate with him about his lifestyle. The events of this night and their aftermath are of crucial importance to the theory under discussion and must be studied in great detail.

As mentioned earlier, the volume edition of *The Picture of Dorian Gray* contained many revisions. The reason generally given for this is that Wilde had decided to tone down the homosexual element in the original version. This may well be so, but there are some changes to which this explanation cannot apply. Moreover, Wilde regarded his revised text as vital in its own right, not as a compromise designed to conceal an earlier indiscretion. This is borne out by a letter he wrote in March 1891 to his friend, Coulson Kernahan, who was also acting as the literary advisor to the publishers, Ward & Lock. In this letter, Wilde gave instructions about the text of his book, which was to appear the following month. His views were unequivocal:

. . . As soon as I get the revise, and pass it, the book may go to press, but I must pass it first. **This is essential**. Please tell (Ward & Lock) so. (Original emphasis.)

Here then is firm evidence that these revisions and alterations were anything but capricious and that Wilde made them with some specific purpose in mind. That purpose, it is suggested here, was to include a coded message about the Ripper's identity.

A crucial change is the date Wilde gave to the final and tragic meeting between Dorian and Hallward. In the Lippincott's version, Wilde begins this encounter with the following single sentence paragraph:

It was on the 7th November, the eve of (Dorian's) own thirty-second birthday, as he often remembered afterwards.

In the final version however, Wilde says this:

It was on the 9th November, the eve of his own thirty-eighth birthday, as he often remembered afterwards.

The '9th November', the date of the last Ripper murder. Clearly, Wilde did not pick this date out of the air; he selected it specifically to mark a crucial moment in his novel. He also changed Dorian's age, from 32 to 38, *the age Miles was when the final draft of the novel was prepared*. What then takes place during this last meeting between Dorian and his artist friend and what relevance does this have to the Ripper murders?

The scene opens with Dorian walking home. The night is 'cold and foggy'. Suddenly a man passes him in the mist, wearing a grey ulster and with a bag in his hand. Dorian recognises him as Basil Hallward. '*A strange sense of fear, for which he could not account, came over him.*' Hallward explains that he is leaving that night for Paris by boat train and that he wishes to speak to Dorian before he goes. Dorian agrees to this and takes Hallward back to his home:

'. . . But won't you miss your train?' said Dorian Gray, languidly, as he passed up the steps and opened the door with his latchkey.

The lamplight struggled out through the fog, and Hallward looked at his watch. 'I have heaps of time', he answered. 'The train doesn't go till twelve-fifteen, and it is only just eleven. In fact, I was on my way to the club to look for you, when I met you. You see I shan't have any delay about luggage, as I have sent on my heavy things. All I have with me is in this bag, and I can easily get to Victoria in twenty minutes.'

Dorian looked up at him and smiled. *'What a way for a fashionable painter to travel! A Gladstone bag and an Ulster!'*

What greater hint can be dropped about a Ripper suspect than to have him emerge from the London fog on 9 November wearing an Ulster coat with a Gladstone bag in his hand? (As already seen, Marie Belloc-Lowndes has her Lodger/Ripper dressed in an 'Inverness cape', a very similar garment to an Ulster.)

The boat train to Paris from Victoria Station is a reminder of the most memorable lines in Wilde's most famous play, *The Importance of Being Earnest*. The driving element in this play is the need of the main character, Jack, to find out who he really is. He was separated from his parents as a baby and does not know who he is by birth. Here is the celebrated explanation he gives to his prospective mother-in-law, Lady Bracknell, of how he came to be found:

Jack: The late Mr. Thomas Cardew, an old gentleman of a very charitable and kindly disposition, found me, and gave me the name Worthing, because he happened to have a first class ticket for Worthing in his pocket at the time. Worthing is a place in Sussex. It is a seaside resort.

Lady Bracknell: Where did the charitable gentleman who had a first class ticket for this seaside resort find you?

Jack (very gravely): In a hand-bag.

Lady Bracknell: A hand-bag?

Jack (very seriously): Yes, Lady Bracknell. *I was in a hand-bag – a somewhat large, black leather hand-bag, with handles to it – an ordinary hand-bag in fact.*

Lady Bracknell: In what locality did this Mr. James, or Thomas, Cardew come across this ordinary handbag?

Jack: *In the cloak-room at Victoria Station. It was given to him in mistake for his own.*

Lady Bracknell: The cloak-room at Victoria Station?

Jack: Yes. The Brighton Line.

To return to Dorian Gray, Hallward, once indoors, harangues his companion about his evil reputation. Dorian becomes impatient and decides to show Hallward his painting, a revelation which horrifies the artist for he realises that everything he has heard about the younger man is true. Hallward's first utterance on seeing the monster his creation had become is profoundly important – 'This is the face of a satyr.'

The face of a satyr! Such, it will be recalled, was the charge levelled against Frank Miles, that he was a man who was sexually insatiable. Such was also the conclusion reached by Dr Thomas Bond in his report on the Ripper, written immediately after the Kelly murder, where Bond stated that the killer 'may be in a condition sexually, that may be called Satyrcisis.'

On hearing Hallward's response, Dorian loses his self control:

. . . The mad passions of a hunted animal stirred within him, and he loathed the man seated at the table, more than in his whole life he had ever loathed anything. He glanced wildly round. Something glimmered on top of the painted chest that faced him. His eyes fell on it. He knew what it was. It was the knife he had brought up some days before, to cut a piece of cord, and had forgotten to take away with him. He moved slowly towards it, passing Hallward as he did so. As soon as he got behind him, he seized it, and turned round. Hallward stirred in his chair as if he was going to rise. *He rushed at him, and dug the knife into the great vein that is behind the ear*, crushing the man's head down on the table, and stabbing again and again.

There was a stifled groan, and the horrible sound of someone choking with blood. Three times the outstretched arms shot up convulsively, waving grotesque stiff-fingered hands in the air. He stabbed him twice more, but the man did not move. Something began to trickle on the floor. He waited for a moment, still pressing the head down. Then he threw the knife on the table, and listened.

Lily Langtry, in her memoirs, linked Miles' fate with a peacock. Was there a hidden message here known only to herself and Wilde? This must be asked, because after murdering Hallward, Dorian 'felt strangely calm, and walking over to the window opened it and stepped out on to the balcony. The wind had blown the fog away *and the sky was like a monstrous peacock's tail*, starred with myriads of golden eyes. . .'

After the murder, Dorian turns to literature in an attempt to compose himself. The piece he chooses is of great relevance, for it is a poem about *Jean Lacenaire, the French forerunner of the Ripper*:

It was Gautier's 'Emaux et Camees', Charpentier's Japanese edition, with the Jaquemart etching. . . As he turned over the pages his eye fell on the poem about the hand of Lacenaire, the cold yellow hand du supplice encore mal lavée, with its downy red hairs and its doigts de faune. He glanced at his own white taper fingers, shuddering slightly in spite of himself, and passed on, till he came to those lovely stanzas upon Venice. . .

To cover up the crime, Dorian burns Hallward's clothes and bag:

A huge fire was blazing. He piled another log upon it. The smell of the singeing clothes and burning leather was horrible. It took him three quarters of an hour to consume everything.

That Wilde should link the date of the last Ripper murder, as far as can be seen the only date given in the entire novel, with the killing of a person by the slicing of the carotid artery and the burning of clothes in a blazing fire is startling enough. But this is not all; there is also the Freemason connection to consider.

As mentioned earlier, previous researchers into the Ripper case have suggested that the murders were carried out in accordance with Masonic ritual, namely the laments of Jubela, Jubelo, and Jubelum who murdered Hiram Abiff, the architect of Solomon's temple, and were later brought to justice. Until now attention has focused on the laments of Jubela and Jubelo for they deal with the cutting of the throat and disembowelment. The present writer though has shown the similarities between Mary Kelly's death and the lament of Jubelum, the man who actually dealt Hiram Abiff the death blow:

O that my body had been severed in two in the midst, and divided to the north and south, my bowels burnt to ashes in the centre and the ashes scattered by the four winds of heaven.

In order to get rid of Hallward's body, Dorian summons to his home Alan Campbell, an old acquaintance with a knowledge of chemistry. This man refuses to help Dorian, but under the threat of blackmail, finally relents. Here are Dorian's exact instructions for the disposal of Hallward's corpse:

> You, Alan, you must change him, and everything that belongs to him, *into a handful of ashes that I may scatter in the air.*

Oscar Wilde, whose father was a Freemason, was initiated into the Apollo Lodge No. 357 in Oxford on 23 February 1875. He took his second degree on 24 April and his third degree (Master Mason) on 25 May. This lodge practised the Scottish rite and Wilde was admitted to the 33rd degree of this on 27 November 1876. *In the Scottish rite, the construction of Solomon's temple and the story of Hiram Abiff play an important part.* There can be no doubt then that Wilde was familiar with the laments of Hiram Abiff's three assassins.

The real importance of the Masonic ritual is that it establishes yet another link between the Ripper murders and the quarrel of Wilde and Miles in 1881. In all probability, the cause of this quarrel was Wilde's *Poems* and his decision to go to America where he hoped to have his play, *Vera or the Nihilists*, staged. The point to note here is that – as Wilde's biographer, Richard Ellmann, makes clear – Wilde used his knowledge of Masonic ritual in both these works.

On the title page of his *Poems*, to which Miles's father objected so strongly, Wilde included a drawing of a Masonic rose which he designed himself. More importantly, Wilde in the first act of his play, *Vera*, based the opening of a Nihilist meeting on the ritual used in his Lodge:

President: What is the word?
First Conspirator: Nabat.
President: The answer?
Second Conspirator: Kalit.
President: What hour is it?
Third Conspirator: The hour to suffer.
President: What day?
Fourth Conspirator: The day of oppression.
President: What year?
Fifth Conspirator: The year of hope.
President: How many are we in number?
Sixth Conspirator: Ten, nine and three.

Clinching evidence that Wilde recognised the Masonic element in the Ripper murders lies in his choice of the name, *Dorian*, for the main character in his novel. This is still an unusual name today, but before the publication of Wilde's book, it was virtually unknown. 'Dorian' means 'of the Doric', a reference either to a Greek tribe or to a form of Greek architecture. *Doric was also the name of the Whitechapel Lodge (No. 933).*

* * * * *

The aftermath of Basil Hallward's murder is of great significance in demonstrating the link between the Ripper murders and *The Picture of Dorian Gray*. While discussing the mysterious disappearance of Basil Hallward with Lord Henry, Dorian suddenly asks, 'What would you say, Harry, if I told you that I had murdered Basil?' This question elicits the following exchange:

'I would say, my dear fellow, that you were posing for a character that doesn't suit you. All crime is vulgar, just as all vulgarity is crime. It is not in you, Dorian, to commit a murder. I am sorry if I hurt your vanity by saying so, but I assure you it is true. Crime belongs exclusively to the lower orders. I don't blame them in the smallest degree. I should fancy that crime was to them what art is to us, simply a method of procuring sensations.'

'*A method of procuring sensations? Do you think then, that a man who has committed a murder could possibly do the same crime again? Don't tell me that?*' (Author's emphasis.)

'Oh! Anything becomes a pleasure if one does it too often,' cried Lord Henry laughing. 'That is one of the most important secrets of life . . .'

It is obviously important that Dorian should raise the possibility of becoming a multiple murderer and that Lord Henry should see such a course as a 'method of procuring sensations' – the essential motivation of a sex murderer, a fact which few Victorians could easily grasp. In fact, to Dorian, 'man was a being with myriad lives and myriad sensations, a complex multiform creature that bore within itself strange legacies of thought and passion, and whose very flesh was tainted with the monstrous maladies of the dead.'

Of further significance is the fate which Lord Henry thinks actually befell Basil Hallward. Lord Henry rejects the notion that Dorian murdered Hallward and maintains that the artist actually reached Paris, as the British police claimed. Here is Lord Henry's explanation of Hallward's fate:

'. . . I dare say he fell into the Seine off an omnibus, and that the conductor hushed up the scandal. Yes: I should fancy that was his end. I see him lying now on his back under those dull-green waters with the heavy barges floating over him, and long weeds catching in his hair.'

The similarity between this solution to Hallward's disappearance and the death of Montague John Druitt is too great to be ignored. A murder on 9 November in Wilde's novel is linked to a drowning in the Seine. The solution favoured by a senior London police officer to the Ripper murders, the last of which took place on 9 November, is that the killer drowned himself in the Thames. Is this an enormous coincidence? Or did Wilde in fact know about the rumours concerning Druitt? This is a question which will be considered in due course.

* * * * *

What of the book which 'poisoned' Dorian, which represented to him his life as written before he had lived it, and which made him see evil 'simply as a mode through which he could realise his conception of the beautiful'? What book is this and what relevance does it have to Frank Miles and the Ripper case?

In a letter to Mr E.W. Pratt in April 1892, Wilde stated that the book in question 'is partly suggested by Huysmans' *A Rebours*'. Wilde though later denied that there was any connection with *A Rebours*. In a letter to a Ralph Payne dated 12 February 1894, he claimed that he had invented the book which 'poisoned, or made perfect' Dorian. Also, when the identity of the book became an issue during his prosecution of the Marquis of Queensbury for criminal libel in 1895, Wilde prevaricated in the witness box. Under persistent questioning from the defence counsel, Edward Carson, Wilde conceded that the book in question was, after all, *A Rebours*, but he was clearly reluctant to discuss the work in detail.[11]

Wilde's evasiveness is strange, not least because the introductory description of the poisonous book in *The Picture of Dorian Gray* is as good a summary of *A Rebours* as one is likely to find:

It was a novel without a plot, and with only one character, being, indeed, simply a psychological study of a certain young Parisian, who spent his life trying to realise in the nineteenth century all the passions and modes of thought that belonged to every century except his own, and to sum up, as it were, in himself the various moods through which the world spirit had ever passed, loving for their mere artificiality those renunciations that men have unwisely called virtue, as much as those natural rebellions that wise men call sin. The style in which it was written was that curious jewelled style, vivid and obscure at once, full of argot and archaisms, of technical expressions and of elaborate paraphrases, that characterises the work of some of the finest artists of the French school of Symbolistes. There were in it metaphors as monstrous as orchids, and as subtle in colour. The life of the senses was described in the terms of mystical philosophy. One hardly knew at times whether one was reading the spiritual ecstasies of some mediaeval saint or the morbid confessions of a morbid sinner.

A Rebours (Against the Grain) by Joris-Karl Huysmans, art critic and novelist, was published in Paris in 1884. Wilde was in the French capital on honeymoon at the time. He read it at once and hailed it on his return home. James McNeil Whistler, Wilde's erstwhile neighbour, read it at the same time and he wrote to Huysmans congratulating him on his 'marvellous book'. There is no doubt then that the book was highly thought of in Tite Street.

Most modern readers will probably find this praise hard to comprehend for *A Rebours* is not a novel in the accepted sense, but rather a claustrophobic and depressing account of one man's attempt at unrestricted self indulgence. The central character in the book, Des Esseintes, is a misanthropic aristocrat who finds himself labouring under an 'ever powering sense of ennui'. He turns to sex in the hope of arresting 'the universal disdain that was rising within him' and even 'plunges into the nether depths hoping to revive his flagging passions by sheer force of contrast, thinking to stimulate his exhausted senses *by the very foulness of the filth and beastliness of low bred vice.*' But to no avail. Sickened by the world, Des Esseintes shuts himself up in his house at Fontenay and there devotes his time to experiencing and reflecting upon the best the world has to offer in art, music, perfume, and other diversions. His hermit-like existence and the intensity of his feelings cause him to fantasise, which only exacerbates his nervous condition. Eventually at his doctor's request, he returns to Paris and to the society he had detested.

His attitude towards that society is made clear in Chapter Six where he puts into effect a scheme which can only be described as diabolical. In this Chapter, Des Esseintes picks up a sixteen-year-old urchin on the street and takes him to an upper-class brothel where he informs the Madame that he will pay for the boy for the next three months. When the Madame enquires into the reason for this generosity, Des Esseintes provides the chilling response, '*the plain fact is I am simply trying to train a murderer.*' Des Esseintes explains that after three months of sampling 'a luxury he had never suspected the existence of', the boy would be unable to live without such pleasure and would therefore resort to crime to finance his trips to the brothel. Des Esseintes hopes that the boy's desperation would be such that he would one day commit murder in order to obtain the money he needs. Then, he exclaims, 'my object will be attained, I shall have contributed, so far as in me lay, to create a scoundrel, an enemy the more for the odious society that wrings so heavy a ransom from us all.'

To create a scoundrel, an enemy the more for the odious society that wrings so heavy a ransom from us all! This sums up what was almost certainly the underlying motive of Jack the Ripper

– to wreak revenge on the society that had wronged and neglected him.

Clearly, Des Esseintes is the sort of man from whom maniacs are made. Perhaps his state of mind is best illustrated by his decision to adorn the walls of his boudoir with prints of Jan Luyken, the Dutch engraver, the description of whose work reads like a blueprint for the murder of Mary Jane Kelly:

> The works he possessed of this artist, at once fantastic and depressing, vigorous and brutal, included the series of his Religious Persecutions, a collection of appalling plates representing all the tortures which the savagery of religious intolerance has invented, plates exhibiting all the horrors of human agony – men roasted over braziers, skulls laid open by sword cuts, pierced with nails, riven asunder with saws, *bowels drawn out of the belly*, and twisted round rollers, finger nails torn out one by one with pincers, eyes put out, eyelids turned back and transfixed with pins, limbs dislocated or *carefully broken bones laid bare and scraped for hours with knives*.[12]
>
> These productions, replete with abominable imaginations, stinking of the stake, reeking with blood, echoing with curses and screams of agony, made Des Esseintes' flesh creep as he stood stifled with horror in the red boudoir. (Author's emphasis.)

The similarities between Miles and Des Esseintes are immediately apparent. Both came from strong religious backgrounds, the Frenchman having been brought up by the Jesuits; both were deeply interested in art and related subjects; both were highly sexed and indiscriminate in their taste with regard to rank and gender; and both had the opportunity to brood and fantasise. The last point is especially important, as Colin Wilson emphasises in his *A Casebook of Murder* where he writes, 'the essence of the sadistic crime is the fantasy beforehand, and fantasy flourishes in a vacuum.' Des Esseintes' vacuum was his great house at Fontenay; Miles had Keats House.

Huysmans was certainly well aware of the nature of his creation for he himself likened Des Esseintes to *Marshall Gilles de Rais, the fifteenth-century French nobleman who killed and disembowelled a great number of children.* Huysmans was so interested in this medieval mass murderer that he wrote a novel about his exploits (*Là Bas,* published in 1891). Robert Baldick, Huysmans' biographer, quotes him as saying that in writing about Gilles de Rais, he was attracted by the problem of explaining 'how this man, who was a good soldier and a good Christian, suddenly turned into a monster of sacrilege and sadism, cruelty and cowardice.' Here too is a parallel with Dorian Gray and Frank Miles, namely how a seemingly gentle and well intentioned man, from a religious background, could become a murderer.

Des Esseintes' attitude towards women is typical of Huysmans and could help explain why the Ripper had a 'down on whores'. In describing the writer's misogyny, Baldick writes:

. . . In all his early novels he had shown how women inflicted untold physical and spiritual suffering on man, *stifling his artistic talent or implanting disease in his body and doubt in his mind* . . . (He asserted that) woman had always fomented evil, that she was 'the great vessel of crime and iniquity, the store house of shame and misery, the mistress of ceremonies who introduced into our souls the ambassadors of all the vices.' And he made no secret of his personal conviction that woman was essentially 'the naked and venomous Beast, the mercenary of the Powers of Darkness, the absolute slave of the Devil.'[13]

A particularly interesting insight into Des Esseintes' attitude towards women is afforded by his viewing of Gustave Moreau's painting of Salome. In considering the significance of the lotus flower in the painting, Des Esseintes wonders if Moreau had been thinking of 'the dancing harlot of all times, the mortal woman the temple of whose body is defiled – cause of the sins and all the crimes'. Perhaps, Des Esseintes speculates, Moreau was recalling the embalming ceremonies of ancient Egypt 'when surgeons and priests stretch the woman's body on a slab of jasper, then with curved needles extract her brains through the nostrils, her entrails through an incision opened in the left side', after which petals of the lotus flower are placed into her sexual parts in order to purify them.

These similarities are intriguing. However, in Chapter Fourteen of *A Rebours*, there is a clear connection with the Ripper case. As has been shown, the Ripper mutilated almost the whole of Mary Kelly's body except her eyes, which he left untouched and which, according to Walter Dew, the police photographed in the hope of detecting the image of her killer. It is suggested here that the Ripper learned of this method of detection from reading Chapter Fourteen of *A Rebours*.

In this chapter, Des Esseintes tires from the powerful literature he has been reading. He finds that he can no longer indulge freely in 'these formidable elixirs' or 'intoxicate himself with the sight of Odilon Redon's gloomy paintings or Jan Luyken's representations of tortures.' In this mood, he decides to turn to the works of Villiers de l'Isle Adam, whose works, with one exception, did not distil in him 'so overwhelming a sense of horror'. The exception is Claire Lenoir. What then horrified Des Esseintes in this work? Huysmans explains:

First published in 1867 in the Revue des lettres et des arts, this Claire Lenoir opened a series of romances included under the generic title of Histoires morose. On a background of obscure speculations borrowed from old

Hegel, moved a phantasmagoria of impossible beings, a Doctor Tribulat Bonhomet, pompous and puerile, a Claire Lenoir, comic and uncanny, wearing blue spectacles, as round and big as five franc pieces, concealing her almost lifeless eyes.

The romance turned on an ordinary adultery, but ended on an unspeakable note of horror, when Bonhomet, uncovering Claire's eyeballs on her death-bed and searching them with hideous probes, beheld distinctly reflected on the retina the picture of the offended husband brandishing in his extended hand the severed head of the lover; and, like a Kanaka savage, howling a war-song of triumph.

Based on the physiological fact, more or less surely verified, *that the eyes of some animals, oxen for instance, preserve till decomposition sets in, in the same way as photographic plates, the image of the persons and things lying at the instant of their death within the range of their last look, the tale evidently derived from those of Edgar Allan Poe, from whom he copied the meticulous and appalling discussion of the details.*

There are though even more links to consider between *A Rebours*, Frank Miles, and the Ripper murders. These links Wilde identified in the volume edition of Dorian Gray, in revisions which, like those describing the crucial final meeting between Dorian and Hallward, serve no immediately obvious purpose. By way of illustration, Wilde wrote that Dorian saw in these chapters '*the awful and beautiful forms of those whom Vice and Blood and Weariness had made monstrous or mad.*' Dorian saw a '*horrible fascination*' in these people. '*He saw them at night and they troubled his imagination in the day.*' (Author's emphasis)

In chapter IX of the original version, which deals with the 'poisonous' book, Wilde writes that Dorian used to read 'one fantastic chapter and the other immediately following' time and time again. In the final version however, Wilde identifies the 'seventh chapter' as the 'fantastic' one and states that Dorian used to read this and 'the two chapters immediately following' 'over and over again'. Clearly these chapters must now be examined. For the purpose of continuity, the seventh chapter will be discussed last.

The relevance of Chapter Eight of *A Rebours* to Frank Miles is obvious from the first line. 'He had always been madly fond of flowers . . .' Des Esseintes though, in his solitude, had developed a new taste. He wanted not 'artificial flowers aping the true' but 'natural flowers imitating the false'. To this end he has delivered to his house a new collection of obscure and exotic flowers. For example, 'the virginale which seemed cut in glazed cloth'; 'the Albane, that looked as if made from the semi-transparent membrane that lines an ox's ribs, or the diaphanous film of a pig's bladder' and 'the Aurora Borealis (with its) broad leaves the colour of raw meat, intersected by striations of a darker red and purplish threads, leaves that seemed swollen and sweating with dark liquor and blood.' Des Esseintes lines up his new collection and is pleased to see that he has achieved his object.

Viewing these monstrosities though produces more fantasy which establishes a clear link with the real fate of Frank Miles in the form of the disease which killed him:

> '*It's all a matter of syphilis*', reflected Des Esseintes, his eyes attracted, riveted on the hideous marking of the Caladiums, lit up at that moment by a shaft of daylight. And he had a sudden vision of the human race tortured by the virus of long past centuries. Ever since the beginning of the world, from sire to son, all living creatures were handing on the inexhaustible heritage, the everlasting malady that has devastated the ancestors of the man of today, has eaten to the very bone old fossil forms which we dig up at the present moment.

Never wearying, it had travelled down the ages, to this day it was raging everywhere, disguised under ordinary symptoms of headache or bronchitis, hysteria, or gout; from time to time, it would climb to the surface, attacking for choice badly cared-for, badly-fed people breaking out in gold pieces, setting, in horrid iron, a Nautch-girls parure of sequins on its wretched victim's brow, inscribing their skin, for a crown to their misery, with the very symbol of wealth and well being.

And Lo! Here it was reappearing, in its pristine splendour, on the bright-coloured petals of the flowers!

Not surprisingly, these thoughts induce terrible nightmares. In one Des Esseintes is attracted to a naked woman but on touching her 'black Amorphophalli sprang up at every side, and made darts at her belly . . .' He fights to free himself but he fails and 'haggard with horror, he saw the Nidularium blossom under her meagre thighs, with its sword blades gaping in blood red hollows.' The nightmares continue in Chapter Nine inflicting on him 'obstinate fits of insomnia and feverish restlessness.' Des Esseintes seeks relief in the study of his Rembrandt and Goya prints, but it is only while reading Dickens that he finds some solution to his distress. The 'exaggerated virtue' of Dickens's characters however has the opposite effect on him. He becomes 'filled with a craving not now for religious conviction, but for the pleasant sins religion condemns' and 'the carnal side of his nature . . . now asserted itself . . .' In the rest of the chapter, Des Esseintes, with the use of a drug, relives some of his previous sexual experiences, with both sexes.

In a nightmare in Chapter Eight, Des Esseintes finds himself in a great forest at dusk with a strange woman at his side. She was 'tall and thin, had pale flaxen hair, a bulldog face, freckled cheeks, irregular teeth projecting below a flat nose. She wore a servant's apron, a long kerchief crossed like a soldier's buff-belt over her chest, a Prussian grenadier's half-boots, a black bonnet trimmed with ruchings and a big bow.' He had never seen the woman before, but knew that she had 'long been an intimate part of his life.'

Suddenly, a figure on horseback appeared in front of them. The rider was an 'ambiguous sexless creature' and from its 'purple lids shone a pair of pale blue eyes, cold and terrible.' These eyes focused on Des Esseintes 'piercing him, freezing him to the marrow of his bones; more terrified still the bulldog woman pressed against him and yelled death and destruction, her head thrown back, her neck stiffened with a spasm of wild terror.' Des Esseintes saw at once the true nature of this threat. 'And lo! In an instant he knew the meaning of the appalling vision. *He had before his eyes the image of the pox.*'

Terrified he runs for his life and takes refuge in the passage of a summer house. The 'bulldog woman' appears beside him and declaring she had lost her teeth in her panic, 'drew from the pocket of her servant's apron a number of clay pipes (and) proceeded to break them and stuff bits of the stems into the holes in her gums.' Des Esseintes points out that the pipes would fall out, but at that moment he hears the horsed figure approach:

A paralysing fear seized Des Esseintes; his limbs failed him. But the sounds of the hooves grew momentarily louder; despair stung him into action like the lash of a whip; he threw himself upon the woman, who was trampling the pipe bowls underfoot, beseeching her to be quiet and not betray him by the noise of her boots. She struggled but he dragged her to the end of the passage, *throttling her to stop her crying out. . .*

Was this nightmare the origin of the Ripper's need to strangle women? Note here the resemblance which this 'bulldog woman' bore to Catherine Eddowes. She too wore a black bonnet and two clay pipes were found in her white apron which the Ripper wrapped around her neck after tearing off a piece to take with him. She also wore a pair of men's boots, which in the nightly silence of Mitre Square would have made a considerable noise.

Before Chapter Seven is discussed, it is best to digress and give the outline of a documented murder case where fantasising played a major part. The case in question, which is discussed in *The Shadow of Violence* by Frederick Wertham, is that of Robert Irwin, an American artist who in 1937 was sentenced to one hundred and thirty years in Sing Sing Prison for murdering two women in New York. At the age of 15, Irwin realised one day how what he came to call 'visualising', that is conjuring up in his mind a detailed image, could help him in his artistic endeavours. He started consciously to develop this power and persuaded his girlfriend to help him. He began to study philosophy and in particular Schopenhauer. This was an event which changed his life. The German philosopher, the arch-pessimist himself, taught him that all life is meaningless and that man's only hope is to live an objective and contemplating existence free from all basic urges and desires. Irwin concluded from this that sex would interfere with his visualising. He broke off his engagement and tried to castrate himself. He spent the next few years of his life in and out of asylums, his condition aggravated by his failure to find work suited to his artistic temperament. Finally, one day, racked by frustration, he committed the double murders for which he was sent to prison. The point made here is the role Schopenhauer played in driving a man of Irwin's mental condition to murder.

In Chapter Seven, Des Esseintes relives the whole of his life. In practical terms, this means re-evaluating his religious upbringing and reconciling what he has been taught by the

Jesuits with what he has learned since leaving school. 'For a brief moment he was a believer, an instructive convert to religion; then after the shortest interval of reflection, all his attraction towards the faith would evaporate. But all the time and in spite of everything, he was anxious and disturbed in spirit.' Soon the fantasising begins:

He beheld a long procession pass before his eyes of prelates, archimandrites, patriarchs, blessing the kneeling multitude with uplifted arms of gold, wagging their white beards in reading of the Scriptures and in prayer . . .

He feels himself weakening against the attraction of religion, but his thoughts on Schopenhauer encourage him to stand firm:

Schopenhauer had seen the truth! What were all the evangelical pharmacopoeias beside his treatises of spiritual hygiene? He made no professions of healing, offered the sick no compensation, no hope; but his theory of Pessimism was, after all, the great consoler of chosen intellects, of lofty souls; it revealed society as it was, insisted on the innate foolishness of women, pointed you out the beaten tracks, saved you from disillusions by teaching you to restrict, so far as possible, your expectations; never, if you felt yourself strong enough to check the impulse, to let yourself come to the state of mind of believing yourself happy at least if only, when you least expected it, heaven did not send crashing on your head some murderous tile from the housetops.

It would appear that Robert Irwin was not the only artist to be pushed over the precipice of sanity by the teachings of

Schopenhauer. An obsession with this philosopher, it would seem, helped bring down a 'murderous tile' onto the head of another artist, this time in the autumn of 1888.

It would seem from Chapter Seven that this 'murderous tile' took the form of 'nervous disturbances' which began to plague Des Esseintes:

> Since his earliest childhood he had been tormented by inexplicable repulsions, shuddering spasms that froze his backbone and clenched his teeth, whenever, for instance, he saw a servant-maid in the act of wringing out wet linen. These instinctive dislikes had never changed, and to that day *it caused him genuine suffering to hear a piece of stuff torn in two, to rub his finger over a lump of chalk, to stroke the surface of watered silk.*

Here at long last in the quest for the Ripper's identity is a tangible link between a suspect and the murders themselves. A chalked message was found after the 'Double Event'. Does the above passage explain why the Ripper chose to carry a piece of chalk on his person? *That message was found above a piece of Eddowes' apron left there by the Ripper.* Also, at the inquest into the death of Elizabeth Stride, Dr Blackwell testified that the victim had a 'check silk scarf round the neck, the bow of which was turned to the left side and pulled tightly.' It had been raining on the night of the murder, which means that the scarf would have been damp. In any case, it would have been soaked by the incision in Stride's neck which passed so close to the scarf as to fray it.

Did this unexpected feel of 'wetted silk' strike a cord in the Ripper's mind as he knelt over Stride's body? Did it remind him of Chapter Seven of 'A Rebours', which according to Wilde, Dorian Gray read over and over again? Did this memory obsess him as, after being disturbed, he hurried off in search of another victim? Did he seize on Catherine

Eddowes, out of all the women available that night, because of the resemblance she bore to the 'bulldog woman' in Des Esseintes' nightmare? And after murdering her, did he act in accordance with Des Esseintes' 'nervous disturbances' *by tearing a piece from her white apron and leaving it beneath a chalked message on a wall, a message with an apparent Masonic meaning?*

* * * * *

PART THREE

A DIVERSION

If Frank Miles was Jack the Ripper, how did the name of Montague John Druitt end up in Macnaghten's memoranda? *The simple answer could be that Macnaghten originally learned of Druitt from his Tite Street neighbour, Oscar Wilde.*

When Macnaghten returned to London from India in the late 1880s, he went to live at No. 9 Tite Street. This fact appears in *The Post Office London Directory* for 1888, which means that Macnaghten moved into this address in 1887, *when Wilde and Miles were staying at Tite Street.* The London Directories show that Macnaghten remained at this address until 1891.

That Macnaghten, a member of the drama orientated Garrick Club, would have enjoyed, indeed sought, the company of Oscar Wilde, there is no doubt. Macnaghten's obituary (or to be an exact 'An Appreciation' of his life) which appeared in *The Times* on 17 May 1921 reported:

Sir Melville was a man of many and diverse interests; in his early years an amateur actor of no mean ability, he was a constant and enthusiastic theatre goer; always a considerable reader, he never lost his love of the Classics, and on a long voyage in the last 10 months of his life made a translation of the 'Ars Poetica' into English verse, which showed both skill and scholarship. . .

Extraordinary as it may be, it was in this very street – Tite Street, Chelsea – that there reverberated the spine chilling shouts to which Macnaghten refers in his 1915 autobiography. 'Even now I can recall the foggy evenings, and hear again the raucous cries of the newspapers: Another horrible murder, murder, mutilation, Whitechapel!'

Marie Belloc Lowndes, *who visited Oscar Wilde in Tite Street and who had with him a self confessed 'very real link'*, includes a scene in her novel which is highly reminiscent of Macnaghten's. She begins *The Lodger* with Mr Bunting, the landlord in her story, hearing 'boys crying the late afternoon editions of the evening papers.' On listening more closely, 'Bunting's brain pierced the loud, indistinct cries into some sort of connected order. Yes, that was it – "Horrible murder! Murder at St. Pancras!"'

There is further reason to credit the notion that Macnaghten and Marie Belloc Lowndes shared a common source. In her novel, Belloc Lowndes briefly mentions a literary figure. This takes place when Mrs Bunting, the landlady in the story, attends an inquest into one of the murders. As she arrives, she scrutinises a group of men who are waiting outside the Coroner's Court:

Many of the gentlemen – they mostly wore tall hats and good overcoats – standing round and about her looked vaguely familiar. She picked out one at once. He was a famous journalist, whose shrewd, animated face was familiar to her owing to the fact that it was widely advertised in connection with a preparation for the hair – a preparation which in happier, more prosperous days Bunting had great faith in, and used, or so he always said, with great benefit to himself. This gentleman was the centre of an eager circle, half a dozen men talking to him, listening deferentially when he spoke, and each of these men, so Mrs. Bunting realised, was a somebody.

There is little doubt that the 'famous journalist' to whom Marie Belloc Lowndes was alluding here was George R. Sims, who was called 'Tatcho' by his friends through his advertising of a hair restoring product which apparently went by that name. Sims was very interested in the Ripper murders and he did indeed frequent inquests and courtrooms in his profession as a journalist. This identification leads to another important connection.

Sims was an acquaintance of **both** *Oscar Wilde and Melville Macnaghten.* He and Wilde attended a banquet organised by the Society of Authors at the Criterion Hotel on 25 July 1888, just weeks before the Ripper murders started. (Wilde would later express concern that his *Ballad of Reading Gaol* was too similar to *Christmas Day in the Workhouse*, Sims's most famous work.) As for Melville Macnaghten, he and Sims frequented the Crimes Club, probably the leading criminological society in the United Kingdom.

It will be recalled that Sims gives two conflicting accounts of the Ripper's identity. In several instances, he alludes to a body being found in the Thames, an obvious reference to Druitt, although Sims mistakenly refers to him as a doctor, an understandable error in view of the fact that Macnaghten described him as such. However, in his *Mysteries of London* (1906), Sims describes the Ripper *as a former inmate of an asylum* who travelled to Whitechapel by the underground, 'often late at night.' According to Sims, the Ripper was a man of 'birth and education' who could 'keep himself without work' and who for 'a whole year at least was a free man, exercising all the privileges of freedom', a description which clearly does not apply to Druitt.

In fact, Sims combines (or perhaps confuses) these two accounts. In his memoirs, he states that the Ripper 'was undoubtedly a doctor who had been in a lunatic asylum and developed homicidal mania of a special kind.' In a much neglected article entitled *Who was Jack the Ripper?* in *Lloyd's Weekly News* on 22 September 1907, Sims provides more important detail. The article is clearly based on Macnaghten's memorandum, although no names are provided. After rejecting two suspects, a 'Polish Jew' and a 'Russian doctor', Sims turns his attention to his prime suspect:

> The third man was a doctor who lived in a suburb about six miles from Whitechapel and who suffered from a horrible form of homicidal mania, a mania which leads the victim to look upon women of a certain class with frenzied hatred.
>
> The doctor had been an inmate of a lunatic asylum for some time and had been liberated and regained his complete freedom.

This description is clearly an amalgamation of Montague Druitt and **another man**, a man who had been released, or allowed to escape, from an asylum and who lived in a suburb of London about six miles from Whitechapel. Frank Miles was an inmate of an asylum and he was a resident of Chelsea, a London suburb around six miles from Whitechapel.

How then did Montague Druitt enter the Ripper case? Did Oscar Wilde bring this drowned barrister to the attention of his neighbour, Melville Macnaghten? Was Wilde the source of Macnaghten's much debated 'private information' which labelled Druitt Jack the Ripper?

Here, the focus must turn to Wilde's short story, *Lord Arthur Savile's Crime*, which appeared initially not in volume form, but in *The Court and Society Review* in May 1887. Subtitled

A Study of Duty, it is a black comedy about a young man, Lord Arthur Savile, who is told by Mr Podgers, a chiromantist (a palm reader), that his destiny is to commit murder. The young man is engaged to be married, but such is his sense of honour that he feels he must postpone the marriage until he has committed the prophesised crime. He is however totally inept in his attempts and he never comes close to success until one night, while out for a walk, he spots the fortune teller and decides on the spur of the moment to murder him, which he does. His problem 'solved', Lord Savile goes on to wed his sweetheart.

One of Savile's intended victims is his uncle, the Dean of Chichester. Savile sends him a clock with a bomb in it, but learns in a letter from the Dean's family that the bomb had failed to explode (and had remained undetected). The letter begins with the line, 'Thank you so much for the flannel for the Dorcas society.' The relevance here is that Macnaghten's wife, Dora (hence the reference to the Dorcas society?), *was the daughter of a Canon of Chichester*.

Another connection lies in Wilde's choice of names. Macnaghten and his wife were to have four children. By 1887 however, only two had arrived, Charles Melville and Julia Mary Melville, who was to inherit her father's notes on the Ripper case. In his short story, Wilde calls Lord Savile's prospective mother-in-law, *Lady Julia*.

It will be recalled that when Macnaghten returned to England in 1887, he looked to his old India friend, James Monro, for a job with the Metropolitan Police. There are certain jibes in Wilde's story which can be seen as evidence that he knew of Macnaghten's plans. For example, when wondering how to make a bomb, Lord Arthur 'felt that there was little use in going to Scotland Yard about it, as they never seemed to know anything about the movements of the dynamite faction till after an explosion had taken place, and not much even then.' Savile finally locates a German bomb maker living in London, but this man wishes to know for whom the bomb is intended:

'. . . If it is for the police, or for anyone connected with Scotland Yard, I am afraid I cannot do anything for you. The English detectives are really our best friends, and I have always found that by relying on their stupidity, we can do exactly what we like. I could not spare one of them.'

'I assure you,' said Lord Arthur, 'that it has nothing to do with the police at all. In fact, the clock is intended for the Dean of Chichester.'

'Dear me! I had no idea that you felt so strongly about religion, Lord Arthur. Few young men do nowadays.'

Sceptics may well feel inclined to dismiss all of this as coincidence. But they would be rash to do so without first considering the murder of the palm reader, for the relevance of this to Druitt – and via that – to the identity of the Ripper, is such that it simply cannot be ignored.

The murder follows immediately after Savile receives the letter telling him of his failure to kill the Dean of Chichester. He sinks into depression and goes for a walk late at night along the Thames Embankment. As he is strolling between Blackfriars and Cleopatra's needle he sees the fortune teller in front of him and realises at once how his destiny could be fulfilled:

Lord Arthur stopped. A brilliant idea flashed across him, and he stole softly up behind. In a moment he had seized Mr. Podgers by the legs, and flung him into the Thames. There was a coarse oath, a heavy splash, and all was still. Lord Arthur looked anxiously over, but could see nothing of the chiromantist but a tall hat, pirouetting in an eddy of moonlit. After a time it also sank, and no trace of Mr. Podgers was visible. . .

For the next few days, Savile lives in a state of nervous excitement. And then when reading a newspaper in his club, he spots the following article:

Suicide of a Chiromantist

Yesterday morning, at seven o'clock, the body of Mr. Septimus R. Podgers, the eminent chiromantist, was washed on shore at Greenwich, just in front of the Ship Hotel. The unfortunate gentleman had been missing for some days, and considerable anxiety for his safety had been felt in chiromantic circles. It is supposed that he committed suicide under the influence of a temporary mental derangement, caused by overwork, and a verdict to that effect was returned this afternoon by the coroner's jury. Mr. Podgers had just completed an elaborate treatise on the subject of the Human Hand, that will be shortly be published, when it will no doubt attract attention. The deceased was sixty-five years of age, and does not seem to have left any relations.

Obviously, it can be seriously argued that Wilde was prompted by his own story to convey to his Tite Street neighbour information he had learned about Druitt. What greatly strengthen this argument are, once again, the contents of *The Picture of Dorian Gray*, where, it will be recalled, Lord Henry Wotton suggested that *Basil Hallward, who disappeared on 9 November – the date of the last Ripper murder – actually drowned in the Seine.*

Wilde was certainly in a position to learn of Druitt's death. In late 1888, he had a connection with Chiswick, where Druitt's body was fished from the Thames on the last day of the year, in the form of his erstwhile friendship with William Ernest Henley, the former editor of the *Magazine of Art*, who lived there at No. 1 Merton Place (Lord Arthur Savile's fiancée, the girl for whose honour he was prepared to commit murder, was called Sybil *Merton*). In October 1888, Henley unsuccessfully proposed Wilde for membership of the *Savile* Club, shades of the blackballing Wilde had received at the hands of the Oxford Union. A much more important connection exists in the form of Thomas Seymour Tuke, who ran the Chiswick asylum to which Druitt is believed to have gone in vain after being sacked in November 1888, and where Druitt's mother was placed in 1890. Tuke was an Oxford contemporary of Wilde and Evelyn Ruggles Brise, as well as Montague and William Druitt. Moreover, Tuke and Wilde joined the Apollo Freemason Lodge in Oxford in February 1875. *It is totally credible, therefore, that Wilde heard about Druitt's suicide from his Masonic brother, who was probably the doctor who declared Druitt 'sexually insane.'*

Knowledge of Druitt's death is one thing. There is, though, something much more important to consider – the likelihood *not just that Wilde knew Druitt, but that the two men were actually lovers.*

The trail of evidence begins with the works of Druitt's uncle, Robert Druitt (1814–83), who, like Wilde's father, Sir William Wilde (1815–76), was one of the leading medical figures of the mid-Victorian period. Robert Druitt[14] is best known as the author of *The Surgeon's Vade-Mecum* which first appeared in 1839 and became recognised as a standard work in its field. It is inconceivable that a copy of this seminal work would not have found its way into the library of Wilde's father in Dublin. Doubtless, Robert Druitt's other works would also have been accorded a place there.

These other works included *The Medical Times and Gazette* which Druitt edited from 1862 to 1872. In Druitt's first year in the post, the Gazette carried four articles on Wilde's father. There was also a lengthy review of his latest work, *An Essay on the Malformations and Congenital Diseases of the Organs of Sight*. On 28 June, a speech which William Wilde had delivered on the condition of the blind in Ireland was published in full. In 1863 and 1864, reports which Wilde's father had produced on the *Vital Statistics of Ireland* were printed. In February, the Gazette reported on the knighting of the distinguished Irish surgeon.

The list could go on, but the point is surely made that Wilde almost certainly knew of Druitt's family. What is particularly significant about this is the fact that Wilde was a contemporary at Oxford of **both** Montague John Druitt and his elder bother, William Harvey, the man who gave evidence at the inquest into Montague's death.

Wilde and William Druitt entered Oxford in October 1874. The two men went to different Colleges, Wilde to Magdalen and Druitt to Trinity. However the Archives of the Oxford Union Society show that they both served as Probationary members of the Union at the same time, which would have brought them together in a group of some 150 students, *making it virtually certain that they met at some point*. William Druitt was successfully elected to the Union in January 1875. Wilde, it will be recalled, was rejected by the Union, almost certainly because he had already started to live an 'evil life'.

William left Oxford in 1877, a year before Wilde. The Census Returns of 1881 show that William Druitt, spelled Drewitt, was living at that time as a lodger with a Mrs Mary Wilson of No. 59 Palace Gardens Terrace, Kensington, which is in the same London borough as Tite Street, Chelsea where Wilde was then staying with Miles. (William's uncle, the surgeon Robert Druitt, was also living in Kensington in 1881 at No. 8 Strathmore Gardens). Perhaps then, when William visited London from Bournemouth in January 1889 to give evidence into his brother's death, Wilde met up with him as an old Oxford friend and learned of the fears the Druitt family had about Montague's state of mind. Among these fears was, it appears, the suspicion that Montague had been the Ripper.

Here is a plausible explanation of how Wilde could have become equipped with the 'private information' which Macnaghten quoted. There is though also Wilde's relationship with Montague himself to consider.

Montague John Druitt entered Oxford University (New College) in October 1876. It is clear that he did so with enthusiasm. In a letter dated September 1876 to his uncle Robert, the prominent surgeon mentioned above, he invited his uncle to visit him in Oxford and ended with the line, 'I hope soon to earn something independently.' The *Stranger's Book* of the Oxford Union (O22/12/A4/1) shows that he had visited Oxford on 12 April 1875, while still a schoolboy at Winchester, and that he was signed into the Union by his brother, William, then a new member. Montague was a keen debater at his school, serving as the Treasurer to the Debating Society in his final year, and it is reasonable to assume therefore that he was looking forward eagerly to his time in what had become the most famous debating society in the world. To that end, he registered as a Probationary member of the Union in the autumn of 1876, paying a subscription of £1 5s.

It must have been therefore a bitter blow for Montague to learn that he had failed his Probationary period and that he was prevented from joining the Union. This is revealed in the Probational Members Subscriptions (*sic*) in the Union Archives (O22/8/F2/1) where the pencilled 'E' for 'Elected' does not appear beside Druitt's name and confirmed by the Index of Members (O22/8/A2/1) where the name of Montague John Druitt is not to be found. In Druitt's group of Probationary members, some 143 secured election, while only 28, including Druitt himself, were refused admission. Montague's brothers – William in 1875 and Arthur in 1883 – were both elected to the Union, which shows beyond doubt that the decision to reject Montague was a personal one and that the problem lay, as far as the

University Establishment was concerned, with Montague's character and behaviour. In short, Montague, like Wilde, led an 'evil life'.

These revelations serve virtually to confirm that Montague was homosexual, indeed the sort of privileged man who led the vice-driven life described by Wilde in *The Picture of Dorian Gray*. First, he never married. Secondly, a few days prior to his suicide, he got into serious trouble at the Blackheath School where he taught and was dismissed. Before it became known that he had drowned himself in the Thames, the minutes of his cricket club recorded that he had 'gone abroad' and should be removed from his post as Honorary Secretary, virtual confirmation that his fellow sportsmen believed he had left the country as a result of a sex scandal at school. Thirdly, Macnaghten described him as 'sexually insane,' almost identical to the 'sexual insanity' used by Wilde to describe his own carnal urges. *This wording probably had a common source in Dr Thomas Tuke, Wilde's Masonic brother.*

There is clearly good reason therefore to assert that at Oxford, Montague John Druitt was already a practitioner of the 'love that dares not speak its name', which in turn makes it highly likely that at some time during the two years they shared at university, he and Wilde, as members of a small, close-knit gay community, became intimate. After all, birds of a feather flock together.

This would explain the factual error in Macnaghten's memorandum where he states that Druitt was 'said to be a doctor'. For obvious reasons, Macnaghten simply would not have wanted to record, even in a confidential police document, that a child molester, let alone one he suspected of being Jack the Ripper, had been a teacher at a boys' boarding school. Given the established attitude towards homosexuality in Victorian Britain, such a statement would have unjustly tainted the boys concerned and seriously damaged their careers and marriage prospects. The inaccuracies in Macnaghten's memorandum must be seen therefore not as evidence of ignorance or incompetence, as students of the Ripper case have until now assumed, but as 'white lies' designed to protect young innocents. *Quel beau geste!*

Druitt is mentioned nowhere in the published letters of Oscar Wilde. In April 1878, though, during an Easter break from Oxford, Wilde visited Bournemouth, a city with which the Druitt family had strong links. From the Royal Bath Hotel, Wilde wrote to Florence Balcombe, a young Dublin girl, 'I have a delightful friend (a *new* friend) with me and have written one sonnet so am not so misanthropic as usual.' (Original emphasis) Was this new friend Montague John Druitt showing his family to Wilde, as Miles had done two years before?

Florence Balcombe, the recipient of the Bournemouth letter, is likely to have learned at a later date the identity of this new friend, for Wilde was then wooing her with a view to marriage. She rejected his advances however and in December 1878 married instead an Irish Civil Servant with literary ambitions, by the name of Bram Stoker, who was later to achieve fame as the author of *Dracula. His brother, Tom, was the grandfather of Daniel Farson, the first Ripper researcher to be allowed access by Lady Aberconway to her father's notes on Jack the Ripper which named Druitt as a suspect.*

This amazing set of circumstances can surely not be ascribed to coincidence. It can be seriously argued that Lady Aberconway, *who was born in Tite Street*, knew that Oscar Wilde had something to do with her father's 'private information' and that the playwright had once had a relationship with a woman who married into Dan Farson's family. In 1959, Lady Aberconway was anxious to rebut charges that her father had destroyed proof of the Ripper's identity. The best way to do this, it would have seemed to her, was to produce her father's papers. It follows then that Dan Farson, who approached her on the subject of the Ripper, would have appeared as the sensible choice to reveal to the world what she doubtless sincerely believed to be her father's actual views on the Ripper case.

* * * * *

Evidence that Macnaghten, an avid theatre goer, was influenced by Wilde in the writing of his memorandum goes beyond Druitt. There are in fact strong grounds for believing that Wilde played a role, so to speak, in Macnaghten's selection of Michael Ostrog, the 'mad Russian doctor', as a suspect.

A Michael Ostrog did exist in Victorian Britain. This man, born around 1833, was a petty thief who used many aliases and who lived until the early years of the twentieth century. There is reason to believe that he was in a French prison at the time of the Ripper murders, an ascertainable point which would rule him out conclusively as a Ripper suspect. Nevertheless, this man is clearly identical with Macnaghten's suspect. Why though did Macnaghten select him for mention in his memorandum when he appears so unsuitable? Is there evidence of any external influence which led him to select this habitual, but non-violent, criminal out of all the other possibilities? There is indeed.

It is suggested here that Macnaghten's Ostrog is modelled on a character in Wilde's play, *Vera or the Nihilists*, the work which, it was argued earlier, caused so much trouble between Wilde and Miles in 1881. When considering the identity of Jack the Ripper in *The Sunday Referee* on 2 December 1888, George Sims, *the friend of both Wilde and Macnaghten*, remarked:

'The "Russian" theory of the atrocities is worth thinking out. . . We have all seen how political fanaticism will drive a *Nihilist* to the commission of murder, but it is not so generally known that religious fervour drives some sects to the most horrible self-mutilation. . .' (Author's emphasis)

Macnaghten called Ostrog 'a homicidal maniac' whose 'antecedents were of the very worst type'. (As far as is known, the real Ostrog was a simple con man.) In his private notes, he said that Ostrog was in the habit of carrying on his person surgical knives and other instruments. Arthur Griffiths, whose source was without doubt Macnaghten, wrote that the insane Russian doctor had been a convict both in England and Siberia. He also stated that this suspect had been in hiding at the time of the murders, whereas Macnaghten had merely said that Ostrog's whereabouts at the time of the killings had never been ascertained.

One of the leading conspirators in *Vera* is called 'Michael'. He fits the man described by Macnaghten and Griffith far more accurately than the real Ostrog. He can aptly be described as a homicidal maniac in that he kills the Czar and calls for the immediate murder of the Czarevitch (antecedents of the worst possible type?). Indeed, he is obviously obsessed with violence as the following selection from his lines shows:

I think little of pen and ink in revolutions.
One dagger will do more than a hundred epigrams.

They have spoken to us by the sword, and by the sword we shall answer.

To kill all tyrants is our mission!

There should be none here but men whose hands are rough with labour or red with blood.

Of particular interest is:

The curing of Russia is surgeon's business,
and must be done by the knife.

As shown earlier, Wilde based the opening of a Nihilist meeting in *Vera* on Masonic ritual with which he was familiar. Immediately after this, Michael is asked to recite the oath which he does:

To strangle whatever nature is in us; neither to love nor to be loved, neither to pity nor to be pitied, neither to marry nor to be given in marriage, till the end is come; *to stab secretly by night*; to drop poison in the glass; to set father against son, and husband against wife; without fear, without hope, without future, to suffer, to annihilate, to revenge. (Author's emphasis)

The Siberian connection may be explained by the following lines:

Prince Paul: This is the ninth conspiracy I have been in, in Russia. They always end in a *voyage en Siberie* for my friends and a new decoration for myself.
Michael: It is your last conspiracy, Prince.

And what of the other addition to Macnaghten's text made by Griffiths, namely the claim that Ostrog had been *in hiding* at the time of the murders? The real significance of this is to be found, once again, in Wilde's play, *Vera*. When, after murdering the Czar, Michael eventually rejoins his fellow conspirators and is asked where he had been for the past three days, he replies:

Michael: Hiding in the house of the priest Nicholas at the crossroads.

These similarities are all compelling, but most persuasive of all is Michael's surname which Wilde mentions only once in the entire play. This is in the Third Act when Michael returns after killing the Czar to receive the congratulations of his fellow conspirators:

Password: Vae tyrannis!
Answer: Vae victis! (enter Michael Stroganoff.)
President: Michael, the regicide! Brothers, let us do honour to a man who has killed a king.

Now if an 'O' is added to the beginning of this surname, a verbal expedient which would have readily occurred to an Irishman like Wilde, and the last two syllables of the name dropped, the result is '**Michael Ostrog**'.[15]

There is yet another link, a strong thread of evidence which ties Ostrog, Wilde, Druitt and Macnaghten all tightly together. This is that in 1864, Michael Ostrog was charged with stealing property from Reverend George Fredrick Price, a Fellow of New College, Oxford, *the very College where Montague Druitt studied*. Revd Price, who received his prestigious position through his kinship with William of Wykeham, the College's fourteenth-century founder, attended Winchester, Montague's school, and obtained his MA degree in 1880, the same year in which Montague graduated, all of which makes it virtually certain that the two men knew of one another. That in turn makes totally convincing the argument that Melville Macnaghten discussed *both* Druitt and Ostrog with the same source, namely his neighbour Oscar Wilde, a contemporary of Druitt at Oxford and the author of *Vera*.

That *Vera* should have caused a split between Miles and Wilde and inspired the Masonic mutilation of the Ripper victims are matters of valid speculation. But that Wilde's play should also have provided the model for a second suspect in

Macnaghten's list can hardly be labelled a chance occurrence. As Lady Bracknell herself might have said – to lose one suspect may be regarded as a misfortune; to lose two has got nothing to do with carelessness.

* * * * *

In the light of **all** that has been said above, can it be seriously challenged that Macnaghten was somehow fed information on his Ripper suspects in order to divert attention away from the real killer, Frank Miles? After all, there is no smoke without fire and the above material raises several columns of smoke, the thickest over Tite Street, Chelsea, where Miles, Wilde and Macnaghten all lived and where Wilde was visited by his friend, Marie Belloc-Lowndes, the authoress of *The Lodger*.

It must be stressed though that if there was a cover-up, the people involved in it would have acted out of what they saw as the best of motives and in the interests of British society as a whole. This author emphasises that he casts no aspersions whatsoever on the character of Melville Macnaghten, who was without doubt a dedicated policeman and a man of the highest integrity. Indeed, as has already been shown, the factual inaccuracies in Macnaghten's memorandum can be attributed to a desire on the policeman's part, irrespective of the harm it did to his professional reputation, to protect the boys at Druitt's school. It must also be remembered that Macnaghten did not join the Metropolitan police until the summer after the Ripper murders and therefore could have played no role in the decision to return Miles to the asylum.

Nevertheless, there are some question marks hanging over Macnaghten, doubts made all the more nagging by the crime writer, Hargrave Adam, who claimed that Macnaghten had once told him that he had destroyed documentary proof of the Ripper's identity. This was, as Adam states, 'An astonishing thing, surely, for a police official to do!' (Interestingly, Adams, in his *Police Encyclopaedia* of 1920, states his belief that the Ripper suffered from venereal disease, which Frank Miles did.)

Why, for example, did Macnaghten write in his Home Office Memorandum that the Ripper was never seen, when George Hutchinson's statement, which was supported by Inspector Abberline, strongly suggests otherwise. Was it because what Hutchinson saw was Frank Miles picking up Mary Kelly, a woman Miles knew as his former model and whose adopted French name, *Marie Jeanette*, was so strikingly similar to that of *Jeanne Marie*, the product of Lily Langtry's adultery with a member of the Royal family?

Why did Macnaghten leak his list of 'suspects' to his friend, Arthur Griffiths, and allow him to publish this information, minus the actual names? This is a very important question for Macnaghten is hardly likely to have taken this step without official approval. To have acted without such approval would most likely have cost Macnaghten his job. It is therefore difficult to resist the conclusion that a conscious decision was made to lay a false scent and throw the public and amateur sleuths off the Ripper's trail. If this was the case, the ruse worked, for the great Ripper legends of the drowned doctor, the Polish Jew and the mad Russian can all be traced to the publication of Griffiths' book, *Mysteries of Police and Crime* in 1898.

Why did Macnaghten feel the need in his memoirs to comment on the recently published novel, *The Lodger*, by a close friend of Oscar Wilde? In the relevant chapter of his book, *Laying the Ghost of Jack the Ripper* (a clear statement of his intent), Macnaghten rejected the views of Belloc Lowndes and asserted that the Ripper had never been in an asylum, nor lived as a lodger. Did Macnaghten go out of his way to criticise *The Lodger* because he knew Wilde to be the source for that book and that what Belloc Lowndes wrote there was too close to the truth for comfort?

Another important question concerns the 'Dear Boss' letter in which the name 'Jack the Ripper' appeared for the first time. Why is it that Macnaghten and Robert Anderson differed publicly over the Ripper's identity but were at one in denouncing this letter as a hoax? Was it because they knew the origin of the name and its significance, namely that it was a reference to the Lily Langtry and her illegitimate Royal offspring? Was this why they disparaged the letter and labelled it the work of a mischievous (and unidentified) journalist, an accusation which, as already mentioned, is far from convincing. Indeed, could the idea for this accusation have come from Oscar Wilde, who, it will be recalled, was himself a Fleet Street journalist during the Ripper murders? This would have been fitting in view of the strong possibility that Wilde was the model for the character 'Jack' in the *Truth Magazine* article on Lily Langtry which contains the line, 'He said, "she's ripping", and for Jack to say this *she* must be very good.'

For his part, Oscar Wilde, once alerted to the guilt of his former lover, would doubtless have done all he could to ensure Miles's recapture. Afterwards, however, his silence would have been expected by the Establishment, although, given his character, it is entirely credible that Wilde would have felt compelled to write a veiled account of the Whitechapel murders in *The Picture of Dorian Gray*, just as he could not resist the temptation, around the same time, to base his play, *Lady Windermere's Fan*, on Lily Langtry's affair with Prince Louis of Battenberg.

The need for the cover up is certainly understandable. The public revelation of Langtry's illegitimate child would have been damaging to the monarchy at any time. But to have this affair publicly linked to a series of horrific murders was something which the authorities could simply not contemplate. Such disclosures could have damaged the framework of society and done untold harm to British interests abroad. In a Europe governed by dynasties, who knows what trouble such a scandal could have caused, or where it would have ended?[16]

This was a concern of which the British government in late 1888 would have needed no reminding, for earlier that year it had to deal with a crisis over the desire of Prince Alexander of Battenberg, the *brother* of Lily Langtry's former lover, to marry the daughter of the new German Kaiser. Bismarck, the German Chancellor, was strongly opposed to this and threatened to resign if the marriage went ahead. He said such a match would anger the Russian Czar (because Prince Alexander had been the ruler of Bulgaria). The real reason for his opposition though was probably his desire to put the new Empress, who was Queen Victoria's daughter, in her place. Her husband was dying of throat cancer and Bismarck doubtless saw her as a threat to the influence he intended to wield over his son, the future Kaiser Wilhelm II. When Queen Victoria travelled to Berlin, she found herself agreeing with the persuasive Chancellor. The marriage plans were abandoned and Bismarck, the great manipulator, once more had his way.

Victoria certainly had cause to worry, not just about Louis of Battenberg, but also her son, Edward, Prince of Wales. If the Battenberg/Langtry affair was made public, it would only have been a matter of time before Edward's own relationship with Langtry became an issue. (It must not be forgotten that the last Ripper murder took place on 9 November, the Prince's birthday, a date which could have been deliberately chosen by the Ripper to draw attention to this very relationship.) By 1888, the Prince of Wales had survived several sex scandals largely untarnished – *including the divorce of Lady Mordaunt, who named the Prince as one of her lovers only to be conveniently declared insane and incarcerated in an asylum for the rest of her life.* Whether he would have emerged with his position intact from the full disclosure of Langtry's activities and her suggested connection with the Ripper murders is another matter. After all, these earlier scandals lacked the physical element of Langtry's illegitimate daughter and a rampaging murderer in Whitechapel.

Edward, Prince of Wales, had much the same sexual character as Charles II, of whom it was said that while he might not have been the father of his people, he was certainly the father of a good number of them. However Edward did not have the same freedom of action as his Stuart predecessor. Charles II, 'the Merry Monarch', could flaunt his sexual escapades with political impunity, indeed to his political advantage (providing he stuck to Protestant whores). Edward could do no such thing. He was training to become a constitutional monarch and Governor of the Church of England, and as such he was expected, publicly at least, to behave in an irreproachable manner by which the moral standards of the nation would be set. He could never forget that he was there on tolerance and that if he failed in his duties, he would be called to task by his people through Parliament.

It is in the context of such weighty matters as these that the suggested cover-up must be seen. As for the killer, all that mattered was that he harmed no one else and that his name be kept secret, an exercise helped greatly by the fact that, thanks to the false obituaries, Miles, at the time of the Ripper murders, was a 'dead man'. He would have been detained shortly after the last murder, and, in due course, returned to the confinement from which, it seems, he had emerged, or perhaps escaped. There he would have been left to sink deeper into dementia until he found the final release, which took place on 15 July 1891.

* * * * *

But is there any reason to believe that Miles was arrested shortly after Kelly's murder? There is indeed.

Steward Hicks, a Ripper historian, has quoted the wife of Sir Robert Anderson as saying that the Ripper was detained in an asylum near 'Stone'. There are several towns in England called Stone, and Lady Anderson did not specify which one she was referring to. However, it is important to note here that there is a town in Gloucestershire called Stone, and that according to local oral tradition, Jack the Ripper once lived there.[17]

About 15 miles south of this Stone is Brislington asylum where Miles died. Less than ten miles to the west of Stone stands Almondsbury where Miles is buried.

There is a further fascinating piece of evidence which has been virtually ignored since it appeared many years ago in a book entitled, *Great Unsolved Crimes*.[18]

In this book, there is an article by a Dr Harold Dearden who relates a tale told to him in a trench on the Somme in November 1918 by a brother officer who was celebrating his fortieth birthday. This officer claimed that his father, who ran a private asylum on the outskirts of London, had promised to take him to a pantomime on his tenth birthday which fell on 9 November, the day of the last Ripper killing. While the boy and his father were at dinner that evening, a 'violent and noisy' patient arrived with a 'huddle of attendants'. So important was this patient that the boy's birthday treat had to be cancelled. The boy later got to see quite a lot of this patient, whom he believed to be the son of an old friend of his father. He had this to say about his strange friend, whom he later assumed to be the Jack the Ripper:

He had, it appeared, a marvellous gift for drawing and would cover literally reams of paper with fantastically conceived, but perfectly executed, pictures of tiny animals, birds and butterflies, which miraculously ran or marched or flew to form a definite orderly design. And in the execution of this delicate task he showed equal facility with either hand.

* * * * *

Thomas Tuke, who ran the Chiswick asylum on 'the outskirts of London', seems to hold the key to the Ripper mystery. Tuke's links with the Druitts have already been established. He attended Oxford with both Montague and William Druitt and was presumably the doctor who declared Montague 'sexually insane'. Druitt probably visited Tuke's asylum before drowning himself nearby and it was there that Ann Druitt died in 1890. There is now another link to consider.

Tuke attended Brasenose College at the same time as Audley C. Miles. Tuke and Miles were members of Oxford's sporting Vincent's Club, *as was Evelyn Ruggles Brise, considered Macnaghten's main source on Druitt.* Moreover, the families of both Tuke and Miles stemmed from the Bristol area. *What is pertinent here is that Audley Miles was the cousin of Frank Miles. Tuke, it will be recalled, knew Oscar Wilde, Frank's friend.*

All roads in the Ripper case lead, apparently, to Tuke's Manor House Asylum in Chiswick. To there, it seems, Miles was brought (temporarily) right after the last Ripper murder and Druitt rushed in a vain attempt to save himself, *which could mean that Tuke treated both men simultaneously.*

Now there's a thought.

NOTES

1   See Rubert Croft-Cooke, *The Unrecorded Life of Oscar Wilde*, W.H. Allen 1972, pp. 44–5.

2   Wilde was friendly with the entire Sickert family, but he seemed to be especially close to Helena. In view of this relationship, it is surely noteworthy that Walter Sickert should be credited with spreading a story that is very similar to that of *The Lodger*, a novel about the Ripper murders by another of Wilde's friends, Marie Belloc Lowndes. Walter Sickert was accused of being the Ripper by Patricia Cornwell in her 2002 book, *Portrait of a Killer – Jack the Ripper, Case Closed*.

3   See Richard Ellmann, *Oscar Wilde*, Hamish Hamilton (London) 1987 (hereafter Ellmann), pp. 141–2.

4   Wilde was so keen to have *Vera* staged that he had it printed privately. His plans to see it produced during his first American tour came to nothing. According to Hesketh Pearson in his biography of Wilde (p. 76), this was partly because Wilde refused to alter his play in any way. *Vera* eventually had its debut in New York on 20 August 1883. However, the reviews were less than favourable and the play was withdrawn eight days later. In an attempt to save *Vera*, Wilde was invited by the producers to play the part of Prince Paul. He declined the offer.

5   In the early 1930s, the Nottinghamshire historian, S. Race, who was then carrying out research into Frank Miles, wrote to Wilde's friend, Coulson Kernahan, for information on the artist. In his reply, dated 21 March 1934, Kernahan said that he seemed to remember an artist by the name of Miles who sometimes visited Wilde at his home at

No. 16 Tite Street. However, Kernahan had no clear recollection of Miles, although he had the impression that Mrs Wilde 'was not greatly taken with him.'

Kernahan was an old man when he wrote this letter and he could easily have confused Miles with someone else. Nevertheless, the letter is at least further evidence of how well Wilde 'compartmentalised' his friends.

6   As a young man Sherard knew Hugo well. During his exile from Napoleon III's France, Hugo shared a house in Guernsey with Sherard's father who served there as an Anglican priest.

7   Samuel Edwards, *Victor Hugo*, New English Library (London), 1970, pp. 105–6.

8   'Fairy Fay' is a mystery within a mystery. During the Ripper scare in late 1888, several newspapers and pamphlets stated as a fact that an 'unknown' woman had been murdered on Boxing Day 1887. However, to date no official documentary evidence has surfaced to substantiate these reports.

9   As mentioned earlier, the source for the date of Miles's entry into Brislington asylum is the *Dictionary of National Biography*. The Electoral Register for 1888 lists Miles as the occupant of No. 26 Tite Street, as does the *Post Office London Directory* for that year. This information of course relates to the previous year, 1887. The *Post Office London Directory* for 1889 shows that Miles had left Keats House and that the address was occupied by a Miss Dixon.

10   The reference to outlawed noblemen and perverted telegraph boys alludes to the Cleveland Street scandal of 1889 in which the Earl of Euston and Lord Somerset fled the country after a police raid on a homosexual brothel off the Tottenham Court Road where telegraph boys were being used as male prostitutes. Released government files suggest that the Duke of Clarence, grandson of Queen Victoria, was involved in the scandal. Interestingly, Inspector Abberline handled the case.

11   Wilde initially intended to call the book, *Le Secret de Raoul par Catulle Sarrazin*, but deleted the title from the manuscript he had sent to *Lippincott's Monthly Magazine*. There is no doubt that Dorian's book was inspired by a number of works, including Walter Pater's *Studies in the*

Renaissance. However, as explained in the text, the dominant influence by far was Huysmans' *A Rebours.* See the Explanatory Notes by Isobel Murray to *The Picture of Dorian Gray* in the *Oxford English Novel* series, 1974.

12 The detailed separate report by Dr Thomas Bond on the Kelly killing, which was returned to Scotland Yard only in 1987, says of the mutilations done to Kelly's legs:

> ... The right thigh was denuded in front to the bone, the flap of skin, including the external organs of generation & part of the right buttock. The left thigh was stripped of skin, fascia & muscles as far as the knee.

This is confirmed by the police photograph of Kelly as she was found in Miller's Court which shows clearly that the Ripper had scraped her right thigh bone clean of flesh. Her left thigh is not visible in the photograph.

13 Robert Baldick, *The Life of J.K. Huysmans,* Oxford 1955, pp. 144–5.

14 Father of the Lionel Druitt suggested by Daniel Farson as the author of the article, 'The East End Murderer – I knew him'.

15 There is evidence that Wilde was fond of such wordplay. For example, it will be recalled that he devised the name 'Keats House' from Miss Skeates, who owned a dwelling which had stood on the site of Miles' new home.

16 A classic example of what is meant here is the death in the Mayerling hunting lodge in January 1889 of the Crown Prince of the Austro-Hungarian Empire and his mistress. These deaths were recorded as suicide and have been described as such in history books. Recently though, a member of the Austrian royal family, the Hapsburgs, revealed that the couple had been murdered for political reasons.

17 See *The Jack the Ripper A To Z,* p. 168.

18 *Great Unsolved Crimes,* Hutchinson & Co. (London), pp. 172–3.

Select Bibliography

DOCUMENTS
Public Record Office
Mepo 3/140-142
HO 144/220/A49301, A 49301B
HO 144/221/A49301, C-K
MH 94/105

Nottinghamshire Record Office
S. Race collection

Oxfordshire Record Office
Records of the Oxford Union Society

SECONDARY SOURCES
Adam, H.L., *The Trial of George Chapman*, Hodge, 1930.
Anderson, Robert, *The Lighter Side of My Official Life*, Hodder & Stoughton, 1910.
Aronson, Theo, *The King in Love*, John Murray, 1988.
Baldick, Robert, *The Life of J.K. Huysmans*, Oxford, 1955.
Begg, Paul, *Jack The Ripper, The Facts*, Robson Books, 2006.
Begg, Paul, Fido Martin, and Skinner, Keith, *The Jack The Ripper, A to Z*, 1991.
Cornwell, Patricia, *Portrait of a Killer – Jack the Ripper, Case Closed*, 2002.
Croft-Cooke, Rupert, *The Unrecorded Life of Oscar Wilde*, W.H. Allen, 1972.
Cullen, Tom, *Autumn of Terror*, Bodley Head, 1965.
Daft, Richard, *Kings of Cricket*, Bristol, 1893.

Deardon, Harold, 'Who was Jack the Ripper?' in *Great Unsolved Crimes*, by A.J. Alan and others, Hutchinson, 1935.

Dew, Walter, *I Caught Crippen*, Blackie & Sons, 1938.

Edwards, Samuel, *Victor Hugo*, New English Library, 1970.

Ellmann, Richard, *Oscar Wilde*, Hamish Hamilton, 1987.

Evans, Steward P., and Keith Skinner, *Jack the Ripper: Letters from Hell*, Sutton, 2001.

Farson, Daniel, *Jack The Ripper*, Michael Joseph, 1972.

Felberman, Heinrich, *The Memoirs of a Cosmopolitan*.

Fido, Martin, *The Crimes, Detection & Death of Jack The Ripper*, Weidenfield & Nicholson, 1987.

Griffith, Arthur, *Mysteries of Police & Crime*, Cassell, 1898.

Hart-Davis, Rupert ed., *The Letters of Oscar Wilde*, 1962 and *Selected letters of Oscar Wilde*, Oxford University Press, 1979.

Harris, Frank, *My Life & Loves*, Corgi Edition, 1966.

Harris, Melvyn, *Jack The Ripper, The Bloody Truth*, Columbus Books Ltd, 1987.

Harrison, Michael, *Clarence*, W.H. Allen, 1972.

Holland, Merlin, *Irish Peacock & Scarlet Marquess, The Real Trial of Oscar Wilde*, Fourth Estate, 2004.

Howells, Martin, and Keith Skinner, *The Ripper Legacy: The Life and Death of Jack the Ripper*, Sidwick & Jackson, 1988.

Huysmans, J.K. *Against The Grain*, Dover Publications Ltd (New York), 1969.

Hyde, H. Montgomery, *Oscar Wilde*, Eyre Methuen, 1976.

—— (ed.), *The Trials of Oscar Wilde*, 1962.

——, *Cleveland Street Scandal*, 1976.

Jones, Elwyn and Lloyd, John, *The Ripper File*, Arthur Barker, 1975.

Kelly, Alexander, *Jack the Ripper: A Bibliography and Review of the Literature*, Association of Assistant Librarians, 1973, 1984.

Knight, Stephen, *Jack The Ripper, The Final Solution*, Harrap, 1976.

Krafft-Ebbing, *Aberrations of Sexual Life*, Staples Press, 1959.

Langtry, Lily, *The Days I Knew*, 1925

Leighton, D.J., *Ripper Suspect, The Secret Lives of Montague Druitt*, Sutton, 2006.

Le Qeuex, William, *Things I know about Kings, Celebrities and Crooks*, Nash and Grayson, 1923.

Lowndes, Marie Belloc, *The Lodger*, Methuen, 1913.

Lowndes, Susan (ed.), *Diaries and Letters of Marie Belloc Lowndes*, Chatto and Windus, 1971.

Macnaghten, Sir Melville, *Days of My Years*, Edward Arnold, 1915.

McCormick, Donald, *The Identity of Jack the Ripper*, Arrow books, 1970.

McKenna, Neil, *The Secret Life of Oscar Wilde*, Arrow books 2004.

Matters, Leonard, *The Mystery of Jack the Ripper*, Hutchinson, 1929.

Odell, Robin, *Ripperology, A Study of the World's First Serial Killer and a Literary Phenomenon*, The Kent State University Press, 2006

——, *Jack the Ripper in Fact and Fiction*, Harrap, 1965.

Pearson, Hesketh, *Oscar Wilde*, 1946.

Rumbelow, Donald, *The Complete Jack The Ripper*, Penguin, 1988.

Sherard, Robert, *The Real Oscar Wilde*, 1911.

Sims, George, *The Mysteries of Modern London*, Pearson, 1906.

Smith, Lt Col Sir Henry, *From Constable to Commissioner*, Chatto & Windus, 1910.

Stewart, William, *Jack the Ripper*, Quality Press, 1939.

Sugden, Philip, *The Complete History Of Jack The Ripper*, Robinson, 2006.

Thomson, Sir Basil, *The Story of Scotland Yard*, Grayson, 1935.

Ward, E.A., *Recollections of a Savage*.

Wensley, Frederick Porter, *Detective Days*, Cassell, 1931.

Wertham, Frederick, *The Shadow of Violence*.

Whittington-Egan, Molly, *Frank Miles and Oscar Wilde, Such White Lillies*, Rivendale Press, 2008.

Wilde, Oscar, *Complete Works*, Hamlyn Publishing, 1963.

——, *The Picture of Dorian Gray*, ed. Isobel Murray, Oxford English series, 1974.

Williams, Watkin Wynn, *The Life of Sir Charles Warren by his gransdson*, Blackwell, 1941.

Wilson, Colin, *A Casebook of Murder*, Leslie Frewin, 1969.

—— and Odell, Robin, *Jack the Ripper, Summing Up and Verdict*, Bantam Press 1987.

Winslow, Dr Lyttleton Stewart Forbes, *Recollections of Forty Years*, Ousley, 1910.

DIRECTORIES

Dictionary of National Biography
Post Office Directory of London
The Dictionary of Victorian Painters by Christopher Wood.
Dictionnaire critique et documentaire des Peintres, Sculpteurs, Dessinateurs et Graveurs by E. Benezit.
Masonic Records

MAGAZINES AND NEWSPAPERS

Court And Society
The Criminologist
The Daily Telegraph
The Glasgow Herald
The Illustrated Police News
The Lancet
Lippincott's Monthly Magazine
Lloyd's Weekly News
Magazine of Art
The Medical Times and Gazette
The Nottingham Guardian
The Nottingham Journal
The Scotsman
The Star
The Times
Truth
The Woman's World